THE
BONDAGE
BREAKER®

Neil T. Anderson

HARVEST HOUSE PUBLISHERS

EUGENE, OREGON

Cover by Terry Dugan Design, Minneapolis, Minnesota

The names of certain persons mentioned in this book have been changed in order to protect the privacy of the individuals involved.

THE BONDAGE BREAKER is a registered trademark of The Hawkins Children's LLC. Harvest House Publishers, Inc., is the exclusive licensee of the federally registered trademark THE BONDAGE BREAKER.

THE BONDAGE BREAKER®
Copyright © 2000 by Neil T. Anderson
Published by Harvest House Publishers
Eugene, Oregon 97402
www.harvesthousepublishers.com

Library of Congress Cataloging-in-Publication Data
Anderson, Neil T., 1942-
    The bondage breaker / Neil T. Anderson.—2nd ed.
        p. cm.
    Includes bibliographical references.
    ISBN 0-7369-0241-4
    1. Spiritual warfare. 2. Anderson, Neil T., 1942- I. Title.
    BV4509.5 .A523 2000
    235'.4—dc21   00-022238

Printed in the United States of America.

05 06 07 08 09 10 / BP / 16 15

Contents

Acknowledgments

I AM SO THANKFUL THAT Harvest House agreed to do a second edition on the tenth anniversary of this book. A lot of water has passed under the bridge since *The Bondage Breaker* was first published ten years ago. I had no idea that this book and *Victory Over the Darkness* (Regal Books) would launch an international ministry and prompt the writing of over thirty books, including youth editions and study guides—especially since I never wanted to write a book!

In those ten years I have gained a lot more experience and, I hope, maturity in the Lord. For this reason I believe this second edition is a much better book than the first edition. The basic message is the same, but now I can say it much better, because it has been passed by hundreds of doctoral students and ministry colleagues.

No person helps me more in this area than my dear colleague, Dr. Robert Saucy. I am fully aware of my need to be accountable to others, not just for moral reasons, but for credibility of the message and the integrity of the ministry. Bob, you have been my rudder (and sometimes my anchor when I was tempted to proceed without due reflection) in the sea of spiritual conflicts. I'm indebted to you and so is the body of Christ. It was a privilege to coauthor *God's Power at Work in You* (Harvest House) with you. It helped to crystallize my thinking on sanctification.

I also want to thank Dr. Bruce Ware, Dr. Millard Erickson, and Dr. Bruce Demarest, who graciously agreed to read five of my books related to this subject. They have offered important suggestions to help me refine the message of Freedom in Christ.

I want to acknowledge all the good people who shared their lives with me. I was privileged to see God set you free in Christ. There were many emotional moments remembering the pain and torment you suffered. I have learned from every one of you as you shared your spiritual journeys with me. How wonderful to see God demonstrate His sufficient grace in your lives!

Carolina, a Talbot School of Theology student, put the original content of the manuscript on disk, and Ed Stewart helped immensely with the first edition. The editorial crew at Harvest House has been very helpful and supportive—as you have been with all my books.

No two people have been more helpful to me and this ministry than Jerry and Sally Friesen. You are my partners in ministry, and I dedicate this book to you. Thank you for believing in me and committing yourself so faithfully to Freedom in Christ Ministries. I love you both.

—Neil T. Anderson

For information concerning training and resource material write to:

Freedom in Christ Ministries
9051 Executive Park Dr. Ste. 503
Knoxville, TN 37923
Phone: (865) 342-4000 – Fax: (865) 342-4001
E-mail: info@ficm.org
Website: www.ficm.org

Free at Last!

A FEW YEARS AGO I was speaking in a Southern California church on the subject of the New Age movement. My text was 1 Timothy 4:1: "The Spirit explicitly says that in later times some will fall away from the faith, paying attention to deceitful spirits and doctrines of demons." After my message I was surrounded at the front of the sanctuary by hurting people.

Sitting about halfway back in the sanctuary was a 22-year-old woman who had been weeping uncontrollably since the service ended. Several people had tried to comfort her, but she wouldn't allow anyone to get near her. Finally a church staff member cut through the crowd around me and said, "I'm sorry, folks, but we need Dr. Anderson back here right away."

As I approached the young woman, I could hear her sobbing, "He understands! He understands!" We were able to get her out of the sanctuary and into a private office. After she calmed down, I scheduled an appointment with her for the next week.

When Nancy arrived for her appointment, her face was marked by ugly, open scratch wounds. "I've been scratching myself like this ever since last week, and I can't control it," she admitted sheepishly.

Nancy described her horrible childhood, which included an abusive father and a grandmother who identified herself as a black witch. "When I was three years old I received my guardians—spirit guides," she continued. "They were my companions, telling me how to live and what to say. I never questioned whether having spirit guides was anything but normal until my mother took me to Sunday school. Then I began to suspect that my spirit guides might not be good for me. When I asked my parents about it, my father beat me. I never asked again!"

In order to cope with the increasing torment that her spirit guides brought to her life, Nancy resorted to rigid personal discipline. In her high school years she trusted Christ as her Savior. But instead of leaving, her "guardians" continued to harass her.

After high school Nancy turned to the epitome of discipline: the Marines. Determined to become the toughest of the lady leathernecks, she won awards for her discipline. But her spiritual torment kept pushing her mind and emotions to the edge. She refused to tell anyone about her mental battle for fear that she would be labeled insane. Finally the pressure overcame her, and she snapped. Nancy quietly accepted a medical discharge and retreated to a lonely existence of inner turmoil and pain. This was Nancy's condition when she came to church and heard me talk about deceiving spirits.

"Finally someone understands me!" Nancy concluded tearfully.

"Would you like to get rid of your spirit guides?" I asked.

There was a long pause. "Will they really leave, or will I go home and be thrashed by them again?"

"You will be free," I assured her.

Two hours later Nancy *was* free—and was hugging us with an openness she had never known before. "Now I can have people over to my house!" she exclaimed joyfully.

The Reality of the Dark Side

There was time when I thought Nancy's experience was an unusual exception to the norm. Although the degree of her problem was somewhat exceptional, I have come to realize that Paul had in mind every believer when he wrote, "Our struggle is not against flesh and blood, but against the rulers, against the powers, against the world forces of this darkness, against the spiritual forces of wickedness in the heavenly places" (Ephesians 6:12). After more than 30 years of ministry as a pastor, seminary professor, and conference speaker, I have ministered to thousands of Christians all over the world who are being deceived and are living defeated lives. This is a real tragedy, because their heavenly Father desires for them to live a free and productive life in Christ.

My own journey into this realm of ministry did not come by choice. I was a left-brained aerospace engineer before God called me into ministry. Even as a Christian layman I was never curious about demon activity or the occult. The lure of esoteric knowledge and occultic power never appealed to me. I had no interest in them, nor any experience with them.

On the other hand, I have always been disposed to believe what the Bible says about the spiritual world even when it seems to conflict with Western rationalism and naturalism. As a result, for the past 25 years the Lord has been bringing Christians like Nancy to see me. They have been dominated by thought patterns, habits, and behaviors which have kept them from living free and productive lives in Christ. My seminary training had not adequately prepared me to help them. I fumbled my way through a lot of failure in my early attempts to minister to them, but with each attempt I gained new insight. I kept going back again and again to Scripture, looking for the truth that would set them free.

Through years of learning and ministering I have a better understanding of how the truth sets us free and of the need to resist the devil as well as submit to God (James 4:7). Psychotherapeutic ministries that ignore the reality of the spiritual world don't have an adequate answer, but neither do some deliverance ministries that see the problem as only spiritual.

God is reality, and He relates to us as whole people—and His Word provides a comprehensive answer for all those who live in this fallen world.

God Wants You Free and Growing in Christ

Since the first release of this book, I have coauthored (with Dr. Robert Saucy) a book on sanctification entitled *God's Power at Work in You* (Harvest House). Understanding the process of sanctification is critical since God's will for our lives is our sanctification (1 Thessalonians 4:3). "We are to grow up in all aspects into Him, who is the head, even Christ…to a mature man, to the measure of the stature which belongs to the fullness of Christ" (Ephesians 4:15,13). If God has given us everything we need to mature in Christ (2 Peter 1:3), then why aren't more Christians growing in Christ? Some are no more Christlike now than they were 20 years ago. Paul says, "The goal of our instruction is love from a pure heart and a good conscience and a sincere faith" (1 Timothy 1:5). We should be able to say every year of Christian life, "I have grown in my faith, and now I love God and others more this year than I did last year." If we can't say that, then we are not growing.

Part of the reason for this carnality is given in 1 Corinthians 3:2,3: "I gave you milk to drink, not solid food; for you were not yet able to receive it. Indeed, even now you are not yet able, for you are still fleshly. For since there is jealousy and strife among you, are you not fleshly, and are you not walking like mere men?" According to Paul, some Christians are not even able to receive good biblical instruction because of unresolved conflicts in their lives. What is needed is some way to resolve these personal and spiritual conflicts through genuine repentance and faith in God. That is the purpose of this book; however, it focuses more on the spiritual side of the problem.

My first book, *Victory Over the Darkness* (Regal Books), focuses on the personal side of the believer's life in Christ and walk by faith. The book deals with the foundational issues of your identity in Christ and outlines practical steps on how to live by faith, walk according to the Spirit, renew your mind, manage your emotions, and resolve the emotional traumas of your past through faith and forgiveness. To see the complete picture, I strongly suggest that you work through the second edition of *Victory Over the Darkness* together with your study of this book. Either book can be accompanied by the video or audiotape series entitled *Resolving Personal and Spiritual Conflicts,* which may be purchased in Christian bookstores or from the office of Freedom in Christ Ministries.

Before we received Christ, we were slaves to sin. Now because of Christ's work on the cross, sin's power over us has been broken. Satan has no right of ownership or authority over us. He is a defeated foe, but he is committed to keeping us from realizing that. The father of lies can block your effectiveness as a Christian if he can deceive you into believing that you are nothing but a product of your past—subject to sin, prone to failure, and controlled by your habits.

Paul said, "It was for freedom that Christ set us free; therefore keep standing firm and do not be subject again to a yoke of slavery" (Galatians 5:1).You are free in Christ, but you will be defeated if the devil can deceive you into believing you are nothing more than a sin-sick product of your past. Nor can Satan do anything about your position in Christ, but if he can deceive you into believing what the Scripture says isn't true, you will live as though it isn't. People are in bondage to the lies they believe. That is why Jesus said, "You will know the truth, and the truth will make you free" (John 8:32).

I don't believe in instant maturity. It will take us the rest of our lives to renew our minds and be conformed to the image of God. But it doesn't take long to help people resolve their personal and spiritual conflicts and find their freedom in Christ. Being alive and free in Christ is part of positional sanctification, which is the basis for progressive sanctification. In other words, we are not trying to *become* children of God, we *are* children of God who are becoming like Christ. Once people are established alive and free in Christ through genuine repentance and faith in God, watch them grow! They have a new thirst for the Word of God, and they know who they are in Christ because "the Spirit Himself testifies with our spirit that we are children of God" (Romans 8:16).

In this book I have attempted to clarify the nature of spiritual conflicts and outline how they can be resolved in Christ. Part One explains your position of freedom, protection, and authority in Christ. Part Two warns of your vulnerability to temptation, accusation, and deception. Part Three presents the Steps to Freedom in Christ, which will enable you to submit to God and resist the devil (James 4:7).

The contrast between bondage and freedom in a believer's life is powerfully illustrated in the following letter from a professional man. Unlike Nancy, to all appearances this man was a normal, churchgoing Christian who appeared to be living a very successful life in both his family and career. But he wasn't experiencing his freedom in Christ.

> Dear Neil,
>
> I contacted you because I had been experiencing a host of seemingly inexplicable "psychologically related" attacks. My emotional troubles were probably rooted in my childhood experiences with horror movies, Ouija boards, and so on. I clearly remember fearing a visit from devilish forces after I saw the movie titled *The Blood of Dracula*.
>
> My father had a pretty hot temper and was given to emotional outbursts. My survival response was to sulk and blame myself for upsetting him. Bottling my emotions inside became a way of life. As I grew into adulthood I continued to blame myself for any and all personal shortcomings and misfortunes.

Then I accepted Christ as my personal Lord and Savior. I grew spiritually over the next several years, but I never enjoyed complete peace. There was always a lingering doubt about my relationship with God, whom I saw as distant and stern. I had difficulty praying, reading the Bible, and paying attention to the pastor's sermons. I seriously questioned the purpose of life. I experienced horrible nightmares that woke me up screaming.

It was during my time of prayer with you that I finally found freedom in Christ. I realized that God is not a harsh, aloof disciplinarian, but a loving Father who takes joy in my accomplishments. I experienced a great release when I prayed through the final Step.

Now when I read God's Word I understand it like never before. I have developed a more positive attitude, and my entire relationship with my Lord has completely changed. Since our meeting I haven't had one nightmare.

Neil, I'm afraid there are many Christians like me out there leading lives of "quiet desperation" due to the attack of demonic forces. If I can fall prey to these forces and seem all right, so can others.

Are you one of those Christians who lives in bondage to fear, depression, habits you can't break, thoughts or inner voices you can't elude, or sinful behavior you can't escape? God has made every provision for you to be alive and free in Christ. Throughout these pages I want to introduce you to the One who has already overcome the darkness and secured your freedom: Jesus Christ, the Bondage Breaker!

Part One

Take
Courage!

You Don't Have to Live in the Shadows

In MY EARLY YEARS OF understanding, I was asked by a local Christian counselor if I could provide some spiritual assessment of one of his clients. He had given her several psychological tests but never got to the root of her problem. After four years of counseling with no results, he finally considered the possibility that his client could be in some kind of spiritual bondage. During those early years of counseling, she wrote the following prayer to God, then ten minutes later tried unsuccessfully to kill herself with an overdose of pills:

> Dear God,
>
> Where are you? How can you watch and not help me? I hurt so bad, and you don't even care. If you cared you'd make it stop or let me die. I love you, but you seem so far away. I can't hear you or feel you or see you, but I'm supposed to believe you're here. Lord, I feel them and hear them. They are here. I know you're real, God, but they are more real to me right now. Please make someone believe me, Lord. Why won't you make it stop? Please, Lord, please! If you love me you'll let me die.
>
> —A Lost Sheep

The kingdom of darkness was far more real to her than the presence of God. Over the past 20 years I have encountered hundreds of Christians like the woman who wrote this heartrending note. Most of them didn't attempt suicide, but many of them talked about dark impressions to do so. And nearly all of them admitted to the presence of "them"— inner urges or voices which badgered them, tempted and taunted them, accused them, or threatened them. I often warn people who make appointments to talk with me that they will "hear" messages such as "Don't go; he can't help you,"—or they will think disruptive thoughts in first-person singular like "I don't want to go" or "I've tried this before and it didn't work." One person wrote: "Every time I try to talk to you, or even think about talking to you, I completely shut down. Voices inside literally yell at me: 'No!' I've even considered killing myself to end this terrible battle going on inside. I need help!"

Many other Christians I deal with don't complain about hearing voices as such, but their minds are filled with such confusion that their daily walk with Christ is unfulfilling and unproductive. When they try to pray, they begin thinking about a million other things they should be doing. When they sit down to read the Bible or a good Christian book, they can't concentrate, or they read for several minutes and suddenly realize that their thoughts have been a million miles away. When they have an opportunity to serve the Lord in some way, they are brought up short by discouraging thoughts of self-doubt: "I'm not a strong Christian"; "I don't know enough about the Bible"; "I'm still plagued by sinful thoughts"; or "I don't have many spiritual gifts." Instead of being victorious, productive, joy-filled Christians, they trudge through life under a cloud just trying to hang on until Jesus comes. Some of this is certainly because of lack of mental discipline and patterns of the flesh, but it can also reflect deception from the enemy. I have seen thousands of people freed from this kind of mental torment.

Common Misconceptions About Bondage

Where do these "voices" come from, and what is the cause of all the mental confusion that plagues so many lives? One of the main reasons I fumbled and failed in my early days of ministering to people in bondage was because I didn't know the answers to these questions. Moving from my Western worldview to a biblical worldview has required several paradigm shifts. I labored under a number of misconceptions about the spiritual world which had to be dispelled. Perhaps you are struggling with some of these same faulty ideas that keep Christians in darkness.

1. *Demons were active when Christ was on earth, but their activity has subsided.* Christians who hold this view are not embracing the whole counsel of God in light of what His Word says, nor are they facing reality. The New Testament clearly states that believers will wrestle "against the rulers, against the powers, against the world forces of this darkness, against the spiritual forces of wickedness in the heavenly places" (Ephesians 6:12). Paul goes on to itemize the pieces of spiritual armor that we are to put on in order to defend ourselves against "the flaming missiles of the evil one" (verses 13-17). In 2 Corinthians 10:3-5 Paul again specifies that believers are engaged in a spiritual battle against forces which stand against the knowledge of God. If dark spiritual powers are no longer attacking believers, why would Paul alert us to them and insist that we arm ourselves against them? Surely the armor of God is for the believer, not the unbeliever.

The powers and forces that Paul wrote about in the first century are still evident at the dawn of the twenty-first century. We still have the usual cults and occultic practices, but witness the rise of the New Age movement. There is nothing new about the New Age of course. People are practicing the same old spiritism mentioned in the Old Testament. All they have done is change terms from medium to channeler, and from demon to spirit guide.

The kingdom of God is a major theme of the Bible, but it has to be understood in contrast to the kingdom of darkness. The battle from Genesis to Revelation is between those two kingdoms, between the Christ and the Antichrist, between the Spirit of Truth and the father of lies, between the prophets of God and the false prophets, between the wheat (sons of the kingdom) and the tares (sons of the evil one—see Matthew 13:38). Wrestling against dark spiritual forces is not a first-century phenomenon, nor is it merely optional for the Christian today. The kingdom of darkness is still present, and the devil still "prowls around like a roaring lion, seeking someone to devour" (1 Peter 5:8). In light of this, Peter instructs us to "be of sober spirit, be on the alert...resist him, firm in your faith, knowing that the same experiences of suffering are being accomplished by your brethren who are in the world" (1 Peter 5:8,9). If your biblical worldview does not include the kingdom of darkness, then either God or you will have to take a bum rap for all the corruption Satan is foisting on you and the rest of the world.

2. *What the early church called demonic activity we now understand to be mental illness.* Such statements undermine the credibility of Scripture. Divine revelation is infallible. The first demonically plagued Christian I counseled was diagnosed paranoid schizophrenic by medical doctors. After several attempts at medication and many hospitalizations, the medical establishment finally gave up on her. The diagnosis was based on her symptoms. She was nearly paralyzed by fear and was plagued by condemning thoughts, as is almost anybody who is under spiritual attack.

Any diagnosis based on observed or client revealed symptoms offers by itself no explanation for the cause. Terms such as schizophrenia, paranoia, psychosis, and so on are merely labels classifying symptoms. But what or who is causing the symptoms? Is the cause spiritual, psychological, hormonal, or a neurological chemical imbalance? Certainly all these options must be explored. But what if no physical or psychological cause is found?

We should not be surprised when secular psychologists limited to a natural worldview attempt to offer natural explanations for mental problems. Their worldview does not include God or the god of this world. Even many Christians who vociferously reject the scientific community's explanation for the origin of the species naively accept the secular psychologist's explanation of mental illness. Research based on the scientific method of investigation of human spiritual problems is not wrong; it's just incomplete. It ignores the influence of the spiritual world, because neither God nor the devil submit to our methods of investigation. To be effective Christian counselors, we have to learn to distinguish between organic or psychological mental illness and a spiritual battle for the mind. I have attempted to do this in my recent book on depression, *Finding Hope Again* (Regal Books). Depression is a body, soul, and spirit problem that requires a balanced body, soul, and spirit answer.

3. *Some problems are psychological and some are spiritual.* I believe such thinking creates a false dichotomy that implies a distinct division between the human soul and spirit. There is no inner conflict which is not psychological, because there is never a time when your mind, emotions, and will are not involved. Similarly, there is no problem which is not spiritual. There is no time when God is not present. "He... upholds all things by the word of His power" (Hebrews 1:3). The Bible presents the unseen spiritual world just as real as the natural world which we see with our eyes, "for the things which are seen are temporal, but the things which are not seen are eternal" (2 Corinthians 4:18). Nor does the Bible refer to any time when it is safe to take off the armor of God. As long as we are living on planet earth, the possibility of being tempted, accused, or deceived is continuous. If we can accept that reasoning, we will stop polarizing toward medical

answers only, or psychological answers only, or spiritual answers only.

Dr. Paul Hiebert, who teaches at Trinity Evangelical Divinity School, contends that as long as believers accept "a two-tier worldview with God confined to the supernatural and the natural world operating for all practical purposes according to autonomous scientific laws, Christianity will continue to be a secularizing force in the world."[1]

4. *Christians cannot be affected by demons.* Some evangelicals believe that Christians cannot be affected or influenced by demons. Even the suggestion that demonic influence can be part of the problem prompts the hasty disclaimer, "Impossible! I'm a Christian!" Such thinking removes the church from the position of having an adequate answer and helping those who are under attack, and it leaves such people without hope, because we are the only ones who can help them.

Nothing has done greater damage to diagnosing spiritual problems than this untruth. If Satan can't touch the church, why are we instructed to put on the armor of God, to resist the devil, to stand firm, and to be alert? If we aren't susceptible to being wounded or trapped by Satan, why does Paul describe our relationship to the powers of darkness as a wrestling match? Those who deny the enemy's potential for destruction are the most vulnerable to it. (Our vulnerability to demonic intrusion and influence is the subject of Part Two of this book.)

5. *Demonic influence is only evident in extreme or violent behavior and gross sin.* I labored under this kind of thinking for years when I was a pastor and therefore missed the subtle deceptions that rendered many Christians fruitless. Although there are some cases today like the wild demoniac called "Legion" in Luke 8, most deceived Christians lead relatively normal lives while experiencing personal and interpersonal problems for which no cause or solution has been found.

Since they relegate satanic involvement only to the cases of mass murderers or violent sex criminals, these ordinary problem-plagued individuals wonder what's wrong with them and why they can't just "do better."

Satan's first and foremost strategy is deception. Paul warned: "Satan disguises himself as an angel of light. Therefore it is not surprising if his servants also disguise themselves as servants of righteousness" (2 Corinthians 11:14,15). It is not the few raving demoniacs who are causing the church to be ineffective, but Satan's subtle deception and intrusion into the lives of "normal" believers. One Christian psychotherapist who attended my conference "Living Free in Christ" said, "I had never seen any evidence of demonism in my 15 years of counseling until I came to your conference. When I returned to my practice I discovered that two-thirds of my clients were being mentally deceived—and so was I."

6. *Freedom from spiritual bondage is the result of a power encounter with demonic forces.* Freedom from spiritual conflicts and bondage is not a power encounter; it's a truth encounter. Satan is a deceiver, and he will work undercover at all costs. But the truth of God's Word exposes him and his lie. His demons are like cockroaches that scurry for the shadows when the light comes on. Satan's power is in the lie, and when his lie is exposed by the truth, his plans are foiled.

When I was a boy on the farm, my dad, my brother, and I would visit our neighbor's farm to share produce and labor. The neighbor had a yappy little dog that scared the socks off me. When it came barking around the corner, my dad and brother stood their ground, but I ran. Guess who the dog chased! I escaped to the top of our pickup truck while the little dog yapped at me from the ground.

Everyone except me could see that the little dog had no power over me except what I gave it. Furthermore, it had no inherent power to throw me up on the pickup; it was my *belief* that put me up there. Because I chose to believe a lie,

I essentially allowed that dog to use my mind, my emotions, my will, and my muscles, all of which were motivated by fear. Finally I gathered up my courage, jumped off the pickup, and kicked a small rock at the mutt. Lo and behold, it ran!

Satan is like that yappy little dog: deceiving people into fearing him more than God. His power is in the lie. He is the father of lies (John 8:44) who deceives the whole world (Revelation 12:9), and consequently the whole world is under the influence of the evil one (1 John 5:19). He can do nothing about your position in Christ, but if he can deceive you into believing his lies about you and God, you will spend a lot of time on top of the pickup truck! You don't have to outshout him or outmuscle him to be free of his influence. You just have to *out-truth* him. *Believe, declare, and act upon the truth of God's Word*, and you will thwart Satan's strategy.

This concept has had a dramatic effect on my counseling. Previously when I exposed a demonic influence in a counseling situation it would turn into a power encounter. With such a process, I saw counselees become catatonic, run out of the room, or become suddenly disoriented. I would attempt to take authority over the demon. My first approach was to get the demon to expose itself; then I would command it to leave. This exchange often resulted in a great deal of trauma for the counselee. Although some progress was made, the episode would usually have to be repeated.

But I have learned from the Scriptures that *truth* is the liberating agent, and that has proven to be the case in every successful counseling session. Jesus is the Truth, and He is the One who sets the captive free. Power for the believer comes in knowing and choosing the truth. We are to pursue *truth*, because we already have all the power we need in Christ (see Ephesians 1:18,19). Furthermore, people in bondage are not liberated by what I do as the pastor/counselor, but by what they choose to believe, confess, renounce, and forgive. Notice the progressive logic of Scripture:

You shall know the truth, and the truth shall make you free (John 8:32).

I am the way, and the truth, and the life (John 14:6).

But when He, the Spirit of truth, comes, He will guide you into all the truth (John 16:13).

I do not ask Thee to take them out of the world, but to keep them from the evil one....Sanctify them in the truth; Thy word is truth (John 17:15,17).

Stand firm therefore, having girded your loins with truth (Ephesians 6:14).

Finally, brethren, whatever is true...let your mind dwell on these things (Philippians 4:8).

When God first disciplined the early church in Acts 5, He did so in a dramatic way. What was the issue: drugs—sex? No, the issue was *truth* or the lack of it. Peter confronted Ananias and Sapphira: "Why has Satan filled your heart to lie to the Holy Spirit?" (verse 3). God wanted the church to know Satan the deceiver can ruin us if he can get us to believe and live a lie. That's why it is so important that we take "every thought captive to the obedience of Christ" (2 Corinthians 10:5). If I could infiltrate a church, a committee, or a person undetected, and deceive them into believing a lie, I could exert some measure of control over their lives!

Can a good Christian be deceived? Eve had never previously sinned when she was deceived and believed a lie. The final book of the Bible depicts the struggle in the latter days. It is not a book about dysfunctional families, sexual addiction, drug abuse, crime, or any other corruption. In fact the word sin doesn't even occur in the Book of Revelation. The battle between the Christ and the anti-Christ (Satan) is revealed again, and *deception* is the key strategy of the evil one. In between these two periods of history is "the church of the living God, the pillar and support of the truth" (1 Timothy

3:15), and we the church have been called to preach the good news, and speak the truth in love (Ephesians 4:15).

Setting Captives Free

One of the common objections to the ministry of setting captives free that was performed by Jesus and the apostles is the apparent lack of instruction on the subject in the epistles. To my knowledge there are no specific instructions in the epistles to cast demons out of someone else. Let me offer my perspective, which may help clarify the issue, and let me suggest how we should confront demonic influence in our own lives and minister to others in bondage.

Prior to the cross, divinely empowered agents—such as Jesus and His specifically appointed apostles—were necessary to take authority over demonic powers in the world. Notice the first thing Jesus said when He commissioned the twelve disciples to go on a training mission. "And He called the twelve together, and gave them power and authority over all the demons, and to heal diseases" (Luke 9:1). At that time Satan was not a defeated foe, and believers were not seated with Christ in the heavenlies.

But something radical happened at the cross and in the resurrection that changed the nature of spiritual conflicts forever. First, Jesus' death and resurrection triumphed over and disarmed the rulers and authorities of the kingdom of darkness (Colossians 2:15). Jesus proclaimed, "All authority has been given to Me in heaven and on earth" (Matthew 28:18). Because of the cross Satan is a defeated foe, and he has no authority over those who are alive together with Christ and seated with Him in the heavenly places (Ephesians 2:5,6). Affirming the truth of Christ's victory and Satan's defeat is the primary step to successfully stand against the enemy's attempts to intimidate you.

Second, since you are alive in Christ and seated with Him in the heavenlies, you no longer need an outside agent to effect authority for you. You now reside "in Christ," who has all authority. In order to resist the devil, you first need to understand and appropriate your identity, position, and authority in Christ. Freedom in Christ is your inheritance as a Christian. That's why Paul wrote:

> I pray that the eyes of your heart may be enlightened, so that you may know what is the hope of His calling, what are the riches of the glory of His inheritance in the saints, and what is the surpassing greatness of His power toward us who believe. These are in accordance with the working of the strength of His might which He brought about in Christ, when He raised Him from the dead, and seated Him at His right hand in the heavenly places, far above all rule and authority and power and dominion, and every name that is named, not only in this age, but also in the one to come (Ephesians 1:18-21).

There is no need for the Christian to defeat the devil. Christ has already accomplished that. We just need to believe it. When we read through the epistles, it is obvious that Jesus has already delivered us from Satan and sin. That was the good news Paul conveyed in his prayer. God has done all He needs to do for us to live a victorious life in Christ—now we have to assume our responsibility.

It is your individual responsibility as a believer to repent and believe the truth that will set you free. Nobody else can do that for you. I can't put on the armor of God for you, believe for you, repent for you, forgive others for you, and take every thought captive to the obedience of Christ for you, but I can help you. Finding your own freedom in Christ and helping others do the same is the focus of Part Three of this book.

The woman who called herself "A Lost Sheep" finally gained some measure of freedom. She was sitting in church one Sunday four years after she wrote her desperate prayer when she sensed God's leading to write His response to her. This is what she wrote:

> My Dear Lost Sheep,
>
> You ask Me where I am. My child, I am with you and I always will be. You are weak, but in Me you are strong. I love you so much that I can't let you die. I am so close that I feel everything you feel.
>
> I know what you are going through, for I am going through it with you. But I have set you free and you must stand firm. You do not need to die physically for my enemies to be gone, but be crucified with Me and I will live in you, and you shall live with Me. I will direct you in paths of righteousness. My child, I love you and I will never forsake you, for you are truly mine.
>
> —Love, God

Finding Your Way in the World

IN THE PAST SEVERAL YEARS I have spoken on a number of university campuses in the United States and Canada. Flyers were distributed inviting students to attend meetings on the topic of demonic influences in the world today. The eventual purpose was to share the claims of Christ. To my surprise, several hundred students filled each auditorium. These were not fad-seeking teenagers or argumentative hecklers (although a group of Satanists did gather outside one meeting to chant!). Nor did they come to hear Neil Anderson, because they had no idea who I was. These people had a curiosity about demonic influences.

The Western world is experiencing a massive paradigm shift in its worldview, best seen in the rise of the New Age movement, the acceptance of parapsychology as a science, the growing popularity of the supernatural, and the increasing visibility of Satanism in our culture. New Age mysticism, which gathered its greatest strength with the influx of Eastern religions in the 1960s, has been popularized by a host of celebrities. Turn on late-night television and witness the number of psychic hot lines promising everything Christianity promises—except the forgiveness of sins and new life in Christ.

The New Age movement is not just a celebrity issue. New Age philosophy is making significant inroads into business, education, and even religion across our nation. Two seminary students attended (for the sake of research) a New Age conference being held two blocks from Biola University. When they arrived at the door and discovered the cost to be 65 dollars each, they started to walk away. But two strangers approached them saying, "We were told to give you these tickets." The surprised students took the tickets and walked in.

They reported that one of the speakers led conference participants in a meditation exercise. He challenged everyone to imagine a spirit guide coming alongside. The speaker concluded the exercise by saying, "Now invite your spirit guide to come in." I could hardly believe it. The devil was giving altar calls just two blocks from Biola University!

The Two-Tier Worldview

The Western world sees reality in two tiers (see Figure 2a). The upper tier is the transcendent world where God, ghosts, and ghouls reside, a world which is understood through religion and mysticism. The lower tier is the empirical world, which is understood through science and the physical senses. In two-tier mentality, the spiritual world has no or little practical bearing on the natural world; we have practically excluded it from our understanding of reality. Humanists reject the upper tier altogether. Most attempts at integrating theology and psychology include only God and humanity (fallen and redeemed) and exclude the activity of Satan and demons.

In stark contrast to Western rationalism and naturalism, other inhabitants of the world have a different view of reality. The reality of the spiritual world is part of their culture and worldview. Animistic and spiritistic cultures appease their gods with peace offerings and perform religious rituals to ward off evil

spirits. In many Third World nations, religious practice or super-
stition has more practical relevance in daily life than science does.

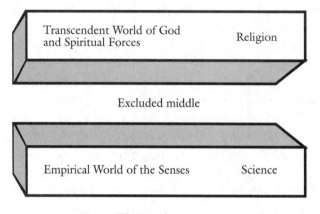

Figure 2a

It is easy for those who are educated in the West to dismiss
Eastern worldviews as inferior on the basis of our advanced
technology and economic success. But why then do we have
the highest crime rate of any industrial nation and the greatest
distribution of pornographic filth? Neither worldview reflects
biblical reality.

Between the two tiers is what Dr. Paul Hiebert calls the
"excluded middle," the real world of spiritual forces active on
earth. We must include the kingdom of darkness in our
worldview because in reality there is no excluded middle!
When Paul talks about the spiritual battle in the heavenlies, he
is not referring to some distant place like Mars or Pluto. He
is referring to the spiritual realm, the kingdom of darkness
that is all around us and governed by the ruler of this world.

To illustrate how this secular, two-tier mentality has
affected the thinking of some Western Christians, let me tell
you about a bright young woman named Dee, a pastor's
daughter. Dee developed physical symptoms which were later
diagnosed as multiple sclerosis. When I heard about Dee's

condition and the prospect of her life with this debilitating disease, I felt the inner pain her parents must have felt. I prayed for Dee, but I couldn't get her off my mind. The next time I had an opportunity to see her, I took it.

"When did you first become aware of the symptoms?" I asked.

"I started feeling the first tingling sensations right after a special time of devotions I had with the Lord," Dee replied.

"What was so special about your devotions that day?"

"I was feeling a little sorry for myself because I haven't achieved the spiritual stature of my parents. My devotions were in 2 Corinthians 12 that day, and I read the passage where Paul told about his thorn in the flesh. Paul said God's power was perfected in his weakness, and I wanted God's power in my life too. So I asked God to give me a thorn in the flesh."

"You asked God for a thorn in the flesh?"

"Yes."

"Do you know what Paul's thorn in the flesh was?"

"Some sort of physical problem, wasn't it?"

"Well, we're not told how it was manifested, but 2 Corinthians 12:7 clearly states that it was a 'messenger of Satan,' literally an angel of Satan—a demon! Paul never asked for it. In fact, he prayed three times that it be removed. Dee, I strongly recommend that you renounce your request for a thorn in the flesh and pray that any influence by Satan be removed from your life."

Dee received my counsel and we prayed together. She began to feel better almost immediately. The symptoms disappeared and she resumed her normal activities. Several months later the symptoms began to reappear. At that time I led her through the Steps to Freedom in Christ (the "Steps") described in Part Three of this book and located in chapter 13. Today Dee is free.

Most doctors and psychologists would not even consider Dee's condition to be a spiritual problem. They would argue that Dee's "recovery" was remission of a physical disease instead of freedom from a demonic attack. But even modern medicine proclaims that the majority of people are sick for psychosomatic reasons. To say there is no spiritual basis for those psychosomatic reasons is biblically unwarranted. Psychosomatic problems originate in our thinking. We shall see later that the primary spiritual battle is in the mind.

Many Christians either exclude the supernatural from their worldview altogether or consign it to the transcendental tier where it will have no effect on their lives. By doing so they not only exclude God's power from their theology and practice, but they also explain all human failure—even that which is induced by demonic influence, such as Dee's symptoms—as the result of psychological or natural causes.

Living in the Excluded Middle

The Christian worldview perceives life through the grid of Scripture, not through culture or experience. And Scripture clearly teaches that supernatural, spiritual forces are at work in this world. For example, approximately one-fourth of all the healings recorded in the Gospel of Mark were actually deliverances. The woman whom Jesus healed in Luke 13:11,12 had been the victim of a "sickness caused by a spirit" for 18 years.

People often complain during counseling sessions of physical symptoms, which disappear after they resolve their personal and spiritual conflicts and find their freedom in Christ. The most common symptoms I have seen are headaches, dizziness, and general pain throughout the body. Some feel as if they need to vomit. I have counseled three people who have been diagnosed with multiple sclerosis (MS), who were set free in Christ after going through the Steps. Apparently there are two types of MS. One is a very progressive degenerative disease, which I believe is a physical problem. The other has MS symptoms which seem to come and go, which was the case for the three mentioned above.

Some problems are clearly physical, such as a broken leg. In this case, go see your doctor, and he will set the break. Then have the church pray for a speedy recovery. Other problems are clearly spiritual, such as bitterness, guilt, and shame. Go see your pastor and get right with God. The difficulty lies with the twilight in-between problems when the doctors can observe physical symptoms but can't find any physical cause for your illness. For instance, remember 20 years ago when everybody was struggling with hypoglycemia? I must confess that as a pastor I got caught up in it. I recommended a glucose tolerance test for every fourth person I counseled. These people all came back and said they were borderline glucose-intolerant! So what happened to hypoglycemia? Then along came chronic fatigue syndrome—and now every other child and some adults have attention deficit disorder (ADD or ADHD).

I am convinced that some Christians battle physical symptoms unsuccessfully through natural means when the essence of the problem and the solution is psychological and spiritual. In our Western world we have been conditioned to look for every possible natural or physical explanation first, and if that doesn't work we say, "There is nothing left to do but pray." Jesus said we should "seek first His kingdom and His righteousness" (Matthew 6:33). Why don't we first submit to God and resist the devil (James 4:7)? The *first* thing a Christian should do about anything is pray. Why not submit our bodies to God as living sacrifices which we have been urged to do (Romans 12:1)? "If the Spirit of Him who raised Jesus from the dead dwells in you, He who raised Christ Jesus from the dead will also give life to your mortal bodies through His Spirit who dwells in you" (Romans 8:11).

The fact that Jesus left us "in the world" (John 17:11) to wrestle against "spiritual forces of wickedness in the heavenly places" (Ephesians 6:12) is a present-day reality. Supernatural forces are at work on planet earth. We live in the natural world, but we are involved in a spiritual war. The "excluded middle" is only excluded in our secularized minds, not in reality.

Getting Spiritual Without God

Over the last four decades people in the West have begun to think there is more to life than what science can explain and what they can discern through their five physical senses. On the surface this new hunger may sound encouraging to those of us with a Christian worldview, but in fact many of the same people who are disillusioned with the materialistic world are also disillusioned with established religion. Instead of turning to Christ and His church, they are filling their spiritual void with old-fashioned occultism dressed in the modern garb of parapsychology, holistic health, Eastern mysticism, and the numerous cults marching under the banner of the New Age movement.

Attempting to meet spiritual needs apart from God is nothing new. Christ encountered a secularized form of Judaism during His earthly ministry which was bound to its traditions instead of to the God of Abraham, Isaac, and Jacob. The religious leaders of the day didn't recognize the Messiah as their spiritual deliverer. They perceived the oppressor to be Rome, not Satan, the god of this world. But Jesus tied the two tiers together when "the Word became flesh" (John 1:14). He came to undo the works of *Satan* (1 John 3:8), not Caesar.

Now, as then, the center of the secular worldview is self: What will *I* get out of this? Who will meet *my* needs? I'm doing *my own* thing. Even a Christian who operates in this sphere is motivated by selfish ambition and pride.

The apostle Peter is a glaring example of the struggle between self- and Christ-centered living. Only moments after Peter confessed the fundamental truth that Jesus Christ is the Messiah, the Son of the living God (Matthew 16:13-16), he found himself in league with the powers of darkness. Having just blessed Peter for his noble confession, Jesus announced to him and the other disciples the suffering and death which awaited Him at Jerusalem. "And Peter took Him aside and began to rebuke Him, saying, 'God forbid it, Lord! This shall never happen to You'"(verse 22).

Jesus responded: "'Get behind Me, Satan! You are a stumbling block to Me; for you are not setting your mind on God's interests, but man's'" (verse 23).

Jesus' memorable rebuke seems mercilessly severe. But the fact that He identified Satan as the source of Peter's words describes precisely and appropriately the character of the advice Peter tried to give. Peter's advice was satanic in principle, for Satan's primary aim is to promote self-interest as the chief end of man. Satan is called the prince of this world because self-interest rules this world. He is called the accuser of the brethren because he does not believe that even a child of God has a higher motive than self-service. You can almost hear him hissing: *Save yourself at all costs. Sacrifice duty to self-interest, the cause of Christ to personal convenience. All men are selfish at heart and have their price. Some may hold out longer than others, but in the end every man will prefer his own things to the things of God.*

Such is Satan's creed, and unfortunately the lives of all too many people validate his claims. Satan has deceived them into thinking they are serving themselves when in fact they are serving the world, the flesh, and the devil.

But the Christian worldview has a different center. Jesus confronts our self-sufficiency and offers a different perspective—the perspective from the cross. Only when you live from God's perspective can you escape the bondage of the one whose sole intent is "to steal, and kill, and destroy" (John 10:10).

The View from the Cross

Together with his wife Eve, Adam was the first mortal to entertain the notion that he could "be like God" (Genesis 3:5), which is the essence of the self-centered worldview that Satan promotes. Countless others since Adam have been seduced by Satan into believing that they are their own gods, and today the New Age movement is promoting this lie on a grand and international scale.

However, the biblical account of creation clearly establishes that only the Creator is truly God. Adam and his ancestors are not gods; we are created beings which cannot exist apart from God. Adam became a living being when God breathed into him the breath of life. Adam was physically and spiritually alive, but he was not a god. God told him that if he ate of the tree of the knowledge of good and evil, he would surely die. But Satan told him that God didn't know what He was talking about, that eating the forbidden fruit would unlock his godlike potential. Adam ate and died—not physically at first, but spiritually. His sin separated him from God, and he was expelled from the Garden of Eden.

Since Adam, every person coming into the world is born physically alive but spiritually dead (Ephesians 2:1). Being separated from God, human beings sought to make a name for themselves and determine their own purpose in life through the natural order of things. They became their own little gods, and their lives were characterized by pride, self-exaltation, and independence from the God who made them. They proclaimed, "We are the captains of our souls and the masters of our destinies." The diabolical idea that people are their own gods is the heartbeat of this fallen world and the primary link in the chain of spiritual bondage to the kingdom of darkness.

The problem with any attempt at being our own gods is that we were never designed to occupy that role. We lack the necessary attributes to determine our own destiny. Even sinless, spiritually alive Adam in the garden of Eden wasn't equipped to be his own god, much less his fallen descendants, who come into the world physically alive but spiritually dead. Contrary to what New Agers tell us, we never had nor ever will have the potential to be God or even a god. There is only one infinite Creator, and all the rest is finite creation.

If you desire to live in freedom from the bondage of the world, the flesh, and the devil, this primary link in the chain must be smashed. The self-centered worldview which Satan and his emissaries are promoting must be replaced by the perspective that Jesus introduced to His disciples in the wake of Peter's self-preserving rebuke:

> If anyone wishes to come after Me, let him deny himself, and take up his cross, and follow Me. For whoever wishes to save his life shall lose it; but whoever loses his life for My sake shall find it. For what will a man be profited if he gains the whole world and forfeits his soul? Or what will a man give in exchange for his soul? For the Son of Man is going to come in the glory of His Father with His angels, and will then recompense every man according to his deeds (Matthew 16:24-27).

This passage is the central message of all four Gospels. I call the absence of understanding this message "the great omission." In writing *Rivers of Revival* (Regal Books) with Dr. Elmer Towns, I came to the conclusion that self-sufficiency is the number-one dam that is holding back the rivers of revival. We are trying to do God's work in our way with our resources, and we can't. The following six guidelines from Jesus' statement constitute the view from the cross. They are the foundational guidelines for those who want to be free from the bondage of the world system and the devil who inspires it. Stay within the light of the cross, and you will successfully find your way in this dark world.

Deny Yourself

Denying yourself is not the same as self-denial. Every student, athlete, and cult member practices self-denial, restricting themselves from substances and activities which keep them from reaching their goals. But the ultimate purpose of that kind of self-denial is self-promotion: to receive the top grade, to break a record, to achieve status and recognition.

To deny ourselves is to deny self-rule. Dying to self is the primary battle of life. The flesh scrambles for the throne and struggles to be God. Jesus doesn't enter into that battle; He's already won it. He occupies the throne and graciously offers to share it with us. But for some deceptive reason, we want to be king and rule our own lives. Until we deny ourselves that which was never meant to be ours—the role of being God in our lives—we will never be at peace with ourselves or with God, and we will never be free.

You were not designed to function independent of God, nor was your soul designed to function as a master. "No one can serve two masters" (Matthew 6:24). When you deny yourself, you invite God to take the throne of your life, to occupy what is rightfully His, so that you may function as a person who is spiritually alive in Christ. Denying yourself is essential to spiritual freedom.

Pick Up Your Cross Daily

The cross we are to pick up on a daily basis is not our *own* cross but *Christ's* cross. Paul wrote, "I have been crucified with Christ; and it is no longer I who live, but Christ lives in me; and the life which I now live in the flesh I live by faith in the Son of God, who loved me and gave Himself up for me" (Galatians 2:20). His cross provided forgiveness from what we have done and deliverance from what we were. We are forgiven because He died in our place; we are delivered because we died with Him. We are both justified and positionally sanctified as a result of the cross.

To pick up the cross daily means to acknowledge every day that we belong to God. We have been purchased by the blood of the Lord Jesus Christ (1 Peter 1:18,19). When we pick up the cross we affirm that our identity is not based in our physical existence but in our relationship with God. We are children of God (1 John 3:1-3). Our life is in Christ, because He is our life (Colossians 3:3,4).

Follow Christ

Seeking to overcome self by self-effort is a hopeless struggle. Self will never cast out self, because an independent self which is motivated by the flesh still wants to be god. We must follow Christ by being led by the Holy Spirit: down the path of death to the old nature we had in Adam, into the new nature we now have in Christ. "We who live are constantly being delivered over to death for Jesus' sake, that the life of Jesus also may be manifested in our mortal flesh" (2 Corinthians 4:11).

This may sound like a dismal path to walk, but I assure you that it is not. It is a tremendous experience to be known by the great Shepherd and to follow Him as His sheep (John 10:27). The fact that we are led by the Spirit of God, even when it results in death to self, is our assurance of sonship (Romans 8:14). We were not designed to function independent of God. Only when we are dependent on Him and intent on following Christ are we complete and free to prove that the will of God is good, acceptable, and perfect (Romans 12:2).

Sacrifice the Lower Life to Gain the Higher Life

If you want to save your natural life (that is, find your identity and sense of worth in positions, titles, accomplishments, and possessions, and seek only worldly well-being), you will lose it. At best you can only possess these things of temporal value for a few years, only to lose everything for eternity. Furthermore, in all your efforts to possess these earthly treasures, you will fail to gain all that can be yours in Christ. Shoot for this world and that's all you'll get, and eventually you will lose even that. But shoot for the next world, and God will throw in the benefits of knowing Him now. Paul said it another way: "Bodily discipline is only of little profit, but godliness is profitable for all things, since it holds promise for the present life and also for the life to come" (1 Timothy 4:8).

Sacrifice the Pleasure of Things to Gain the Pleasure of Life

What would you accept in trade for the fruit of the Spirit in your life? What material possession, what amount of money, what position or title would you exchange for love, joy, peace, patience, kindness, goodness, faithfulness, gentleness, and self-control? To think that worldly positions and possessions can give you love, joy, peace, and so on is to believe the lie of this world. For some reason we want to be happy as animals rather than be blessed as children of God. The fruit of the Spirit is possible only as we abide in Christ.

Jesus discussed this very conflict with two of His closest friends, Mary and Martha (Luke 10:38-42). Martha was "worried and bothered about so many things" (verse 41) and was focused on meal preparation and service, while Mary centered her attention on Jesus and His words. Martha's tendency was to love things and use people, but Jesus indicated that Mary had chosen "the good part" (verse 42) by loving people and using things. We have won a degree of victory over self when we have learned to love God and others.

Sacrifice the Temporal to Gain the Eternal

Possibly the greatest sign of spiritual maturity is the ability to postpone rewards. Hebrews 11:24-26 says: "By faith Moses, when he had grown up, refused to be called the son of Pharaoh's daughter; choosing rather to endure ill-treatment with the people of God than to enjoy the passing pleasures of sin, considering the reproach of Christ greater riches than the treasures of Egypt; for he was looking to the reward." It is far better to know that we are the children of God than to gain something in this world which we will eventually lose. Even if following Christ results in hardships in this life, He will make it right in eternity.

Satan's ultimate lie is that you are capable of being the god of your own life—and his ultimate bondage is the attempt to live as though his lie were truth. Satan is out to usurp God's place in your life. Every temptation is an endeavor by him to get you to live your life independent of God. Whenever you focus on yourself instead of Christ or prefer material and temporal values over spiritual and eternal values, the tempter has succeeded. The message of this fallen world is to inflate the ego while denying God the opportunity to take His rightful place as Lord. Satan couldn't be more pleased—that was his plan from the beginning.

You Have Every Right to Be Free

Lᴅɪᴀ ɪꜱ ᴀ ᴍɪᴅᴅʟᴇ-ᴀɢᴇᴅ ᴡᴏᴍᴀɴ who was dealt a bad hand. Memories of ritual and sexual abuse that she suffered as a young child had haunted her continually throughout her Christian life. When she came to see me her damaged self-image seemed beyond repair. As she told me her story, Lydia displayed little emotion, but her words reflected total despair.

"Lydia, who do you think you are? I mean, how do you perceive yourself?" I asked.

"I think I'm evil," she answered stoically. "I'm just no good for anybody. People tell me I'm evil, and all I do is bring trouble."

"As a child of God, you're not evil. You may have done evil things, but at the core of your very being is a desire to do what is right, or you wouldn't be here," I argued. I handed her the following list of Scripture which shows who she is in Christ:[1]

 In Christ

I am accepted:
- John 1:12
- John 15:15
- Romans 5:1

I am God's child
I am Christ's friend
I have been justified

- 1 Corinthians 6:17   I am united with the Lord and one with Him in spirit
- 1 Corinthians 6:20   I have been bought with a price—I belong to God
- 1 Corinthians 12:27   I am a member of Christ's body
- Ephesians 1:1   I am a saint
- Ephesians 1:5   I have been adopted as God's child
- Ephesians 2:18   I have direct access to God through the Holy Spirit
- Colossians 1:14   I have been redeemed and forgiven of all my sins
- Colossians 2:10   I am complete in Christ

I am secure:
- Romans 8:1,2   I am free from condemnation
- Romans 8:28   I am assured that all things work together for good
- Romans 8:31-34   I am free from any condemning charges against me
- Romans 8:35-39   I cannot be separated from the love of God
- 2 Corinthians 1:21,22   I have been established, anointed, and sealed by God
- Colossians 3:3   I am hidden with Christ in God
- Philippians 1:6   I am confident that the good work that God has begun in me will be perfected
- Philippians 3:20   I am a citizen of heaven
- 2 Timothy 1:7   I have not been given a spirit of fear but of power, love, and a sound mind
- Hebrews 4:16   I can find grace and mercy in time of need
- 1 John 5:18   I am born of God and the evil one cannot touch me

I am significant:
- Matthew 5:13   I am the salt and light of the earth

- John 15:1,5   I am a branch of the true vine, a channel of His life
- John 15:16   I have been chosen and appointed to bear fruit
- Acts 1:8   I am a personal witness of Christ's
- 1 Corinthians 3:16   I am God's temple
- 2 Corinthians 5:17-20 I am a minister of reconciliation
- 2 Corinthians 6:1   I am God's coworker
- Ephesians 2:6   I am seated with Christ in the heavenly realm
- Ephesians 2:10   I am God's workmanship
- Ephesians 3:12   I may approach God with freedom and confidence
- Philippians 4:13   I can do all things through Christ who strengthens me

"Would you read these statements aloud right now?" I asked. Lydia took the list and began to read the first statement aloud: "I am G-G-God's ch-ch..." Suddenly her whole demeanor changed, and she sneered, "No way, you dirty son of a———!"

It is never pleasant to see the evil one reveal his ugly presence through a victim like Lydia. I calmly exercised Christ's authority and led Lydia through the Steps to Freedom in Christ. She was able to gain a new perspective of who she really is in Christ. Realizing that she was not just a product of her past, but rather a new creation in Christ, she was able to throw off the chains of spiritual bondage and begin living according to who she really is, a child of God.

Later she told me that the list I asked her to read appeared to go blank as she started to read it. Was there something special about the paper or the statements printed on it? No, it was only ink on paper. But there was something infinitely significant about Lydia realizing who she is in Christ. Satan had deceived her into believing she was worthless and evil, which was a lie. He didn't want her to know the truth of who she was in Christ, nor how Jesus meets her needs for life, identity, acceptance, security, and significance. He knew that God's truth would disarm his lie just as surely as the light dispels the darkness. And he wasn't about to give up without a fight.

You Are a Child of God

Nothing is more foundational to your freedom from Satan's bondage than understanding and affirming what God has done for you in Christ and who you are as His child. Your attitudes, actions, responses, and reactions to life's circumstances are greatly affected by what you believe about yourself. If you see yourself as the helpless victim of Satan and his schemes, you will probably live like a victim and be in bondage to his lies. But if you see yourself as a dearly loved and accepted child of God, you will have a better chance of living like one. I think that is what John is saying in 1 John 3:1-3: "See how great a love the Father has bestowed on us, that we would be called children of God; and such we are....Beloved, now we are children of God...and everyone who has this hope fixed on Him purifies himself, just as He is pure."

Every defeated Christian I have worked with has had one thing in common. None of them have known who they were in Christ or have understood what it means to be a child of God. Scripture is very clear. "But as many as received Him, to them He gave the right to become children of God" (John 1:12). "The Spirit Himself bears witness with our spirit that we are children of God, and if children, heirs also, heirs of God and fellow heirs with Christ...so that we may also be glorified with Him" (Romans 8:16,17).

In this chapter I want to highlight several critical aspects of our identity and position in Christ. Many of you have already internalized the biblical truths summarized here, but others may find this section to be a little on the heavy side because of its doctrinal content. But I urge you not to skip over this review on your way to the more practical chapters.

These concepts are foundational to your freedom from spiritual conflict as a child of God. The issue of spiritual identity and maturity in Christ is so vital that I again suggest you work through *Victory Over the Darkness* (Regal Books) together with your reading of this book. (For a more in-depth theological study of positional and progressive sanctification, see the book *God's Power at Work in You,* which I mentioned earlier in this book.)

You Are Spiritually and Therefore Eternally Alive

The basic nature of mankind is composed of two major parts: your material self and your immaterial self or the outer man and the inner man (2 Corinthians 4:16). The material self is your physical body, and the immaterial self is your soul/spirit. Because we are created in the image of God, we have the ability to think, feel, and choose (<u>mind, emotions, and will are often collectively identified as the soul</u>), and the ability to relate to God (if we are spiritually alive). As a Christian, your soul/spirit is in union with God at the moment of your conversion, and that makes you spiritually alive. You are physically alive when your body is in union with your soul/spirit. (Note: I use the term "soul/spirit" because theologians don't perfectly agree whether the human soul and the spirit are separate entities or fundamentally the same. Trying to distinguish one from the other is not necessary for our discussion.)

When God created Adam, he was both physically and spiritually alive. Because of Adam's sin and subsequent spiritual death, every person who comes into this world is born physically alive but spiritually dead (Ephesians 2:1). When you were born again, your soul/spirit was united with God, and you came alive spiritually. You are no longer "in Adam"—you are "in Christ." For every verse that says Christ is in you there are ten verses saying you are "in Christ" or "in Him." Since the life of Christ is eternal, the spiritual life you now have in Christ is eternal. Eternal life is not something you get when you physically die; it is something you get the moment you are born again! "He who has the Son has the life; he who does not have the Son of God does not have the life" (1 John 5:12).

Contrary to what Satan would like you to believe, he can't ever take away your eternal life because he can't take Jesus away from you, who promised never to leave you or forsake you (Hebrews 13:5). And you don't have to physically die to get rid of tormenting spirits, which is a lie that deceived people commonly believe. You can submit to God and resist the devil, and he will flee from you (James 4:7).

You Are a New Creation in Christ

If you don't fully understand your identity and position in Christ, you will likely believe there is little distinction between yourself and non-Christians. Satan, the accuser, will seize that opportunity, pour on the guilt, and question your salvation. As a defeated Christian you will confess your sin and strive to do better, but inwardly you will think, "I'm just a sinner saved by grace, hanging on until the rapture. Having my sins forgiven was the only thing that happened at salvation. I am still the same person I was before."

That is how Paul describes who you were *before* you came to Christ: "You were dead in your trespasses and sins, in which you formerly walked according to the course of this world, according to the prince of the power of the air...and were by nature children of wrath" (Ephesians 2:1-3). You were by nature a child of wrath, but now you have become a partaker "of the divine nature, having escaped the corruption that is in the world by lust" (2 Peter 1:4).

As a born-again child of God you are no longer "in the flesh"; you are now "in Christ." You were a sinner, but you are now a saint according to the Bible. You had a natural and finite beginning, but now you are eternally united with Christ. Paul said: "You were formerly darkness, but now you are light in the Lord; walk as children of light" (Ephesians 5:8); "If any man is in Christ, he is a new creature" (2 Corinthians 5:17). In the face of Satan's accusations, we must believe and live in harmony with the truth that we are eternally different in Christ.

The New Testament refers to the person you were before you received Christ as your old self (old man). At salvation your old self, which was motivated to live independent of God and was therefore characterized by sin, died (Romans 6:6); and your new self, united with Christ, came to life (Galatians 2:20). Being spiritually alive means your soul is in union with God and you are identified with Him:

- Romans 6:3;   In His death
  Galatians 2:20;
  Colossians 3:1-3
- Romans 6:4   In His burial
- Romans 6:5,8,11   In His resurrection
- Ephesians 2:6   In His ascension
- Romans 5:10,11   In His life
- Ephesians 1:19,20   In His power
- Romans 8:16,17;   In His inheritance
  Ephesians 1:11,12

Your old self had to die in order to sever your relationship with sin which dominated it. Being a saint or a child of God doesn't mean that you are sinless (1 John 1:8). But since your old self has been crucified and buried with Christ, you no longer *have* to sin (1 John 2:1). You sin when you choose to believe a lie or act independently of God.

You Can Be Victorious over Sin and Death

Death is the end of a relationship, not the end of existence. Sin is still alive, strong, and appealing, but the power and authority it had over you have been broken. "Therefore there is now no condemnation for those who are *in Christ Jesus*. For the law of the Spirit of life *in Christ Jesus* has set you free from the law of sin and of death" (Romans 8:1,2 emphasis added). The law of sin and the law of death are still present, and that is why Paul used the word "law." You cannot do away with a law, but you can overcome it with a greater law, which is the "law of life in Christ Jesus."

Furthermore, the flesh is still present after salvation. You still have learned habit patterns of thought and previously conditioned responses ingrained in your brain that prompt you to focus on your own interests. However, you are no longer *in the flesh* as your old self was; you are now *in Christ*. But you can still choose to *walk according to the flesh* (Romans 8:12,13), complying with those old urges which were conditioned to respond independent of God.

Paul teaches in Romans 6:1-11 that what is true of the Lord Jesus Christ is true of us in terms of our relationship to sin because we are "in Christ." God the Father "made Him who knew no sin to be sin on our behalf, so that we might become the righteousness of God *in Him*" (2 Corinthians 5:21 emphasis added). When He died on the cross, our sins were placed on Him. But when He rose from the grave, there was no sin on Him. When He ascended to the Father, there was no sin on Him. And today, as He sits at the Father's right hand, there is no sin on Him. Since we are seated in the heavenlies in Christ, we too have died to sin.

When we find a promise in the Bible, the only appropriate response is to claim it. When we find a commandment in Scripture, we should obey it. But when the Bible tells us the truth about who we already are and what Christ has already done, there is only one appropriate response—and that is to believe it. I point this out only because the verses in Romans 6:1-10 are not commandments to be obeyed; they are truths to be believed. Christ has already died to sin, and because you are in Him, you also have died to sin. You cannot do for yourself what Christ has already done for you. Notice the use of the past tense in Romans 6:1-11 (emphasis added): "We who *died* to sin" (verse 2); "All of us who *have been baptized* into Christ Jesus *have been baptized* into His death" (verse 3); "We *have been buried* with Him" (verse 4); "Our old self *was crucified* with Him, that our body of sin might be done away with, that we should no longer be slaves to sin" (verse 6); "For he who *has died* is freed from sin" (verse 7); "If we *have died* with Christ, we believe that we shall also live with Him" (verse 8). The verbs in these verses are past tense, indicating what is already true about us. Our only response is to believe them.

Verse 11 tells us what to believe about our relationship with sin and our position in Christ: "Even so consider yourselves to be dead to sin, but alive to God in Christ Jesus." Paul uses a present tense verb because we are to continuously believe this truth. Believing it doesn't make it true. It is true whether we believe it or not. You may not feel dead to sin, but you are to *consider* it so because it *is* so. A wrong response to this verse is to ask, "What experience must I have in order for this to be true?" The only necessary experience is that of Christ on the cross, which has already happened; and the only way to appropriate that truth is to believe it. In a similar fashion, some Christians try to put the old self to death and can't do it. Why not? Because the old self has been crucified and is therefore already dead.

We don't make anything true by our experiences. We choose to believe what God says is true, then live accordingly by faith; and the truth works out in our experience. It is not what we do that determines who we are. It is who we are that determines what we do. I don't labor in the vineyard with the hope that God may one day accept me. God has already accepted me, and that is why I labor in the vineyard. I don't do the things I do with the hope that God may one day love me. God loves me, and that is why I do what I do.

Since we are alive in Christ and dead to sin, how can we as believers still be associated or connected with sin? Paul answers in Romans 6:12,13: "Do not let sin reign in your mortal body that you should obey its lusts, and do not go on presenting the members of your body to sin as instruments of unrighteousness; but present yourselves to God as those alive from the dead, and your members as instruments of righteousness to God." Sin is a sovereign master that demands service from its subjects. You are dead to sin, but you still have the capacity to serve it by putting your body at sin's disposal. It's up to you to choose whether you're going to let your body be used for sin or for righteousness. Satan, who is at the root of all sin, will take advantage of anyone who tries to remain neutral.

To illustrate, suppose your pastor asks to use your car to deliver food baskets to the needy, and a thief asks to use it to rob a bank. It's your car and you can choose to lend it however you want, for good or for evil. Which would you choose? There should be no question!

Your body is also yours to use to serve either God or sin and Satan, but the choice is up to you. That's why Paul wrote so insistently: "I urge you therefore, brethren, by the mercies of God, to present your bodies a living and holy sacrifice, acceptable to God, which is your spiritual service of worship" (Romans 12:1). Because of Christ's victory over sin, you are free to choose not to sin. It is your responsibility not to let sin reign in your mortal body.

Let's apply this to the struggle that many have with sexual sins. Could you commit a sexual sin without using your body as an instrument of unrighteousness? I don't know how you could. Therefore, if you commit a sexual sin, you have used your body as an instrument of unrighteousness, and you have thus allowed sin to reign in your mortal body. If we commit a sexual sin with another person, the two of us become one flesh according to 1 Corinthians 6:15,16. Simple confession will probably not resolve the conflict. We need to renounce that use of our bodies, give our bodies to God as living sacrifices, and then be transformed by the renewing of our minds. That is precisely the order of Romans 12:1,2. (For a complete discussion on how to overcome sexual strongholds, see my book *A Way of Escape,* published by Harvest House.)

You Can Be Free from the Power of Sin

"Not allowing sin to reign in my body sounds wonderful, Neil, but you don't know how hard my battle with sin is," you may be thinking. "I find myself doing what I shouldn't do and not doing what I should do. It's a constant struggle."

Believe me, I know how hard the battle is; I've faced it myself. So did the apostle Paul. In Romans 7:15-25 he is struggling with the same feelings of frustration. This passage clearly shows that the law is incapable of setting us free. I believe it also reveals what the struggle would be like if we allowed sin to reign in our mortal bodies. (Some believe this passage refers to Paul's preconversion experience. I disagree because every disposition of Paul's heart is toward God. The natural man does not "joyfully concur with the law of God" and "[confess] that the Law is good".)

I invite you to listen in as I walk through this passage with Dan, who is struggling to overcome the power of sin in his life:

> *Neil:* Dan, let's look at a passage of Scripture that seems to describe what you are presently experiencing. Romans 7:15 reads: "For that which I am doing, I do not understand; for I am not practicing what I would like to do, but I am doing the very thing I hate." Would you say that this verse describes you?
>
> *Dan:* Exactly! I desire to do what God says is right, but sometimes I find myself doing just the opposite.

Neil: You probably identify with verse 16 as well: "But if I do the very thing I do not wish to do, I agree with the Law, confessing that it is good." Dan, how many personalities or players are mentioned in this verse?

Dan: There is only one person, and it is clearly "I."

Neil: It is very defeating when we know what we want to do, but for some reason can't do it. How have you tried to resolve this in your own mind?

Dan: Sometimes I wonder if I'm even a Christian. It seems to work for others, but not for me. Often I wonder if the Christian life is even possible or if God is really here.

Neil: If you and God were the only players in this scenario, it would stand to reason that you would either blame God or yourself for your predicament. But now look at verse 17: "So now, no longer am I the one doing it, but sin which indwells me." How many players are there now, Dan?

Dan: Apparently two, but I don't understand.

Neil: Let's read verse 18 and see if we can make some sense out of it: "For I know that nothing good dwells in me, that is, in my flesh; for the wishing is present in me, but the doing of the good is not."

Dan: I learned that verse a long time ago. It has been easy to accept the fact that I'm no good.

Neil: That's not what it says, Dan. In fact, it says the opposite. *Whatever it is that is dwelling in you* is not *you.* If I had a wood splinter in my finger, it would be "nothing good" dwelling in me. But the "nothing good" isn't me; it's the splinter. It is also important to note that this "nothing good" is not even my flesh, but it is dwelling *in* my flesh. If we saw only ourselves in this struggle, it would be hopeless to live righteously. These passages are going to great lengths to tell us that there is a second party involved in our sin struggle whose nature is different from ours.

You see, Dan, when you and I were born, we were born under the *penalty* of sin. And we know that Satan and his emissaries are always working to keep us under that penalty. When God saved us, Satan lost that battle, but he didn't curl up his tail or pull in his fangs. He is now committed to keep us under the *power* of sin. We also know that he is going to work through the flesh, which remains after salvation.

Let's read on to see if we can learn more about how this battle is being waged: "For the good that I wish, I do not do; but I practice the very evil that I do not wish. But if I am doing the very thing I do not wish, I am no longer the one doing it, but sin which dwells in me. I find then the principle that evil is present in me, the one who wishes to do good" (verses 19-21).

Dan, can you identify from these passages the nature of that "nothing good" which indwells you?

Dan: Sure, it is clearly evil and sin. But isn't it just my own sin? When I sin I feel so guilty.

Neil: There is no question that you and I sin, but we are not "sin" as such. Evil is present in us, but we are not evil per se. This does not excuse us from sinning, however, because Paul wrote earlier that it is our responsibility not to let sin reign in our mortal bodies (Romans 6:12). Do you ever feel so defeated that you just want to strike out at someone or yourself?

Dan: Almost every day!

Neil: But when you cool down, do you again entertain thoughts that are in line with who you are in Christ?

Dan: Always, and then I feel terrible about lashing out.

Neil: Verse 22 explains this cycle: "For I joyfully concur with the law of God in the inner man." When we act out of character with who we really are, the Holy Spirit immediately brings conviction because of our union with God, and we often take it out on ourselves. But soon our true nature expresses itself again and we are drawn back to God. It's like the frustrated wife who announces that she has had it with her husband. She wants out and couldn't care less about the bum. But after she acknowledges her pain and expresses her emotions, she softens and says, "I really do love him, and I don't want a divorce. But I just don't see any other way out." That's the inner person, the true self, being expressed.

Verse 23 describes the nature of this battle with sin: "But I see a different law in the members of my body, waging war against the law of my mind, and making me a prisoner of the law of sin which is in my members." According to this passage, Dan, where is the battle being fought?

Dan: The battle appears to be in the mind.

Neil: That's precisely where the battle rages. Now if Satan can get you to think you are the only one in the battle, you will get down on either yourself or God when you sin. Let me put it this way: Suppose there is a talking dog on the other side of a closed door and the dog is saying, "Come on, let me in. You know you want to. Everybody is doing it. You will get away with it. After all, who would know?" So you open the door, and the dog comes in and clamps his teeth around your leg. On the other side of the door, the dog plays the role of the tempter, but once you let the dog in, he plays the role of the accuser. "You opened the door! You opened the door!" And what do you do?

Dan: I usually end up confessing because I feel so guilty. But in my struggle with sin, nobody has ever told me about this tempting and accusing dog! I usually end up beating on myself, but now I think I should beat on the dog.

Neil: I find that people eventually get tired of beating on themselves, so they walk away from God under a cloud of defeat and condemnation. On the other hand, just beating on the dog is not enough either. You were right to confess to God, which means you agreed with Him that you did open the door, but that is not enough. Confession is only the first step in repentance. Christians who only do that get caught up in the sin-confess-sin-confess-sin-confess cycle and eventually give up. You submitted to God when you agreed with Him that you opened the door; now you should resist the devil, and he will flee from you (James 4:7). Finally, go back and close the door and don't get suckered into opening it again. Repentance isn't complete until you have truly changed.

Paul expressed this feeling of unresolved conflict in verse 24: "Wretched man that I am! Who will set me free from the body of this death?" He's not saying, *"wicked or sinful* man that I am"; he's saying, *"miserable* man that I am." There is nobody more miserable than the person who knows what is right and wants to do what is right, but for some reason can't. He is defeated because he is in bondage. His attempts to do the right thing are met with defeat. He wonders, "Is there any victory?"

The answer starts to appear in verse 25: "Thanks be to God through Jesus Christ our Lord! So then, on the one hand I myself with my mind am serving the law of God, but on the other, with my flesh the law of sin." Now let's read Romans chapter eight and see how Paul overcomes the law of sin by the law of life in Christ Jesus.

Dan: I think I'm getting the picture. I've been feeling guilty for my inability to live the Christian life without really understanding how to live it. I have tried to overcome this sin by myself, and I have never really understood the battle for my mind.

Neil: You're on the right track. Condemning yourself won't help because there is no condemnation for those who are in Christ Jesus (Romans 8:1,2). Let's see if we can resolve your conflict with genuine repentance and faith in God. With your permission, I would like to walk you through these Steps to Freedom. Then we can talk about how to win that battle for your mind and see if we can learn to walk by faith in the power of the Holy Spirit. Then you will not carry out the desires of your flesh (Galatians 5:16).

You Can Win the Battle for Your Mind

H<small>E RESCUED US FROM THE</small> domain of darkness, and transferred us to the kingdom of His beloved Son, in whom we have redemption, the forgiveness of sins" (Colossians 1:13,14).

"If anyone is in Christ, he is a new creature; the old things passed away; behold, new things have come" (2 Corinthians 5:17). "You have died and your life is hidden with Christ in God" (Colossians 3:3).

"If those verses are true, then how come I still struggle with the same thoughts and feelings I did before I became a Christian?" I suspect that every honest Christian has asked that question or at least thought about it. There is a very logical reason why you still think, feel, and too often act as you did before you were born again.

During those early and formative years of your life, you had neither the presence of God in your life nor the knowledge of His ways. Consequently, you learned to live your life independent of God. This learned independence from God is a major characteristic of what Scripture calls the flesh. When you became a new creation in Christ, nobody pushed the delete button in your memory bank. Everything you learned

59

before Christ (and all the feelings that go with it) is still recorded in your memory. That is why Paul said, "Do not conform any longer to the pattern of this world, but be transformed by the renewing of your mind" (Romans 12:2 NIV). Even as believers we can still be conformed to this world by listening to the wrong programs or reading the wrong material.

Strongholds of Self-Defense

In our natural state, we learned many ways to cope with life or defend ourselves which were not always mentally and emotionally healthy. Psychologists refer to these unhealthy patterns of living as defense mechanisms, and they are certainly not congruent with Christianity. For instance, many people have learned to lie in order to protect themselves. Other common defense mechanisms include:

- denial (conscious or subconscious refusal to face the truth)
- fantasy (escaping from the real world)
- emotional insulation (withdrawing to avoid rejection)
- regression (reverting to less threatening times)
- displacement (taking out frustrations on others)
- projection (blaming others)
- rationalization (making excuses for poor behavior)

Defense mechanisms are similar to what Paul calls strongholds. He writes, "Though we walk in the flesh, we do not war according to the flesh, for the weapons of our warfare are not of the flesh, but divinely powerful for the destruction of fortresses. We are destroying speculations and every lofty thing raised up against the knowledge of God, and we are taking every thought captive to the obedience of Christ" (2 Corinthians 10:3-5).

Fortresses (or "strongholds" in the King James Version) are fleshly thought patterns that were programmed into your mind when you learned to live your life independently of

God. Your worldview was shaped by the environment you were raised in. But when you became a Christian, nobody pressed the "CLEAR" button. Your old fleshly habit patterns of thought weren't erased.

What was learned has to be unlearned. If you have been trained wrong, can you be retrained? If you believed a lie, can you renounce that lie and choose to believe the truth? Can your mind be reprogrammed? That is what repentance is: a change of mind. We are transformed by the renewing of our minds. We can be transformed because we have the mind of Christ within us and because the Holy Spirit will lead us into all truth. But the world system we were raised in and our independent flesh patterns are not the only enemies of our sanctification. Even though we are new creations in Christ, we still battle the world, the flesh, and the devil.

Satan's Schemes

Don't think that Satan is no longer interested in manipulating your mind in order to accomplish his purposes. Satan's perpetual aim is to infiltrate your thoughts with his thoughts and to promote his lie in the face of God's truth. He knows that if he can control your thoughts, he can control your life. That is why Paul continues in the present tense with the statement, "And we are taking every thought captive to the obedience of Christ" (2 Corinthians 10:5). In this passage the word "thought" is the Greek word *noema*. To understand this passage, I have found it helpful to see how Paul uses this word elsewhere in this second letter to the Corinthian church.

Paul instructs the church to forgive after the believers carry out church discipline. "One whom you forgive anything, I forgive also; for indeed what I have forgiven, if I have forgiven anything, I did it for your sakes in the presence of Christ, so that no advantage would be taken of us by Satan, for we are not ignorant of his schemes [*noema*]" (2 Corinthians 2:10,11). "Schemes" comes from the same root word, *noema.* Satan does take advantage of those who will not forgive. After helping thousands find their freedom in Christ, I can testify that unforgiveness is the major reason people remain in bondage to the past.

Concerning evangelism, Paul wrote, "If our gospel is veiled, it is veiled to those who are perishing, in whose case the god of this world has blinded the minds [*noema*] of the unbelieving so that they might not see the light of the gospel of the glory of Christ, who is the image of God" (2 Corinthians 4:3,4). How are we going to reach this world for Christ if Satan has blinded the minds of unbelievers? The answer is prayer.

Paul wrote, "I am afraid that, as the serpent deceived Eve by his craftiness, your minds [*noema*] will be led astray from the simplicity and purity of devotion to Christ" (2 Corinthians 11:3). My conversation with a 55-year-old undergraduate student illustrates how a mind could be led astray. Jay came into my office one day and said, "Dr. Anderson, I'm in trouble."

"What's the problem, Jay?"

"When I sit down to study, I get prickly sensations all over my body, my arms involuntarily rise, my vision gets blurry, and I can't concentrate. If this keeps up, I'm going to flunk all my classes. I can't even read my Bible."

"Tell me about your walk with God," I probed.

"I have a very close walk with God," Jay boasted.

"What do you mean by that?" I asked.

"Well, when I leave school at noon each day, I ask God where He wants me to go for lunch. I usually hear a thought like Burger King, so I go to Burger King. Then I ask Him what He wants me to eat. If the thought comes to order a Whopper, I order a Whopper."

"What about your church attendance?" I continued.

"I go every Sunday wherever God tells me to go. And for the last three Sundays, God has told me to go to a Mormon church."

Jay sincerely wanted to do what God wanted him to do, but he was being deceived. God was not directing him to a

Mormon church, and He is too good a nutritionist to suggest Whoppers all the time. Jay was listening to his own subjective thoughts as if they were God's voice instead of "taking every thought captive to the obedience of Christ" (2 Corinthians 10:5). In so doing he had opened himself up to Satan's activity in his life, with the result that his theological studies were being sabotaged. Those deceiving thoughts had convinced him that God was preparing him to be one of the two prophets mentioned in the book of Revelation who were slain in the streets of Jerusalem. He even tried to convince his college roommate that he was the other prophet!

Satan and Our Minds

Scripture clearly teaches that Satan is capable of putting thoughts into our minds. In the Old Testament "Satan rose up against Israel and incited David to take a census of Israel" (1 Chronicles 21:1 NIV). What is wrong with taking a census? Shouldn't David know how many troops he has to take into combat? This really reveals the subtle nature of Satan. He knew that David had a whole heart for God and would not willingly defy the Lord. The strategy was to get David to put his confidence in his resources rather than God's resources. This was the same David who wrote, "A horse is a false hope for victory" (Psalm 33:17). He knew the battle belonged to the Lord, but suddenly he had this "thought" to take a census against the protests of Joab, who knew it was sin. Tragically, 70,000 men of Israel fell as the result of David's sin.

How did Satan incite David? Did he talk audibly to David? No, these were David's thoughts. At least he thought they were. Therein lies the deception. These deceptive thoughts come first person singular in such a way that we think they're our own thoughts. I began to realize this years ago while helping others find their freedom in Christ. The battle for the mind involves more than just "self talk."

Judas also listened to the devil. "During supper, the devil having already put into the heart of Judas Iscariot, the son of Simon, to betray him" (John 13:2). We may be tempted to dismiss this as just a bad decision prompted by the flesh, but Scripture clearly says that the origin of those thoughts was Satan. When Judas realized what he had done, he took his own life. "The thief comes only to steal and kill and destroy" (John 10:10).

In the early church, Satan filled the heart of Ananias to lie to the Holy Spirit (Acts 5:3). F. F. Bruce, the New Testament scholar, says that Ananias was a believer.[1] Ernest Haenchen wrote that he was "a Jewish Christian" and commented: "Satan has filled his heart. Ananias has lied to the Holy Spirit, inasmuch as the Spirit is present in Peter (and in the community). Hence in the last resort it is not simply two men who confront one another, but in them the Holy Spirit and Satan, whose instruments they are."[2]

Martin Luther wrote, "The Devil throws hideous thoughts into the soul—hatred of God, blasphemy, and despair." Concerning himself he reported, "When I awake at night, the Devil tarries not to seek me out. He disputes with me and makes me give birth to all kinds of strange thoughts. I think that often the Devil, solely to torment and vex me, wakes me up while I am actually sleeping peacefully. My night time combats are much harder for me than in the day. The Devil understands how to produce arguments that exasperate me. Sometimes he has produced such as to make me doubt whether or not there is a God."[3] (For other references to the devil putting thoughts into the minds of noted saints, see the book *The Life of the Devil*.[4])

David Powlison, though opposed to the view that demons can invade believers, acknowledges that Satan can put thoughts into one's mind. " 'Voices' in the mind are not uncommon: blasphemous mockeries, spurts of temptation to wallow in vile fantasy or behavior, persuasive lines of unbelief. Classic spiritual warfare interprets these as coming from the evil one."[5] Thomas Brooks in his discussion of Satan's devices continually speaks of Satan presenting thoughts to the soul of believers.[6]

"Not Against Flesh and Blood"

I have counseled hundreds of believers who are struggling with their thought life. Some have difficulty concentrating and reading their Bible, while others actually hear "voices" or struggle with accusing and condemning thoughts. With few exceptions these struggles have proven to be a spiritual battle for their minds. This shouldn't surprise us since we have been warned in 1 Timothy 4:1 (NIV): "The Spirit clearly says that in later times some will abandon the faith and follow deceiving spirits and things taught by demons."

Why don't we as believers in Christ take account of this? For one reason, I can't read your mind, and you can't read my mind. So we really don't have any idea what is going on in the minds of other people unless they have the courage to share with us. In many cases they won't, because in our society many people will assume they are mentally ill. Consequently, they will tell you about their negative experiences; but only with the right person will they dare share what is going on inside. Are they mentally ill, or is there a battle going on for their mind? If we are "ignorant of Satan's schemes," we can only come to the conclusion, "Any problem in the mind must either be a chemical imbalance or a flesh pattern."

Psychologists and psychiatrists routinely see patients who are hearing voices: chemical imbalance is the standard diagnosis. I believe our body chemistry can get out of balance and cause discomfort and hormonal problems can throw our systems off. But I also believe that other legitimate questions need to be asked, such as, "How can a chemical produce a personal thought?" and "How can our neurotransmitters involuntarily and randomly fire in such a way that they create thoughts that we are opposed to thinking?" Is there a natural explanation? We have to remain open to any legitimate answers and explanations, but I don't think we will have a comprehensive answer unless we take into account the reality of the spiritual world.

When people say they are hearing voices, what are they actually hearing? The only way we can physically hear with our ears is to have a sound source. Sound waves move from the source through the medium of air and strike our eardrums, which send a signal to our brains. That is how we physically hear. But "voices" that people hear or the "thoughts" that they struggle with are not coming from that kind of source if others around them are not hearing what they hear.

In a similar fashion, when people say they see things (that others don't), what are they actually seeing? The only way that we can naturally see something is to have a light source reflecting from a material object to our eyes, which then send a signal to our brain. Satan and his demons are spiritual beings; they do not have material substance, so we cannot see them or any spiritual being with our natural eyes, nor hear them with our ears. "Our struggle is not against *flesh and blood*, but against the rulers, against the authorities, against the powers of this dark world and against the spiritual forces of evil in the heavenly realms" (Ephesians 6:12 NIV).

Brain vs. Mind

There is much we don't know about mental functioning, but we do know that there is a fundamental difference between our brains and our minds. Our brains are organic matter. When we die physically, we are separate from our bodies, and our brain returns to dust. At that moment we will be absent from our bodies and present with the Lord. But we won't be mindless, because the mind is a part of the soul.

Let me draw an analogy. Our ability to think is similar to how a computer functions. Both involve two separate components: one is the hardware, which is the actual physical computer (the brain); the other is the software (the mind), which programs the hardware. Since the software is nonphysical, if it is removed from the hardware, the hardware still weighs the same. Likewise, if the spirit is removed from the body, the body also remains the same weight. A computer is totally worthless without the software, but neither will the software work if the hardware shuts down.

Our society assumes if something is not functioning right between the ears it must be a hardware problem. On the contrary, I don't believe the primary problem is with the hardware; I think the primary problem is in the software. If a person does have some type of organic brain syndrome, such as Alzheimer's disease, or a congenital condition, such as Down's syndrome, the brain won't function very well. Severe brain damage, however, is relatively rare, and there is little that can be done about it. Romans 12:1,2 says we are to submit our bodies to God (which includes our brain) and be transformed by the renewing of our minds.

After hearing my presentation on this subject, a dear lady wanted some clarification. She said, "I recently visited my daughter on the mission field, and I contracted malaria. I got so sick that I almost died. At the height of my fever, I started to hallucinate. Are you telling me that those hallucinations were demonic?"

"What were you hallucinating about?" I asked.

"Mostly about Pluto, Mickey Mouse, Donald Duck, and Daisy," she replied.

I couldn't help but chuckle. "Did you stop at Disneyland on your way to the mission field?" I inquired.

She responded, "Well yes, I did. How did you know?"

There was certainly nothing demonic about her experience. Her visit to Disneyland was fresh on her mind. When we go to sleep or slip into a coma, our physical brains continue to function, but there are "no hands on the keyboard." If you are still mentally active and pounding away on the keyboard of your mind, you are not asleep. You go to sleep when you stop thinking. But while you are sleeping, your brain will continue to function and will randomly access whatever has been stored in your memory. To illustrate, consider the content of your dreams. Don't they almost always relate to people you know, things you have seen, or places you have been? The stories in your dreams can be rather creative, but the people and places have already been programmed into your memory. For instance, suppose a child watches a horror movie, then goes to sleep and has a nightmare. Chances are the players in the nightmare will be the same ones as in the movie.

But when someone has grotesque nightmares which cannot be traced to something previously seen or heard, then I would say the dream is demonic. When we take people through the Steps to Freedom in Christ, those kind of nightmares stop.

The Battle Is Real

We need to expose this spiritual battle for our minds for what it is, so that we can have a comprehensive answer for those who experience it. Let me illustrate why. What typically happens when frightened children come into their parents' bedroom and say they saw or heard something in their room? The parent would probably go into the child's room, look in the closet or under the bed and say, "There is nothing in your room, honey—now go back to sleep!" If you are an adult, and you saw something in *your* room, would *you* just forget about it and go back to sleep? "But I looked in the room. There was nothing there," you respond. And you would be correct. There never was anything in the room that could be observed by our natural senses. "Then it's not real," says the skeptic. Oh yes, it is! What your child saw or heard was in his or her *mind,* and it was *very real.*

I can't explain the means by which people "pay attention to deceitful spirits." Neither do I know how the devil is able to present himself to our minds, but I don't have to know how he does it in order to believe what Scripture clearly teaches. The spiritual battle for our minds does not operate according to the laws of nature, which we can comprehend. There are no physical barriers that can confine or restrict the movements of Satan. The frightened face of a child testifies that the battle is real. Why not respond to your child as follows?

"Honey, I believe you saw or heard something. I didn't hear or see anything, so that helps me understand. You may be under a spiritual attack, or you could be having bad memories of a movie you saw. Sometimes I can't tell the difference between what is real and a dream I just had. Before I pray for your protection, I want you to know that Jesus is much bigger and more powerful than anything you see or hear that frightens you. The Bible teaches us that greater is Jesus who is living in us than any monsters in the world. Because Jesus is always with us, we can tell whatever it is that is frightening us to leave in Jesus' name. The Bible tells us to submit to God and resist the devil, and he will flee from us. Can you do that, honey? Do you have any questions? Then let's pray together."

Much of what is being passed off today as mental illness is nothing more than a battle for our minds. Proverbs 23:7 says, "As he thinks within himself, so he is." In other words, you don't do anything without first thinking it. All behavior is the product of what we choose to think or believe. We can't see what people think. We can only observe what they do. Trying to change behavior, without changing what we believe and therefore think, will never produce any lasting results.

Since we can't read another person's mind, we have to learn to ask the right questions. Five-year-old Danny was sent to the office of his Christian school for hurting several other children on the playground. He had been acting aggressively toward others and was restless in class. His teacher said, "I'm puzzled by his recent behavior—it isn't like Danny to act this way!" Danny's mother was a teacher at the school. When she asked her son about Jesus, he covered his ears and shouted, "I hate Jesus!" Then he grasped his mother and laughed in a hideous voice!

We asked Danny whether he ever heard voices talking to him in his head. He looked relieved at the question and volunteered that voices were shouting at him on the playground to hurt other kids. The thoughts were so loud that the only way to quiet them was to obey, even though he knew he would get into trouble. We told Danny that he didn't have to listen to the voices anymore. We led Danny through the children's version of the Steps to Freedom described later in this book, having him pray the prayers after us. When we were done, we asked him how he felt. A big smile came onto his face, and with a sigh of relief he said, "Much better!" His teacher noticed new calmness in him the next day—as though he were a different child. He has not repeated his aggressive behavior in school.

A committed Christian couple adopted a young boy and received him into their home with open arms. Their little innocent baby turned into a monster before he was five. Their home was in turmoil when I was asked to talk to him. After some friendly chatting, I asked him if it ever seemed like someone was talking to him in his head.

"Yes," he said, "all the time."

"What are they saying?"

"They're telling me that I'm no good."

I then asked him if he had ever invited Jesus into his life. He replied, "Yes, but I didn't mean it."

I told him if he really did ask Jesus to come into his life, he could tell those voices to leave him. Realizing that, he gave his heart to Christ.

Another husband and wife heard thumping on the wall of their son's room. He had taken a pair of scissors and stabbed the wall several times. They never caught him doing it nor found the scissors. Then the child began to cut up every piece of clothing in the house. Again they never actually caught their son doing it. Huge medical and counseling bills piled up as they desperately tried to find a solution. Finally the parents were introduced to our material and began to consider that this might possibly be a spiritual problem. So they asked their son if he ever had thoughts telling him to do what he was doing. He said, "Yes, and if I didn't do what they told me to do, they said they would kill you (the father)!" The little boy thought he was saving his father's life!

The need to distinguish between organic mental illness and a spiritual battle for your mind is graphically illustrated in this testimony:

> I wanted to thank you for showing me how to be free of something I always suspected was spiritual, but I was never quite sure about it. For years, ever since I was a teenager (I am now 36), I had these "voices" in my head. There were four in particular, and sometimes what seemed like loud choruses of them. When the subject of schizophrenia would come up on television or in a magazine I would think to myself, "I know I am not schizophrenic, but what is this in my head???"

> I was tortured, mocked, and jeered. Every single thought I had was second-guessed, and consequently I had zero self-esteem. I often wished the voices would be quiet, and I always wondered if other people heard voices as well and if it was "common."

> When I started to learn from you about taking every thought captive to the obedience of Christ, and when I read about other people's experiences with these voices, I came to recognize them for what they were, and I was able to make them leave.

> This was an amazing and beautiful thing—to be fully quiet in my mind, after so many years of torment. I do not need to explain further all the wonderful things that come with this freedom of the mind—it is a blessing you seem to know well.

Taking Every Thought Captive

How do we know whether those negative, lying, and condemning thoughts are from the evil one or are just our own flesh patterns? In one sense it doesn't make any difference. We are to take *every* thought captive to the obedience of Christ; that is, <u>if it isn't true, don't believe it</u>. But you will know such thoughts did not originate from you if you work through the Steps to Freedom and those thoughts are no longer there. Flesh patterns don't just leave. They are slowly replaced or overcome as we renew our minds. Paul says we are not to be anxious (double-minded) about anything. Rather we are to turn to God in prayer, "and the peace of God, which surpasses all comprehension, will guard your hearts and your minds [*noema*] in Christ Jesus" (Philippians 4:7). The next verse says we are to let our minds dwell on those things which are true, pure, lovely, and right.

Our relationship with God is personal, and as in any relationship there are certain issues that have to be resolved in order for the relationship to work. We can't expect God to bless us if we are living in open rebellion against Him. "Rebellion is like the sin of divination, and arrogance like the evil of idolatry" (1 Samuel 15:23 NIV). If we are proud, God is opposed to us (James 4:6). If we are bitter and unwilling to forgive, God will turn us over to the torturers (Matthew 18: 34). These issues have to be resolved first, since only God can bind up the brokenhearted and set the captive free.

Perhaps a testimony from a veteran missionary will illustrate this point. She was seeing her psychiatrist, psychologist, and pastor once a week just to hold her life together. The next step was hospitalization. I spent one Friday afternoon with her, and two-and-a-half months later, I received this letter.

> I've been wanting to write to you for some time, but I've waited this long to confirm to myself that this is truly "for reals" (as my four-year-old daughter says). I'd like to share an entry from my journal, which I wrote two days after our meeting.

"Since Friday afternoon I have felt like a different person. The fits of rage and anger are gone. My spirit is so calm and full of joy. I wake up singing praise to God in my heart.

"That edge of tension and irritation is gone. I feel so free. The Bible has been really exciting and stimulating and more understandable than ever before. There was nothing 'dramatic' that happened during the session on Friday, yet I know in the deepest part of my being that something has changed. I am no longer bound by accusations, doubts, and thoughts of suicide or murder, or other harm that come straight from hell into my head. There is a serenity in my mind and spirit, a clarity of consciousness that is profound.

"I've been set free!

"I'm excited and expectant about my future now. I know I'll be growing spiritually again and will be developing in other ways as well. I look forward happily to the discovery of the person God has created and redeemed me to be, as well as the transformation of my marriage.

"It is so wonderful to have joy after so long a darkness."

It's been two-and-a-half months since I wrote that, and I'm firmly convinced of the significant benefits of finding freedom in Christ. I'd been in therapy for several months, and while I was making progress, there is no comparison with the steps I'm able to make now. My ability to "process" things has increased manyfold. Not only is my spirit more serene, my head is actually clearer! It's easier to make connections and integrate things now. It seems like everything is easier to understand now.

My relationship with God has changed significantly. For eight years I felt that He was distant from me. Shortly before

I met you, I was desperately crying out to Him to set me free —to release me from this bondage I was in. I wanted so badly to meet with Him again, to know His presence was with me again. I needed to know Him as friend, as companion, not as the distant authority figure He had become in my mind and experience. Since that day two-and-a-half months ago, I have seen my trust in Him grow. I've seen my ability to be honest with Him increase greatly. I really have been experiencing that spiritual growth I'd anticipated in my journal. It's great!

Confronting the Rebel Prince

Mary was a 26-year-old flower child from the 1960s. She was a Christian and a university graduate, but she had severe mental and emotional problems that developed after her father divorced her mother. Within a period of five years, Mary had been institutionalized three times and was diagnosed paranoid schizophrenic. After about three weeks of counseling, Mary finally told me about her struggle with snakes.

"What about the snakes?" I asked.

"They crawl on me at night when I'm in bed," she confessed.

"What do you do when the snakes come?"

"I run in to my mother. But they always come back when I'm alone."

"Why don't you try something different next time?" I continued. "When you're in bed and the snakes come, say out loud, 'In the name of Christ I command you to leave me.' "

"I couldn't do that," Mary protested. "I'm not mature or strong enough."

"It's not a matter of your maturity; it's a matter of your position in Christ. You have as much right to submit to God and resist the devil as I do."

Mary squirmed at the prospect, and I could tell she was afraid. She finally agreed to at least try, since she had nothing to lose. The next week when Mary walked in she said, "The snakes are gone!"

"Great! Why didn't you tell me about them sooner?"

"Because I was afraid you would get them too."

Thinking I would get them was just another part of the deception. If her problem had been neurological, then taking authority over the snakes in Jesus' name wouldn't have worked. But in Mary's case the problem was spiritual, and five years of hospitalization and chemical treatment hadn't worked.

Before we discuss the reality and present activity of Satan and his demons, you need to understand the spiritual power and authority you and every believer have in Christ over the kingdom of darkness.

Carrying Jesus' Badge of Authority

When Jesus was training His disciples, "He called the twelve together, and gave them power and authority over all the demons and to heal diseases. And He sent them out to proclaim the kingdom of God and to perform healing" (Luke 9:1,2). Jesus knew when His disciples began preaching the kingdom of God, there would be demonic opposition. So He specifically gave them power and authority over demons.

Then Jesus sent out 70 of His followers on a similar mission, and they "returned with joy, saying, 'Lord, even the demons are subject to us in Your name' " (Luke 10:17). These missionaries confronted the kingdom of darkness and discovered that demons were subject to them in the name of Jesus. Perhaps they started out on their mission with fear and apprehension, but they came back astonished at the victory they experienced over evil spirits.

But Jesus quickly corrected any wrong conclusions they may have drawn. "I have given you authority to tread on serpents and scorpions, and over all the power of the enemy, and nothing will injure you. Nevertheless do not rejoice in this, that the spirits are subject to you, but rejoice that your names are recorded in heaven" (Luke 10:19,20). The words "serpents" and "scorpions" do not refer to snakes and bugs, because reptiles and insects are not our enemies. Rather, Jesus was metaphorically referring to the devil and his angels. I think He was saying, "Don't rejoice that in the naming of Jesus you have authority over demons. Rejoice in the fact that your name is written in the Lamb's Book of Life. Don't be demon-centered, be Christ-centered. Don't be concerned about the enemy and your authority over him: Be concerned about who you are, and don't let the devil set the agenda." This is consistent with the servant leadership He modeled and in which He would later instruct them.

Understanding the power and authority believers have over the kingdom of darkness could lead some to abuse their position in Christ and step out on their own and "get thrashed." We have no spiritual power or authority apart from our identity and position in Christ. *Who we are* must always take precedence over *what we do;* and we cannot accomplish anything apart from Christ. Even Jesus was tempted by the devil to use His divine attributes independent of His identity in His heavenly Father.

The Right and the Ability to Rule

Jesus gave His disciples both *authority* and *power* over demons. What's the difference? Authority is the *right* to rule; it is based on a legal position. A policeman has the right to stop traffic at an intersection because he has been commissioned by the state which has civil authority (Romans 13:1-5). Jesus said, "All authority has been given to Me in heaven and on earth. Go therefore and make disciples of all the nations" (Matthew 28:18,19). Therefore, Satan has no authority in heaven or on earth.

Power is the *ability* to rule. A policeman may have the authority to stop traffic, but he doesn't have the physical ability to do so. However, you would be able to stop traffic if you moved a 20-foot-square cement block into the middle of the intersection, because it has the power even though you may lack the authority. Believers have both the authority to do God's will because of their position in Christ, and the power to do God's will as long as they walk by the Spirit. "Finally, be strong in the Lord, and in the strength of His might" (Ephesians 6:10).

No good manager would delegate *responsibility* without the *authority* to carry out his directions. Nor would he send his workers on an assignment without enabling them to do it. Even secular leaders talk about the need to empower their employees. Jesus charged His disciples with the *responsibility* to proclaim the kingdom of God. Had He not also given them *authority* and *power* over the kingdom of darkness, the demons would have scoffed at their feeble attempts and sent them running for cover (as they did the seven sons of Sceva in Acts 19).

You may think, as Mary did, that you're not mature enough to resist demonic interference in your life. In the flesh you don't have the ability to resist Satan and his demons, but *in Christ you do*. The Israelites looked at Goliath fearfully and said, "We can't fight him." But young David looked at Goliath and said, "Who is this uncircumcised Philistine, that he should taunt the armies of the living God?" (1 Samuel 17:26), then "took him out" with his slingshot. The army saw Goliath in relation to themselves and trembled; David saw Goliath in relation to God and triumphed. When you encounter the spiritual enemies of your soul, remember: You plus Jesus equal a majority.

People sometimes assume I have some degree of success helping others find their freedom in Christ because of my education, calling, or strength of personality. That's not true at all. A little child and an aged grandmother in Christ have the same authority in the spiritual world that I do. We are to "glory in Christ Jesus and put no confidence in the flesh" (Philippians 3:3).

Pulling Rank

The disciples said, "the demons are subject to us in Your name" (Luke 10:17). "Subject" (*hupotasso* in Greek) is a military term meaning "to arrange under." It pictures a group of soldiers snapping to attention and following precisely the orders of their commanding officer. That is how we should all respond to our Lord, and "every person is to be in subjection to the governing authorities" (Romans 13:1). God is saying to His children, "For your spiritual protection, get in rank and follow Me."

Spiritually defeated Christians don't seem to understand this, however. They see God and His kingdom on one side and Satan and his kingdom on the other side as equal and opposite, and they see themselves stuck in the middle between the two, like the rope in a tug-of-war. On some days God seems to be winning, and on other days the devil appears to have the upper hand. And they don't seem to have anything to say about who wins the battle.

The 70 disciples came back from their mission with a new perspective, a true perspective. Spiritual authority is not a tug-of-war on a horizontal plane; it is a vertical chain of command. Jesus Christ has all authority in heaven and on earth (Matthew 28:18); He's at the top of the chain of command. He has given His authority and power to His servants to be exercised in His name (Luke 10:17); we're under His authority, but we share it for the purpose of doing His will. And Satan and his demons? They're at the bottom, subject to the authority Christ has invested in us. They have no more right to rule your life than a buck private has to order a general to clean the latrine.

Why, then, does the kingdom of darkness exert such negative influence in the world and in the lives of Christians? Because Satan has deceived the whole world, and therefore the whole world lies in the power of the evil one (1 John 5:19). Satan is not an equal power with God; he is a disarmed and defeated foe (Colossians 2:15). But if he can deceive you into believing that he has more power and authority than you do, you will live as if he does! You have been given authority over the kingdom of darkness, but if you don't believe it and exercise it, it's as if you didn't have it.

I experienced this truth during a counseling session with a severely demonized woman. During the session, the woman—who was big and husky—suddenly rose from her chair and walked toward me with a menacing look. At that point I was glad that the weapons of our warfare are not of the flesh, because I would have had a difficult time defending myself against a demonized person of her size.

Instead, I spoke these words based on 1 John 5:18—not to the woman, because she was blanked out at the time, but to the evil spirit controlling her: "I'm a child of God, and the evil one can't touch me. Sit down right now." She stopped in her tracks and returned to her chair. Had I not exercised my authority in Christ, fear would have controlled me, and some kind of power encounter would have ensued. But by taking a stand in Christ's name, I neutralized the demon's hollow show of power and was able to minister to the woman.

It is important to realize that you don't "shout out the devil." Authority doesn't increase with volume. You will not be effective by shouting or screaming at the devil. It is no different than with parental authority. If you are shouting and screaming at your children in order to control their behavior, you are not properly exercising your God-given authority; you are undermining it. You are operating in the flesh.

The episode with the woman was merely a scare tactic from a demon that was hoping I would respond in fear. Fear of anything (other than the fear of God) is mutually exclusive to faith in God. When Satan tries to incite fear, we are to maintain our position in Christ and exhibit the fruit of the Spirit, which includes self-control (Galatians 5:23).

The Riches of Our Inheritance in Christ

We may have an even greater advantage in spiritual warfare than the first disciples did. They were *with* Christ (Mark 3:14,15), but we are *in* Christ. That was Paul's great news in the opening lines of his letter to the church at Ephesus. Notice how many times he mentions our position in Christ (emphasis added):

> Blessed be the God and Father of our Lord Jesus Christ, who has blessed us with every spiritual blessing in the heavenly places *in Christ,* just as He chose us *in Him* before the foundation of the world (verses 3,4)...To the praise of the glory of His grace, which He freely bestowed on us *in the Beloved. In Him* we have redemption through His blood (verses 6,7)...He made known to us the mystery of His will, according to His kind intention which He purposed *in Him* with a view to an administration suitable to the fullness of times, that is, the summing up of all things in Christ (verses 9,10)...*In Him* also we have obtained an inheritance...to the end that we who were the first to hope *in Christ* should be to the praise of His glory. *In Him,* you also, after listening to the message of truth, the gospel of your salvation- having also believed, you were sealed *in Him* with the Holy Spirit of promise (verses 10-13).

Paul wanted to make sure that nobody missed his point. He tells us ten times in the first 13 verses that we are "in Christ."

Everything we have is the result of our intimate, personal relationship with the resurrected Christ and His indwelling Spirit. The problem is, we don't see it. So Paul continues:

> I pray that the eyes of your heart may be enlightened, so that you may know what is the hope of His calling, what are the riches of the glory of His inheritance in the saints, and what is the surpassing greatness of His power toward us who believe. These are in accordance with the working of the strength of His might which He brought about in Christ, when He raised Him from the dead, and seated Him at His right hand in heavenly places (Ephesians 1:18-20).

When we don't understand our spiritual heritage, we don't experience the freedom and fruitfulness which is intrinsic to our position in Christ. As long as we fail to perceive our position in Christ and our authority over the kingdom of darkness and authority to do His will, we will fail to carry out our delegated responsibility.

The Depth and Breadth of Authority

In Ephesians 1:19-23, Paul explains the source of Christ's authority as the same power that raised Him from the dead and seated Him at the Father's right hand. That power source is so dynamic that Paul used four different Greek words in verse 19 to describe it: "power" (*dunameos*), "working" (*energeian*), "strength" (*kratous*), and "might" (*ischuos*). Behind the resurrection of the Lord Jesus Christ lies the mightiest work of power recorded in the Word of God. And the same power that raised Christ from the dead and defeated Satan is the power available to us as believers.

Paul also wants to open our eyes to the expansive scope of Christ's authority, which is "far above all rule and authority and power and dominion, and every name that is named, not only in this age, but also in the one to come" (Ephesians

1:21). Think about the most powerful and influential political or military leaders in the world, good and bad. Imagine the most feared terrorists, crime kingpins, and drug barons. Think about the notorious figures of the past and present who have blighted society with their diabolical ways. Think about Satan and all the powers of darkness marshaled under his command. Jesus' authority is not only above all these human and spiritual authorities past, present, and future, but He is *far* above them.

Authority Conferred

Paul is saying that Christ's power and authority has been conferred on "us who believe" (Ephesians 1:19). Paul has already explained that God's supreme act of power and authority occurred when He raised Christ from the dead and seated Him in the heavenlies far above all other authorities (1:19-21). After parenthetically alluding to the sinful state in which we existed prior to salvation (2:1-3), Paul continues his central theme of Christ's authority as it relates to us: "God, being rich in mercy, because of His great love with which He loved us, even when we were dead in our transgressions, made us alive together with Christ (by grace you have been saved), and raised us up with Him, and seated us with Him in the heavenly places, in Christ Jesus" (2:4-6).

Paul wants us to see that when Christ was raised from the dead (1:20), those of us who have believed in Him were also resurrected from our condition of spiritual death and made alive "together with Christ" (2:5,6). The resurrection of Christ from the tomb and our resurrection from spiritual death happened at the same time. It's only logical that the head (Christ) and the body (His church) should be raised together.

Furthermore, when God seated Christ at His right hand and conferred on Him all authority (Ephesians 1:20,21), He also seated us at His right hand (2:6) because we are "together with Christ" (2:5). The moment you receive

Christ, you are seated with Him in the heavenlies. Your identity as a child of God and your authority over spiritual powers are not things you *are* receiving or *will* receive at some time in the future; you have them right now. You are a spiritually alive child of God *right now*. You are seated in the heavenlies with Christ *right now*. You have the power and authority over the kingdom of darkness and to do His will *right now*.

Paul also related this empowerment and life-changing truth in his letter to the Colossians: "In Him [Christ] you have been made complete, and He is the head over all rule and authority" (Colossians 2:10). Notice the verb tense: We *have been* made complete. When? At the death, resurrection, and ascension of Jesus Christ. And since Christ is the God-appointed head over all rule and authority, and since we are seated with Him in the heavenlies, we have the power and authority to do His will.

Paul mentioned something else in Colossians which we need to know: "He...disarmed the rulers and authorities [and] made a public display of them, having triumphed over them through Him" (2:15). Not only were you made alive in Christ, but Satan was disarmed and defeated 2000 years ago. His defeat is not pending, nor is it future; it has already happened. It is not our responsibility to defeat the devil. Jesus has already done that.

If Satan is already disarmed, why don't we experience more victory in our lives? Because the father of lies has deceived the whole world. Satan roams around like a hungry lion, looking and sounding ferocious. In reality his fangs have been removed and he has been declawed, but if he can deceive you into believing that he can chew you up and spit you out, you will live as though he can.

What is the ultimate purpose of this conferring of authority? Paul answers in Ephesians 3:8-12:

> To me, the very least of all saints, this grace was given, to preach to the Gentiles the unfathomable riches of Christ, and to bring to light what is the administration of the mystery which for ages has been hidden in God, who created all things; in order that the manifold wisdom of God might now be made known through the church to the rulers and authorities in the heavenly places. This was in accordance with the eternal purpose which He carried out in Christ Jesus our Lord, in whom we have boldness and confident access through faith in Him.

It is the eternal purpose of God to make His wisdom known through the church to "the rulers and authorities in heavenly places." When it comes to fulfilling this purpose, how is the church doing? Some are still asking, "What rulers and authorities?" How are we going to fulfill our calling in the world if we don't believe what God says about the kingdom of darkness? Some are pleading, "O God, please help us! The devil is roaring at us!" And God responds, "I've done all I'm going to do. I defeated and disarmed Satan at the cross. I conferred all authority on you in Christ. Now open your eyes. Realize who you are and start living accordingly."

Qualified for Kingdom Work

I believe there are four qualifications for living in the authority and power of Christ:

1. *Belief.* Paul talks about "His power toward us who *believe*" (Ephesians 1:19 emphasis added). Imagine a rookie traffic cop approaching a busy intersection to direct traffic for the first time. They told him at the academy that all he had to do was step into the street and hold up his hand and the cars would stop, but he's insecure. He stands on the curb, tweets his whistle weakly, and sort of waves at an oncoming car, which just roars by him. His authority is diminished by his lack of confidence.

Now imagine a seasoned officer doing the same thing. He sizes up the situation, steps into the street carefully but confidently, blows his whistle, and stretches out his hand—and the cars stop. There's no doubt in his mind that he's in control in that intersection, because he has the authority to direct traffic.

In the spiritual realm, if you don't believe you have Christ's authority over the kingdom of darkness, you're not likely to exercise it. As I will explain in later chapters, we have learned how to help people without losing control. A few years back I was helping a young lady who was having a hard time staying focused. Suddenly her countenance changed, and another voice said, "Who the (bleep) do you think you are?" I calmly said, "I'm a child of God, and you have no authority to speak." Immediately the young lady came back to her right mind, and we finished the session. It pays to know who you are!

2. *Humility.* Humility is confidence properly placed. Humility is like meekness, which in the case of Christ was great strength under great control. In exercising our authority, humility is placing confidence in Christ, the source of our authority, instead of in ourselves. Like Paul, we "glory in Christ Jesus and put no confidence in the flesh" (Philippians 3:3). Jesus didn't shrink back from exercising His authority, but He showed tremendous humility because He did everything according to what His Father told Him to do.

Pride says, "I resisted the devil all by myself." False humility says, "God resisted the devil; I did nothing." Humility says, "I assumed my responsibility to resist the devil by the grace of God." Apart from Christ we can do *nothing* (John 15:5), but that doesn't mean we're not supposed to do *something*. We humbly exercise His authority—in His strength and in His name.

3. *Boldness.* It is the mark of a Spirit-filled Christian to be strong and courageous. Joshua was challenged four times to be strong and courageous (Joshua 1:6,7,9,18). "The wicked flee when no one is pursuing, but the righteous are bold as a

lion" (Proverbs 28:1). When the early church prayed about their mission of sharing the gospel in Jerusalem, "the place where they had gathered together was shaken, and they were all filled with the Holy Spirit and began to speak the word of God with boldness" (Acts 4:31). Spirit-inspired boldness is behind every successful advance in the church. "God has not given us a spirit of timidity, but of power and love and discipline" (2 Timothy 1:7).

We are living in an age of anxiety. If you are struggling with any kind of anxiety disorder, I would encourage you to read the book which I coauthored with my colleague Rich Miller, *Freedom from Fear* (Harvest House). The fear of God is not only the beginning of wisdom, it is the one fear that can expel all others. The opposite of boldness is cowardice, fear, and unbelief. Notice what God thinks about these characteristics:

> I am the Alpha and Omega, the beginning and the end. I will give to the one who thirsts from the spring of the water of life without cost. He who overcomes shall inherit these things, and I will be his God and he will be My son. But for the cowardly and unbelieving and abominable and murderers and immoral persons and sorcerers and idolaters and all liars, their part will be in the lake that burns with fire and brimstone, which is the second death (Revelation 21:6-8).

Most of us would not see the cowardly and unbelieving lined up at the lake of fire alongside murderers, sorcerers, and idolaters! Obviously God is not pleased with a cowardly church that limps along in unbelief.

After I had conducted a major conference in the Philippines, a missionary shared her testimony with me. She had been warned about going to a certain village because a "quack" doctor was too powerful for her and the whole village was under his spell. She had believed it, but after the conference she knew it was just a lie. She went to the village and actually led this deceived man to Christ, and within six months the whole village was Christian.

4. *Dependence*. The authority we're talking about is not an independent authority. We have the authority to do God's will, nothing more and nothing less. We don't charge out on our own initiative like some kind of evangelical ghostbusters to hunt down the devil and engage him in combat. God's primary call is for each of us to focus on the ministry of the kingdom: loving, caring, preaching, teaching, praying, and so on. However, when demonic powers challenge us in the course of our pursuing this ministry, we deal with them on the basis of our authority in Christ and our dependence on Him. Then we carry on with our primary task.

Nor is the spiritual authority of the believer an authority to be exercised over other believers. We are to be "subject to one another in the fear of Christ" (Ephesians 5:21). There is a God-established authority on earth which governs the civil and social structures of government, work, home, and church (Romans 13:1-7). It is critically important that we submit to these governing authorities unless they exceed their God-given authority or command us to do something which would be sinful. Then we must obey God rather than man.

Free from Fear

When we boldly and humbly exercise the authority that Christ has conferred upon us over the spiritual realm, we experience the freedom we all have in Christ. After the first edition of this book was published, I received the following testimony:

> For the past 35 years, I have lived from one surge of adrenaline to the next. My entire life has been gripped by paralyzing fears that seem to come from nowhere and every-where—fears which made very little sense to me or anyone

else. I invested four years of my life obtaining a degree in psychology, hoping it would enable me to understand and conquer those fears. Psychology only perpetuated my questions and insecurity. Six years of professional counseling offered little insight and no change in my level of anxiety.

After two hospitalizations, trips to the emergency room, repeated EKGs, a visit to the thoracic surgeon, and a battery of other tests, my panic attacks only worsened. By the time I came to see you, full-blown panic attacks had become a daily feature.

It has been three weeks since I've experienced a panic attack! I have gone to malls, church services, played for an entire worship service, and even made it through Sunday school with peace in my heart. I had no idea what freedom meant until now. When I came to see you, I had hoped that the truth would set me free, but now I know it has! Friends have told me that even my voice is different, and my husband thinks I'm taller!

When you live in a constant state of anxiety, most of life passes you by, because you are physically/emotionally/mentally unable to focus on anything but the fear which is swallowing you. I could barely read a verse of Scripture at one sitting. It was as though someone snatched it away from my mind as soon as it entered. Scripture was such a fog to me. I could only hear the verses that spoke of death and punishment. I had actually become afraid to open my Bible. These past weeks I have spent hours a day in the Word, and it makes sense. The fog is gone. I am amazed at what I am able to hear, see, understand, and retain.

Before *The Bondage Breaker*, I could not say "Jesus Christ" without my metabolism going berserk. I could refer to "the Lord" with no ill effect, but whenever I said "Jesus Christ," my insides went into orbit. I can now call upon the name of Jesus Christ with peace and confidence...and I do it regularly.

Jesus Has You Covered

CHAPTER 6

I RECEIVED THE FOLLOWING LETTER during a weeklong conference I was conducting on spiritual conflicts. Frances's struggle vividly captures the nature of the spiritual conflict which entangles many Christians:

Dear Dr. Anderson:

I attended your Sunday sessions, but while waiting to talk to you after the Sunday evening meeting I suddenly felt ill. I was burning up like I had a fever, and I got so weak I thought I was going to faint. So I went home.

I need help. I've had more trouble in my life since I became a Christian. I've overdosed on alcohol and drugs so many times I can't count them. I've cut myself several times with razor blades, sometimes very seriously. I have thoughts and feelings and ideas of suicide weekly, like stabbing myself through the heart. I'm a slave to masturbation; I'm out of control, and I don't know how to stop.

On the outside I appear very normal. I have a good job, and I live with an outstanding family in our community. I even work with junior high students at my church. I can't really explain my relationship with God anymore. I've been seeing a psychiatrist for two years. Sometimes I think I'm this way because of a messed-up childhood, or maybe I was born this way.

How can I tell if my problems are in my mind, or the result of sin and disobedience against God, or the evidence of demonic influence? I would like to talk to you during the conference. But I don't want to try another thing that doesn't work.

—Frances

From the fact that Frances' problem was in her mind, and because of the nature of her sin, it was obvious to me that she was in spiritual bondage. I met with her that week, and she was as miserable, frustrated, and defeated as she sounds in her letter. She wanted to serve God with all her heart, and she had the same power and authority to resist Satan as I did, but she didn't know how to resolve her conflicts.

Once Frances began to realize that she was not powerless or defenseless in the battle, and that she could make choices to change her situation, the chains dropped off and she walked free. A year later she wrote:

I was hesitant to write you because I could not believe that my life would be changed or different for any length of time. I'm the girl who has tried to kill herself, cut herself, destroy herself in every possible way. I never believed that the pain in my mind and soul would ever leave so that I could be a consistent, productive servant of the Lord Jesus Christ.

I have given it over a year, and it was the best year I ever had. I have grown in so many different ways since the conference. I feel stable and free because I understand the spiritual battle going on for my life. Things come back at me sometimes, but I know how to get rid of it right away.

God's Protection

Every Christian should know "how to get rid of it right away." If we understood the spiritual battle, and knew the protection we have in Christ, there wouldn't be so many casualties.

Satan's first goal is to blind the mind of the unbelieving (2 Corinthians 4:3,4). But the battle doesn't stop when you become a Christian. He doesn't curl up his tail and pull in his fangs if he fails to keep you from coming to Christ. He is still committed to foul up your life and "prove" that Christianity doesn't work, that God's Word isn't true, and that nothing really happened when you were born again.

Some Christians are a little paranoid about evil powers lurking around every corner looking for someone to devour. That's an unfounded fear. Your relationship to demonic powers in the spiritual realm is a lot like your relationship to germs in the physical realm. You know that germs are all around you: in the air, in the water, in your food, in other people, even in you. But do you live in constant fear of them? No—unless you're a hypochondriac! The only appropriate response to the swarm of germs around you is to eat the right foods, get enough rest and exercise, and keep yourself and your possessions clean— and your immune system will protect you. However, if you didn't believe in germs, you would be less likely to do those things. For instance, before the medical profession discovered the reality and nature of microbes, they saw no need to wear masks, scrub before surgery, or use antibiotics.

It's the same in the spiritual realm. Demons are like little invisible germs looking for someone to infect. We are never told in Scripture to be afraid of them. You just need to be aware of their reality and commit yourself to know the truth and live a righteous life. Remember: The only thing big about a demon is its mouth. Demons are habitual liars. The only real sanctuary you have is your position in Christ, and in Him you have all the protection you need.

In Ephesians 6:10-18, Paul describes the armor of God which He has provided for our protection. The first thing you should understand about God's protection is that our role is not passive. Notice how often we are commanded to take an active role:

> Finally, *be strong* in the Lord and in the strength of His might. *Put on* the full armor of God, that you may *be able* to *stand firm* against the schemes of the

> devil. For our struggle is not against flesh and blood,
> but against the rulers, against the powers, against the
> world forces of this darkness, against the spiritual
> forces of wickedness in the heavenly places. There-
> fore, *take up* the full armor of God, that you may *be
> able* to *resist* in the evil day, and having done every-
> thing, to *stand firm* (verses 10-13 emphasis added).

You may be wondering, "If my position in Christ is secure and my protection is found in Him, why do I have to get actively involved? Can't I just rest in His protection?" That's like a soldier saying, "Our country is a major military power. We have the most advanced tanks, planes, missiles, and ships in the world. Why should I bother with wearing a helmet, standing guard, or learning how to shoot a gun? It's much more comfortable to stay in camp while the tanks and planes fight the war." When the enemy troops infiltrate, guess who will be one of the first soldiers to get picked off!

Our "commanding officer" has provided everything we need to remain victorious over the evil forces of darkness. But He says, "I've prepared a winning strategy and designed effec-tive weapons. But if you don't do your part by staying on active duty, you're likely to become a casualty of war." In her classic book *War on the Saints*, Jessie Penn-Lewis stated: "The chief condition for the working of evil spirits in a human being, apart from sin, is passivity, in exact opposition to the condition which God requires from His children for His working in them."[1] You can't expect God to protect you from demonic influences if you don't take an active part in His pre-pared strategy.

An example of the active role we need to take is our response to nighttime spiritual attacks—sudden unexplain-able awakenings connected with a sense of oppression and dread. These attacks have happened to me a number of times, usually in connection with important ministries. However, they're not frightening experiences for me now, and they shouldn't be for you. John promised, "Greater is He who is in you than he who is in the world" (1 John 4:4). You have authority over Satan's activity, and you have the armor of God to protect you. Whenever Satan attacks, you must "be strong in the Lord, and in the strength of His might" (Ephesians 6:10). Consciously place yourself in the Lord's hands, resist the devil, and go back to sleep.

Please don't assume that every time you awake at night it is because you are under attack. You are probably waking up because of the pickle you ate, or a noise in the house, or just as a natural occurrence. But if you do come under spiritual attack like this, remember that it is not necessarily because you are doing something wrong. It is not a sin to be under attack. You may be experiencing spiritual opposition because you are doing something *right.* In fact, if you are *not* experiencing some spiritual opposition to your ministry, there is a good chance that Satan doesn't see you as any threat to his plans.

Dressed for Battle

Because we are in a spiritual battle, Paul chose to explain our protection in Christ by using the imagery of armor:

> Stand firm therefore, having girded your loins with truth, and having put on the breastplate of right-eousness, and having shod your feet with the preparation of the gospel of peace; in addition to all, taking up the shield of faith with which you will be able to extinguish all the flaming missiles of the evil one. And take the helmet of salvation, and the sword of the Spirit, which is the word of God (Ephesians 6:14-17).

When we put on the armor of God, we are putting on the armor of light, which is the Lord Jesus Christ (Romans 13:12-14). When we put on Christ, we take ourselves out of the realm of the flesh, where we are vulnerable to attack. Satan has nothing in Christ (John 14:30), and to the extent that we put on Christ, the evil one cannot touch us (1 John 5:18). He can only touch that which is on his own level. That's why we are commanded, "Make no provision for the flesh" (Romans 13:14) that would give the devil an opening for attack.

Armor You Have Already Put On

It would appear from the verb tenses in Ephesians 6:14,15 that three of the pieces of armor—belt, breastplate, and shoes—are already on you: "having girded," "having put on," "having shod." These pieces of armor represent the elements of your protection made available when you receive Jesus Christ and in which you are commanded to stand firm. The past tense of the verb, "having," signifies that the action it refers to was completed before we were commanded to stand firm. That's the logical way a soldier would prepare for action: He would put on his belt, breastplate, and shoes before attempting to stand firm. Likewise, we are to put on the full armor of God after having already put on Christ.

The belt of truth. Jesus said, "I am...the truth" (John 14:6). And because Christ is in you, the truth is in you. The belt of truth is our defense against Satan's primary weapon, which is deception. "Whenever he speaks a lie, he speaks from his own nature, for he is a liar and the father of lies" (John 8:44). The belt of truth (which holds the other pieces of body armor in place) is continually being attacked.

I believe that lying is the number one social problem in America. Ironically, most people lie to protect themselves. But Paul says that *truth* is our first line of defense. Truth is never an enemy—it is a liberating friend. Facing the truth is the first step in any recovery program. You have to speak the truth in love (Ephesians 4:15) if you want to live free in Christ and have meaningful relationships.

The only thing a Christian ever has to admit to is the truth. If a thought comes to mind which is not in harmony with God's truth, dismiss it. If an opportunity comes along to say or do something which compromises or conflicts with truth, avoid it. Adopt a simple rule for living: If it's the truth, I'm in; if it's not the truth, count me out.

Jesus prayed, "I do not ask Thee to take them out of the world, but to keep them from the evil one" (John 17:15). How? "Sanctify them in the truth; Thy Word is truth" (verse 17). You overcome the father of lies with divine revelation, not human reasoning or research.

The breastplate of righteousness. When you put on Christ at salvation, you are justified before our holy God (Romans 5:1). It's not *your* righteousness but Christ's righteousness (1 Corinthians 1:30; Philippians 3:8,9). Putting on the breastplate of righteousness is your defense against the accuser of the brethren. So when Satan aims an arrow at you by saying, "You're not good enough to be a Christian," you can respond with Paul, "Who will bring a charge against God's elect? God is the one who justifies" (Romans 8:33).

Even though we stand on our righteous position in Christ, we should be aware of any deeds of unrighteousness. We are saints who sin. Putting on the armor of light means we walk in the light as He is in the light (1 John 1:6-8). Walking in the light is not sinless perfection. It means living in continuous agreement with God. It is part of our growth process. "If we confess our sins, He is faithful and righteous to forgive us our sins and to cleanse us from all unrighteousness" (1 John 1:9). Confession is not saying "I'm sorry." Many people are sorry, but usually they are sorry they got caught, and even then they will only acknowledge as little as they have to. To confess (*homologeo* in Greek) means to acknowledge or to agree. It is very similar to the concept of walking in the light. To confess means you say, "I did it," the moment you are aware you have done something wrong. Covering up anything is the same as walking in the dark.

You can walk in the light because you're already forgiven. You are the righteousness of God in Christ (2 Corinthians 5:21). Your relationship with God and your eternal destiny are not at stake when you sin, but your daily victory is. Your confession of sin clears the way for the fruitful expression of righteousness in your daily life. We should be like Paul, who said, "I also do my best to maintain always a blameless conscience both before God and before men" (Acts 24:16).

The shoes of peace. When you receive Christ, you are united with the Prince of Peace. You have positional peace with God right now (Romans 5:1), but the peace of Christ must also rule in your heart, and that is possible only when you let the Word of Christ richly dwell in you (Colossians 3:15,16).

The shoes of peace become protection against the divisive schemes of the devil when you act as a peacemaker among believers (Romans 14:19). Peacemakers bring people together. Peacemakers encourage fellowship and have a ministry of reconciliation. They understand that fellowship and unity in the body of Christ are based on common heritage. True believers are children of God, and that's enough to bring us together in peace. If you wait to receive someone until you agree perfectly on every point of doctrine, you'll be the loneliest Christian on earth. We need to work at "being diligent to preserve the unity of the Spirit in the bond of peace" (Ephesians 4:3). "Blessed are the peacemakers, for they shall be called sons of God" (Matthew 5:9). We have the promise that "the God of peace will soon crush Satan under your feet" (Romans 16:20).

The Rest of the Armor

Paul mentions three more pieces of armor that we must take up to protect ourselves from Satan's attack: the shield of faith, the helmet of salvation, and the sword of the Spirit, which is the Word of God. The first three are established by our position in Christ; the last three help us continue winning the battle.

The shield of faith. The object of our faith is God and His Word. The more you know about God and His Word, the more faith you will have. The less you know, the smaller your shield will be, and the easier it will be for one of Satan's fiery darts to reach its target. If you want your shield of faith to grow large and protective, your knowledge of God and His Word must increase (Romans 10:17).

These flaming missiles from Satan are nothing more than smoldering lies, burning accusations, and fiery temptations bombarding our minds. Whenever you discern a deceptive thought, accusation, or temptation, meet it head-on with what you know to be true about God and His Word. How did Jesus deflect the missiles of Satan's temptation? By shielding Himself with statements from the Word of God. Every time you memorize a Bible verse, listen to a sermon, or participate in a Bible study, you increase your knowledge of God and enlarge your shield of faith.

The helmet of salvation. Should your shield of faith be a little leaky and your daily victory elusive, be confident that the helmet of salvation guarantees your eternal victory. In the metaphor of armor, the helmet also secures coverage for the most critical part of your anatomy: your mind, where spiritual battles are either won or lost. As you struggle with the world, the flesh, and the devil on a daily basis, stand firm, knowing that your salvation is not based on your good works, but on the good works of Christ. You are a child of God, and nothing can separate you from the love of Christ (Romans 8:35).

The temptation is to doubt our salvation when under attack. But the Christian warrior wears the helmet of salvation in the sense that he is the receiver and possessor of deliverance, clothed and armed in the victory of his Head, Jesus Christ. Since we are joined to the Lord Jesus Christ, the devil has no legitimate claim on us, for Christ has "delivered us from the domain of darkness, and transferred us to the kingdom of His beloved Son" (Colossians 1:13). Be assured of your salvation. "The Spirit Himself testifies with our spirit that we are children of God" (Romans 8:16).

The sword of the Spirit. The Word of God is the only offensive weapon in the armor of God. Paul uses *rhema* instead of *logos* for "word" in Ephesians 6:17 because he wants to emphasize the spoken word of God. There is only one Word of God, but the Greek word *rhema* brings in the idea of proclamation. For instance, Paul says in Romans 10:17, "So faith comes from hearing, and hearing by the word (*rhema*) of Christ." It is appropriate to use *rhema* in this context because the emphasis is on preaching the good news and hearing it.

Our defense against direct attacks by the evil one is to speak aloud God's truth. Why is it so important to speak God's Word, in addition to believing it and thinking it? Because Satan is not omniscient, and he doesn't perfectly know what you're thinking. By observing you, he can pretty well tell what you are thinking, just as any student of human behavior can. But he doesn't know what you're going to do before you do it. If you pay attention to a deceiving spirit (1 Timothy 4:1), he is putting thoughts into your mind, and he will know whether you buy his lie by how you behave. It is not hard for him to tell what you are thinking if he has given you the thought.

If you have read this book, I have put thoughts in your mind. But I can't read your thoughts. Similarly, Satan can try to influence you by planting thoughts in your mind, but he can't perfectly read your thoughts. You are ascribing too much power to Satan if you think he can perfectly read your mind and know the future. Every occultic practice claims to know the mind (or influence it) or predict the future. But only God knows the thoughts and intents of your mind, and only He knows the future. You should never ascribe the divine attributes of God to Satan.

You can communicate silently with God in your mind and spirit because He knows the thoughts and intents of your heart (Hebrews 4:12). You can have unspoken communion with your heavenly Father. However, should you come under a direct attack from Satan, for instance in your room at night, you will need to exercise your authority in Christ by speaking out loud, since the evil one does not have the power to completely know your thoughts. The good news is that most direct attacks occur at night and when you are alone, so verbally resisting Satan won't be a matter of public spectacle.

Paul says, "With the heart a person believes, resulting in righteousness, and with the mouth he confesses, resulting in salvation" (Romans 10:10). Since you know your own thoughts and God also knows them, then why does verbal confession result in salvation? Paul could be saying that saving faith is not complete until the will is exercised, but he could also be implying the need for the god of this world to hear our commitment.

While conducting conferences, I have asked those in attendance the following question: "How many of you have awakened suddenly at night with an overwhelming sense of fear? You may have felt a pressure on your chest or something grabbing your throat. You tried to respond physically but you couldn't say anything." I have never seen less than a third of the people raise their hands, acknowledging that they have experienced a spiritual attack like this.

If we can't seem to speak, how do we resolve this kind of attack? First, to stand against the attack does not require physical effort on our part, because "the weapons of our warfare are not of the flesh, but divinely powerful for the destruction of fortresses" (2 Corinthians 10:4). The initial flesh response to such an attack is usually fear—but it is not the fear of God. You can try to get out of this yourself, but chances are you will only lie there and squirm for awhile. Second, notice the order of Scripture in James: "Submit therefore to God. Resist the devil and he will flee from you" (4:7). You can always turn to God with all your heart and with all your mind, because your heavenly Father is omniscient, and He knows your heart and your thoughts. The moment you call upon the name of the Lord, you will be free to resist the devil. All you have to say is "Jesus." Such times reveal how dependent upon God we really are.

The Protective Power of Prayer

The mother of one of my seminary students was a psychic. She asked her son, "Have you been praying for me?"

"Of course I have, Mother."

"Well, don't," she insisted, "because you're disturbing my aura."

I say, "Pray on!" We may never know the effects of our prayers, but we do know that God includes our prayer as part of His strategy for establishing His kingdom. I was counseling a man who professed to be a high priest in the upper echelons of Satanism. His conversion turned out to be the most dramatic I have ever seen. Six months after he trusted in Christ, he gave his testimony in our church. I asked him, "Based on your experience on 'the other side,' what is the Christian's first line of defense against demonic influence?"

"Prayer," he answered forcefully. "And when you pray, mean it. Fervent prayer thwarts Satan's activity like nothing else."

What is prayer? It is communication with God. God knows what we need in our battle with the powers of darkness, and He is more willing to save us and meet our needs than we are willing to ask. Our attitude in prayer should be, "You are the Lord, not I. You know what's best; I don't. I'm not telling

You what to do; I'm asking. I am totally dependent upon You."

After instructing us to put on the armor that God has provided, Paul wrote: "With all prayer and petition, pray at all times in the Spirit, and with this in view, be on the alert with all perseverance and petition for all the saints" (Ephesians 6:18). We need to be Spirit-led in our prayers, because we don't really know what to pray for or how to pray apart from God. "The Spirit also helps our weakness; for we do not know how to pray as we should, but the Spirit Himself intercedes for us" (Romans 8:26). The word "helps" (*sunantilambano*) in this verse beautifully describes how the Holy Spirit comes alongside, picks us up, and carries us to the throne of grace. Prayer in the Spirit helps us span chasms of need that we don't know how to cross. Any prayer that God the Holy Spirit prompts us to pray is a prayer that God our heavenly Father always answers.

Praying for Spiritual Sight

There are several specific needs we should consider as targets for prayer in spiritual warfare. One need relates to the condition of blindness which Satan has inflicted on unbelievers (2 Corinthians 4:3,4). People cannot come to Christ unless their spiritual eyes are opened. Theodore Epp wrote, "If Satan has blinded and bound men and women, how can we ever see souls saved? This is where you and I enter the picture. Spoiling the goods of the strong man has to do with liberating those whom Satan has blinded and is keeping bound....This is where prayer comes in."[2]

Prayer is a primary weapon in combating spiritual blindness. The apostle John wrote: "If we ask anything according to His will, He hears us. And if we know that He hears us in whatever we ask, we know that we have the requests which we have asked from Him" (1 John 5:14,15). Then he immediately challenged believers to apply this principle by asking God to bring life to unbelievers (verse 16). Our evangelistic strategy must include authoritative prayer that God's light would penetrate satanic blindness.

We also need to pray, as Paul did in Ephesians 1:18,19, that the eyes of believers may be enlightened to understand the spiritual power, authority, and protection which is our inheritance in Christ. As long as Satan can keep us in the dark about our position and authority in Christ, he can keep us stunted in our growth and ineffectual in our witness and ministry. We need to pray for each other continually that Satan's smoke screen of lies will be blown away and that our vision will be crystal clear.

Binding the Strong Man

Another target for authoritative prayer is the "strong man" mentioned in Matthew 12:29. Jesus said, referring to Satan and his demons: "How can anyone enter the strong man's house and carry off his property, unless he first binds the strong man?" He was saying that you cannot rescue people from the bonds of spiritual blindness or demonic influence unless you first overpower their captors. Satan's power is already broken, but he will not let go of anything he thinks he can keep until we exercise the authority delegated to us by the Lord Jesus Christ.

When we pray we are not trying to persuade God to join us in *our* service for Him; prayer is the activity of joining God in *His* ministry. By faith we lay hold of the property in Satan's clutches which rightfully belongs to God, and we hold on until Satan turns loose. C. Fred Dickason, who taught systematic theology at Moody Bible Institute for years, gives several helpful suggestions for how to pray for someone who is being harassed by demons:

1. Pray that the demons may be cut off from all communication and help from other demons and Satan.

2. Pray that the demons would be confused and weakened in their hold on the person.

3. Pray that the person would be strengthened in his faith to understand his position in Christ and to trust and obey God's Word.

4. Pray that the person may be able to distinguish between his thoughts and feelings and those of Satan.

5. Pray that the person might recognize the demonic presence and not be confused, but willingly seek godly counsel and help.

6. Pray that God would protect and guide His child and set angelic forces at work to break up every scheme of the enemy.[3]

Several years ago a personal experience emphasized to me the power of prayer in dealing with people who are in the clutches of the evil one. I was on the staff of a large church at the time. I came back from lunch one day to find several of our secretaries and custodians drinking coffee and chatting in the lounge near the church office. At the other end of the room was a tall man in his mid-twenties, a total stranger to me, standing at the chalkboard writing tiny words and then erasing them. "Who's that?" I asked my coworkers.

"We don't know. He just walked in."

Amazed that someone hadn't already greeted the man, I walked over and said, "Hi, my name is Neil. Can I help you?"

"Oh, I don't know," he answered rather distantly as he put down the chalk. He looked and sounded like his mind had been blown on drugs, so I decided to get him out of the building and just talk to him for awhile. I discovered that his name was Bill and that he worked at a local car wash. I invited him to come to church. After an hour of conversation he left.

A couple of days later Bill came back, and we talked some more. Then about two weeks later on a Sunday afternoon I was in my office getting ready for the evening service when my intercom buzzed. "There's a guy down here named Bill who wants to see you."

"Send him up," I answered.

I really didn't have much time to spend with Bill, but I didn't want to ignore him either. So I got right to the point. "I'm glad you're here, Bill," I began. "May I ask you a personal question?" Bill nodded. "Have you ever trusted in Christ to be your Lord and your Savior?"

"No."

"Would you like to?"

"I don't know," Bill answered with a slightly troubled expression.

I reached for a salvation tract and read through it with him. "Do you understand this, Bill?"

"Yes."

"Would you like to make that decision for Christ right now?"

"Yes."

I wasn't sure he could read, so I said, "I'll pray a simple prayer of commitment, and you repeat it after me phrase by phrase, okay?"

"Okay."

"Lord Jesus, I need You," I began.

Bill began to respond, "Lor-r-r..." Then he locked up completely. I could feel the oppression in the room.

"Bill, there's a battle going on for your mind," I said. "I'm going to read some Scripture and pray out loud for you. I'm going to bind the enemy and stand against him. As soon as you can, you just tell Jesus what you believe."

His eyes confirmed that the battle was raging. I started reading Scripture and praying aloud every prayer I could think of. I was still very new at dealing with demonic powers at the time, so I was grasping at straws.

After about 15 minutes of prayer and Scripture, Bill suddenly groaned, "Lord Jesus, I need You." Then he slumped back in his chair like he had just gone ten rounds with the world heavyweight champion. He looked at me with tear-filled eyes and said, "I'm free." I had never used the word "freedom" with him; that was his expression. But he was free and he knew it, and I could see it.

Understanding the spiritual nature of our world should have a profound effect on our evangelistic strategy. All too often we proclaim the virtues of Christianity to unbelievers like someone standing outside a prison compound proclaiming to the inmates the benefits of living in the outside world. But unless someone overpowers the prison guards and opens the gates, how can the prisoners experience the freedom we're telling them about?

Concerning the lost, there are four things you need to pray for. First, since the field is white unto harvest, we should pray for workers (Matthew 9:37,38). Paul asks, "How will they hear without a preacher?" (Romans 10:14). Ask God to send someone to share the good news with them. Second, the lost are dead in their trespasses and sin, and what Jesus came to do was give them life (John 10:10). Pray that God will give them life (1 John 5:16). Third, pray against the thoughts raised up against the knowledge of God, and for the binding of Satan. Finally, pray that the eyes of lost people would be opened to the truth that will set them free in Christ.

Part Two

Stand Firm!

Manipulating Spirits

I FIRST MET SHARON BEEKMANN when she attended one of my conferences. Several years prior to our meeting, Sharon was a licensed professional counselor who was living a rather normal life. She was married with one child and lived comfortably in the suburban foothills of Denver. But she sensed a spiritual void in her life. Unfortunately she got drawn into the New Age movement and for the next seven years was trained to be a channel for spirit guides. Her becoming a medium eventually led to divorce, and her own lifestyle began to deteriorate.

She finally came to the conclusion she had lost her mind. She didn't want to be a channel for those voices in her head any longer. But when she wouldn't play ball with those "friendly" little spirit guides, they turned against her. She found herself housebound and unable to function. Somehow she knew that the only way to get rid of the voices was to become a Christian. At that point the story Sharon tells in her book, *Enticed by the Light* (Zondervan), becomes a sad commentary on the church in America. She couldn't find a church that would help her become a Christian. After hearing her story, one pastor suggested that she wouldn't feel very comfortable in his congregation.

She finally found a good evangelical pastor who led her to the Lord, but he didn't know how to help her resolve the spiritual conflicts which continued to plague her. She found another church that specialized in spiritual warfare, and they worked with her for two years. They would call up the spirits and dialogue with them and try to exercise their authority over them. They would seem to leave for a while, but there was never any complete resolution.

One day Sharon suddenly realized that these well-intentioned Christian counselors were just trying to manipulate the spirits—which was what she was trying to do when she was a spiritist or medium, although for different purposes. Shortly afterwards she drove to my conference and learned a completely different approach to resolving personal and spiritual conflicts. I was privileged to write the foreword in her book.

Not very many churches are equipped to help people like Sharon, but I think we had better get ready for a flood of requests. The incredible rise of the New Age movement is going to leave a lot of people in bondage to the god of this world.

The Rebel Authority

God originally created Adam and his descendants to rule over the birds of the sky, the beasts of the field, and the fish of the sea, and over all the earth (Genesis 1:26). But Adam forfeited his position of authority when he sinned, and Satan became the rebel holder of authority whom Jesus referred to as "the ruler of this world" (John 12:31; 14:30; 16:11). During Jesus' temptation, the devil offered Him "all the kingdoms of the world, and their glory" (Matthew 4:8) in exchange for His worship. Satan claimed that the earth "has been handed over to me, and I give it to whomever I wish" (Luke 4:6). He took authority when Adam abdicated dominion over God's creation at the fall. Satan ruled from the fall of Adam until the cross. The death, resurrection, and ascension of Christ secured forever the final authority for Jesus (Matthew 28:18). That authority was extended to all believers in the Great Commission so that we may continue His work of destroying the works of the devil (1 John 3:8).

We all were born spiritually dead and subject to the ruler of this world whom Paul called "the prince of the power of the air" (Ephesians 2:2). But when we received Christ, God "delivered us from the domain of darkness, and transferred us to the kingdom of His beloved Son" (Colossians 1:13). Our citizenship was changed from earth to heaven (Philippians 3:20). Satan is the ruler of this world, but he is no longer *our* ruler, for Christ is our Lord.

But as long as we remain on planet earth, we are still on Satan's turf. He will try to rule our lives by deceiving us into believing we are still under his authority. As aliens in a hostile world, we need protection from this evil tyrant. Christ has not only provided protection, but in Christ we have authority over the kingdom of darkness. We also have the indwelling Holy Spirit who is the Spirit of truth (John 14:17), and He will guide us into all truth (John 16:13).

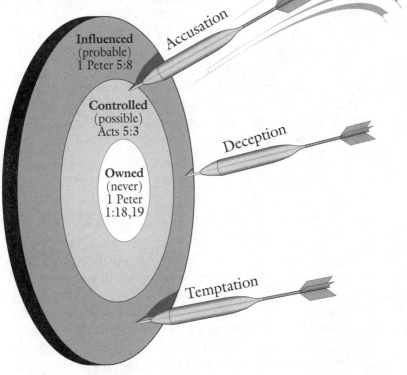

Figure 7a.

Degrees of Vulnerability

Even though we are secure in Christ and have all the protective armor we need, we are still vulnerable to Satan's accusations, temptations, and deceptions (see figure 7a). The fact that we have been instructed to put on the armor of God clearly reveals that we are vulnerable to some degree. Therefore, it is probable that every believer will be influenced by the god of this world. He can gain some measure of control over our lives if we are deceived and believe his lies. I have seen countless numbers of believers who are almost paralyzed by his lies. The oppression is so overwhelming that some can't seem to make the right choices and live responsible lives. They actually *can* make choices, but they don't *think* they can, so they don't.

Ownership is never at stake, however. We belong to God, and Satan can't touch who we are in Christ. We may be demon-oppressed, but we are always "Holy Spirit–possessed." But as long as we are living in these natural bodies in this fallen world, we are the target for Satan's fiery darts. And the answer is not to stick our heads in the sand like an ostrich, because if we do, we will be leaving an incredibly vulnerable target exposed.

The Powers That Be

Belief in a personal devil has always been a creed of the church. That doesn't mean every person has his own personal devil, but that the devil is an actual personage rather than merely an impersonal force. The tendency in our culture is to depersonalize him. It is common to hear someone say of another, "He has his own personal demons." They don't mean that literally. They mean he has his own personal problems. Even many Christians who believe in the devil seem to cringe at the idea of demons being present in this world.

Then how do you think Satan carries on his worldwide ministry of evil and deception? He is a created being. He is not omnipresent, omniscient, or omnipotent. He can't be everywhere in the world tempting and deceiving millions of people at the same moment. He does so through an army of emissaries (demons or fallen angels) who propagate his lies around the world.

Neither disbelief in demonic activity nor an inordinate fear of demons is healthy. In *The Screwtape Letters*, C.S. Lewis wrote: "There are two equal and opposite errors into which our race can fall about the devils. One is to disbelieve their existence. The other is to believe and feel an unhealthy interest in them. They themselves are equally pleased by both errors and hail a materialist or a magician with the same delight."[1]

Paul gives the most complete description of the demonic hierarchy in Ephesians 6:12: "Our struggle is not against flesh and blood, but against the rulers, against the powers, against the world forces of this darkness, against the spiritual forces of wickedness in the heavenly places." Some people have argued that the "rulers" and "powers" mentioned in this verse refer to ungodly human structures of authority instead of a hierarchy of demons under Satan's headship. Some references to rulers and powers in Scripture do designate human authorities (Luke 12:11; Acts 4:26). However, in Paul's epistles these terms are used in reference to supernatural powers (Romans 8:38,39; Colossians 1:16; 2:15). It is clear from the context of Ephesians 6:12 that the rulers, powers, and forces which oppose us are spiritual entities in the heavenlies, that is, the spiritual world. (For a scholarly treatment of this subject, I would encourage you to read *Powers of Darkness* by Dr. Clinton Arnold, which is subtitled *Principalities & Powers in Paul's Letters*, published by InterVarsity Press.)

The Personality of Demons

The Bible does not attempt to prove the existence of demons any more than it attempts to prove the existence of God. It simply reports on their activities as if its first readers accepted their existence. Nor did the early church fathers have a problem with the reality and personality of demons. Origen wrote:

> In regard to the devil and his angels and opposing powers, the ecclesiastical teaching maintains that the beings do indeed exist; but what they are or how they exist is not explained with sufficient clarity. This opinion, however, is held by most: that the devil was an angel; and having apostatized, he persuaded as many angels as possible to fall away with himself; and these, even to the present time, are called his angels.[2]

Luke gives us a helpful view into the personality and individuality of evil spirits. After Jesus cast out a demon which had rendered a man dumb, His detractors accused Him of casting out demons by the power of "Beelzebul, the ruler of the demons" (Luke 11:15). During the discussion of demons which followed, Jesus said:

> When the unclean spirit goes out of a man, it passes through waterless places seeking rest, and not finding any, it says, "I will return to my house from which I came." And when it comes, it finds it swept and put in order. Then it goes and takes along seven other spirits more evil than itself, and they go in and live there; and the last state of that man becomes worse than the first" (Luke 11:24-26).

We can glean several points of information about evil spirits from this passage.

1. *Demons can exist outside or inside humans.* Demons seem to be spirits which find a measure of rest in organic beings, preferring even swine over nothingness (Mark 5:12).

These spirits may take territorial rights and associate with certain geographical locations which have been used for satanic purposes.

2. *They are able to travel at will.* Being spiritual entities, demons are not subject to the barriers of the natural world. The walls of your church building do not establish it as a sanctuary from demonic influence; only prayer and spiritual authority can do that. Remember, the only real sanctuary we have is our position "in Christ."

3. *They are able to communicate.* It is obvious from Luke 11 that evil spirits can communicate with each other. They can also speak to humans through a human subject, such as they did through the Gadarene demoniac (Matthew 8:28-34). Such extreme cases reveal control of the central nervous system. A lesser degree of control comes from paying attention to deceiving spirits (1 Timothy 4:1).

4. *Each one has a separate identity.* Notice the use of personal pronouns in Luke 11: "I will return to my house from which I came" (verse 24). We are dealing with thinking personalities as opposed to impersonal forces. That's why secular methods of research are not going to reveal their existence. Revelation alone is our authoritative source on the reality and personality of evil spirits.

5. *They are able to remember and make plans.* The fact that they can leave a place, come back, remember their former state, and plan reentry with others shows their ability to think and plan.

6. *They are able to evaluate and make decisions.* The fact that the evil spirit found its human target "swept and put in order" (verse 25) clearly indicates that it can evaluate its

intended victim. Demons gain access to our lives through our points of vulnerability. Yet we are not to care what Satan thinks of us; we are to live our lives in a way that is pleasing to God (2 Corinthians 5:9).

7. *They are able to combine forces.* In Luke 11 the one spirit joined with a group of seven others, making the victim's last state worse than his first. In the case of the Gadarene demoniac, the number of demons united for evil was "legion" (Mark 5:9). I have heard many people identify a number of different voices in their mind, describing them as a committee.

8. *They vary in degrees of wickedness.* The first demon in Luke 11 brought back seven other spirits "more evil than itself" (verse 26). Jesus indicated a difference in the wickedness of spirits when He said of one, "This kind cannot come out by anything but prayer" (Mark 9:29). The concept of variations in power and wickedness fits the hierarchy which Paul lists in Ephesians 6:12. I can personally attest that some cases are more difficult than others.

But you need not fear Satan and his demons as long as you cling to God's truth. His only weapon is deception. Irenaeus wrote, "The devil...can only go to this length, as he did at the beginning, to deceive and lead astray the mind of man into disobeying the commandments of God, and gradually to darken the hearts."[3] If you continue to walk in the light, you don't need to be afraid of the darkness.

Running the Gauntlet of Evil

How do these evil spirits interfere with our lives? Let me answer with a simple illustration. Imagine that you are standing at one end of a long, narrow street lined on both sides with two-story apartments. At the other end of the street stands Jesus Christ, and your Christian life is the process of walking down that long street with your eyes on the Author and Finisher of your faith. There is absolutely nothing in the street that can keep you from walking toward Jesus by faith in the power of the Holy Spirit. So when you receive Christ, you fix your eyes on Him and start walking.

But since this world is still under the dominion of Satan, the apartments on either side are inhabited by beings who are committed to keeping you from reaching your goal. They have no power or authority to block your path or even slow your step, so they hang out of the windows and call to you, hoping to turn your attention away from your goal and disrupt your progress. They are like pimps who are trying to lure you into their houses of ill repute.

Some will tempt you by saying, "Hey, look over here! I've got something you really want. It tastes good, feels good, and is a lot more fun than your boring walk down the street. Come on in and take a look."

Others will accuse you by saying, "Who do you think you are? God doesn't love you. You will never amount to anything. Surely you don't believe that bit about being saved." Satan's emissaries are masters at accusation, especially after they have distracted you through temptation. One minute they're saying, "Try this; there's nothing wrong with it." Then, when you yield, they're right there taunting, "See what you did! How can you call yourself a Christian when you behave like that?" Accusation is one of Satan's primary weapons in his attempt to distract you from your goal.

Other remarks which are hurled at you as you walk down the street sound like this: "You don't need to go to church today. It's not important to pray and read the Bible every day. Some of the New Age stuff isn't so bad." That's deception, and it is Satan's most subtle and debilitating weapon. You will often hear these messages in first-person singular: "I don't need to go to church today, pray, read my Bible," and so on.

Satan knows you will be more easily deceived if he can make you think the thought was yours instead of his.

What is the enemy's goal in having his demons jeer you, taunt you, lure you, and question you from the windows and doorways along your path? He wants you to slow down, stop, sit down, and if possible, give up your journey toward Christ. He wants you to doubt your ability to believe and serve God. Remember: He has absolutely no power or authority to keep you from steadily progressing in your walk toward Christ. And he can never again own you, because you have been redeemed by Jesus Christ and you are forever in Him (1 Peter 1:18,19). But if he can get you to listen to the thoughts he plants in your mind, he can influence you. And if you allow him to influence you long enough through temptation, accusation, and deception, he can stop your progress.

The degree of spiritual freedom we experience as Christians is somewhere within a continuum: from the apostle Paul on one end, whose Christian life and ministry were exemplary despite his battle with sin and Satan (Romans 7:15-25; 2 Corinthians 12:7-9), to the Gadarene demoniac on the other end, who was totally controlled by demons (Matthew 8:28-34). Nobody loses control to Satan overnight; it's a gradual process of deception and yielding to his subtle influence. I would estimate that only about 15 percent of the evangelical Christian community is living a free and productive life in Christ. These believers know who they are in Christ, they have meaningful devotions, and they are bearing fruit. How tragic! Being alive and free in Christ is the birthright of *every* child of God. We don't have to live a carnal life—we can live a liberated life in Christ!

Running the Race

There are three ways of responding to the demonic taunts and barbs being thrown at you from those doorways and second-story windows during your daily walk with Christ, and two of these ways are wrong.

First, the most spiritually defeated Christians are those who pay attention to deceiving spirits (1 Timothy 4:1). They weakly give into the temptations and believe the lies and accusations. These Christians are defeated simply because they have been duped into believing God doesn't love them, or they will never be victorious Christians, or they are helpless victims of the past. There is no reason why they can't get up immediately and start walking again, but they have believed a lie, and so they sit there in the middle of the street, defeated.

The second response is just as unproductive. Christians try to argue with the demons: "I am not ugly or stupid. I am a victorious Christian. That is not truth. I rebuke that lie." They think they are fighting the good fight, but in reality, those negative thoughts are still controlling them and setting the agenda. They are standing in the middle of the street shouting at the demons when they should be marching forward. But it doesn't make any difference whether the negative or lying thoughts come from the world, the flesh, or the devil. We take *every* thought captive in obedience to Christ. We are not called to dispel the darkness—we are called to turn on the light.

The third response is this: We overcome the world, the flesh, and the devil by choosing the truth. We are not to believe evil spirits, nor are we to dialogue with them. We are instructed not to pay attention to them. With every arrow of temptation, accusation, or deception they shoot at us, we simply raise the shield of faith, deflect the attack, and walk on. We choose truth in the face of every lie. As we do, we grow with every step.

While I was teaching at Talbot School of Theology, an undergraduate student made an appointment with me. She was researching Satanism and wanted to ask me some questions. I answered some of her questions, but then I stopped. "I don't think you should be researching Satanism," I said.

"Why not?" she asked.

"Because you are not experiencing your freedom in Christ," I responded.

"What do you mean by that?" she protested.

I told her, "I would suspect that you struggle with your Bible classes just trying to pay attention. I would also suspect that your devotional and prayer life are virtually nonexistent. I'm sure your self-esteem is down in the mud somewhere, and you probably entertain a lot of suicidal thoughts."

She told a friend later, "That man read my mind!" I didn't read her mind. I have just been helping people long enough to recognize what is going on with them. That student got permission to take my graduate level class, "Resolving Personal and Spiritual Conflicts" that summer, and this is what she wrote me two weeks later:

> What I've discovered this last week is this feeling of control. Like my mind is my own. I haven't sat and had these strung-out periods of thought and contemplation, that is, conversations with myself. My mind just simply feels quieted. It really is a strange feeling. My emotions have been stable. I haven't felt depressed once this week. My will is mine. I feel like I have been able to choose to live my life abiding in Christ. Scripture seems different. I have a totally different perspective. I actually understand what it is saying. I feel left alone. Not in a bad way. I'm not lonely, just a single person.
>
> For the first time, I believe I actually understand what it means to be a Christian, who Christ is, and who I am in Him. I feel capable of helping people and capable of handling myself. I've been a codependent for years, but this last week I haven't had the slightest feeling or need for someone. I guess I'm describing what it is like to be at peace. I feel this quiet, soft joy in my heart. I have been more friendly with strangers and comfortable. There hasn't been this struggle to get through the day. And then there is the fact that I have been participating actively in life and not passively, critically watching it. Thank you for lending me your hope—I believe I have my own now in Christ.

The Lure of Knowledge and Power

I WAS LISTENING INTENTLY TO ONE of my fellow doctoral students give a presentation on the future of education as it related to the mind. Present in the class were principals of schools, educational administrators, teachers, and a variety of community leaders. The presenter, a principal of an elementary school, was describing such phenomena as astral projection, telekinesis, clairvoyance, and telepathy. That would be less surprising in present-day graduate programs, since the New Age has gained substantial acceptance in secular education. But this was 1980, and such subjects were typically not addressed in doctoral programs.

His New Age presentation certainly piqued the curiosity of my fellow students, who listened intently. They enthusiastically interacted with the lecturer and asked many questions. The lure of knowledge and power has always caught the fancy of those who think there is something out there which their five natural senses can't pick up. I'm not talking about the knowledge gained from disciplined study or research. *Esoteric* knowledge is perceived through a sixth sense (or spiritual sense) and is intended only for the initiated (or anointed ones). Psychics have special powers that are not available to all. There are even licensed or accredited psychics so that the true mediums can be separated from the charlatans.

Two of our country's recent first ladies have consulted psychics. Police have been known to enlist the help of psychics to find missing people or even solve crimes when scientific methods haven't been sufficient. Almost every public newspaper and airline magazine has a daily horoscope. And the public interest in angels has reached an all time high. We are indeed living in a New Age, and it may well be the most dominant religion in America.

Near the end of the class, I asked, "While you were doing your research, did you ever ask yourself whether this new frontier of the mind was good or bad? Is there anything morally wrong with what you are presenting?"

"No," he replied, "I wasn't interested in that."

"I think you should be," I responded, "because nothing you have shared is new. It is as old as biblical history, and God strictly forbids His people from being involved with it."

That brought a swift end to the class, and a number of fellow students gathered around me, wondering what could possibly be wrong with what the presenter was saying.

A Trap As Old As the Bible

The lure of the occult is almost always on the basis of acquiring knowledge and power. Actually, knowledge is power. For example, precognition means to know about something before it happens. Imagine the power you would have if you knew events before they happened. You could be a billionaire just by betting at the race track. To know something before time means that you have tied into some kind of power that can arrange future events. Satan has limited capacity to do that by manipulating deceived people. Everything he does is a counterfeit of Christianity: Clairvoyance is a counterfeit of divine revelation; precognition is a counterfeit of prophecy; telepathy is a counterfeit of prayer; psychokinesis is a counterfeit of God's miracles; and spirit guides counterfeit divine guidance. (Why would you want to have a spirit guide when you can have the Holy Spirit as your guide?)

These finite longings for the infinite can be fulfilled by the knowledge and power which comes from an intimate relationship with *God*. However, Satan is trying to pass off his counterfeits as the real thing. He will gain a foothold in your life if he can lure you into the deceptive world of psychic knowledge and power. The so-called New Age is certainly not new. Moses commanded the people on the eve of their invasion of the Promised Land:

> When you enter the land which the LORD your God gives you, you shall not learn to imitate the detestable things of those nations. There shall not be found among you anyone who makes his son or his daughter pass through the fire, one who uses divination, one who practices witchcraft, or one who interprets omens, or a sorcerer, or one who casts a spell, or a medium, or a spiritist, or one who calls up the dead. For whoever does these things is detestable to the LORD; and because of these detestable things the LORD your God will drive them out before you. You shall be blameless before the LORD your God (Deuteronomy 18:9-13).

This command is as viable for us today as it was for the Israelites under Moses's leadership. We live in a contemporary Canaan where it is socially acceptable to consult spiritists, mediums, palm-readers, psychic counselors, and horoscopes for guidance and esoteric knowledge. This is unfortunately true among Christians also. During a 1990 survey of 1725 professing Christian teenagers, we discovered the following about their activity in the occult:[1]

Occult Activity	Number of Those Surveyed Who Were Involved*
Astral projection	44
Table lifting	149
Fortune telling	180
Astrology	321
Dungeons & Dragons	286
Crystals or pyramids	72
Ouija board	416
Automatic writing	35
Tarot cards	99
Palm reading	192
Spirit guides	37
Blood pact	100
	861 Total Number Involved
	864 Total with No Involvement
	1725 Total Number Surveyed

* Note: Number of involvement per activity add up to greater than 861 because of multiple involvements by some students.

Almost 50 percent of these Christian teenagers indicated some type of involvement! And we never even asked about witchcraft or sorcery, which Moses also mentioned in Deuteronomy 18.

It is hard for some people to believe that young and old alike are actually worshipping Satan. Our police departments are trying to tell parents today, "Wake up! Your kids are not just into drugs and illicit sex. They're into *Satanism*. We've seen the blood and the mutilated animals." The man who was the head of campus security where I taught belonged to a group of security officers from campuses across southern California. This group met once a month. When it was our school's turn to host the meeting, he asked me to speak to the group about spiritual phenomena in our culture. "There aren't many Christians in the group," he said, "but they'll be on our campus, so I want you to speak to them." I agreed to do so.

It was a veteran crowd of former military men and police officers. When I started talking about the rise of Satanism in our community, there wasn't a doubter or a scoffer in the bunch. Every one of them had a story to share about finding grisly evidence of Satanism being active on his own campus. Every security officer was told to cover it up. School administrators don't want the public to know about such things for the same reason they don't like to report rapes.

Every cult or occult practice that Moses warned the Israelites to avoid in Canaan—from "harmless" horoscopes to unthinkable atrocities of animal and human sacrifice—is in place and operating in our culture today.

Knowledge from the Dark Side

The craving for esoteric, "extra" knowledge in our culture was illustrated to me when two conferences, both open to the public, were held in Pasadena, California. One was a major world conference on international missions, and about 600 people attended. At the same time, a New Age conference was being conducted in the Pasadena Civic Center, and more than 40,000 people showed up! That's our society. People don't want to hear what God has to say. They want information and direction from someone else who "knows": a psychic, a channeler, a palm-reader, a card-reader, or the spirit of a dead friend or relative.

God strictly forbade His covenant people from consulting any supernatural source other than Himself. "Do not turn to mediums or spiritists; do not seek them out to be defiled by them....As for the person who turns to mediums and to spiritists, to play the harlot after them, I will also set My face against that person and will cut him off from among his people....A man or a woman who is a medium or a spiritist shall surely be put to death" (Leviticus 19:31; 20:6,27). Anybody who pursued false guidance was to be cut off from the rest, and those who gave false guidance were to be put to death. God still does the former but we don't do the latter.

We do almost the opposite. People are channeling on TV and radio programs, and New Age teachers can propagate their world view while Christian can't. I read recently that more women consult with psychics or New Age practitioners than licensed professional counselors. You can attend a psychic fair in practically any city in our land and pay for a personal spiritual "reading." The reader is either a fake or a spiritual medium who enters a trance and becomes a channel for some demonic spirit. Far from being seen as a blight on society, these people are often revered as highly as ministers and doctors for their "expertise." In fact, maybe one of the greatest spiritual threats to the church is the rapid growth of New Age medicine.

Charlatans and Real Mediums

Where do mediums and spiritists get their "amazing" information and insights? Many of them are "paying attention to deceiving spirits" (1 Timothy 4:1), but some of what is called spiritism and psychic phenomena is no more than clever illusion. These so-called spiritists give what is referred to as "cold readings." These clever charlatans ask the naive a few simple, leading questions. They also observe their clients speech, mannerisms, appearance, and dress. Based on those answers and personal observations, they make general statements which are probably fairly accurate. But the gullible are so impressed with the accuracy of their "revelations" that they start giving more information, which these charlatans fabricate into a "reading." This is not demonic; it's just verbal sleight of hand.

But the mediums and spiritists that God warned against in Leviticus and Deuteronomy were not con artists, but people who possessed and passed on knowledge which didn't come through natural channels of perception. These people have opened themselves up to the spirit world and have become spiritual channels. The charlatan with his phony cold readings is only interested in bilking you of your money. But the false knowledge and direction which comes from Satan through a medium is intended to bilk you of your spiritual vitality and freedom.

I once counseled the victim of a medium. Rory, a sharp-looking man in his late forties who had just gone through a divorce, came into my office and told me his incredible story. One day he took a new lady friend named Bernice on a date to a southern California theme park. While they were walking through the shops they came to a little store advertising a resident psychic. The sign read: "Come in and receive instructions for your life."

Rory and Bernice went inside, and the psychic astounded them with her esoteric knowledge. Whether she was a true medium receiving her information from a familiar spirit or a clever con artist, I don't know. But the effect on the couple was profound. "If you have this kind of power," Rory exclaimed, "what else can you do for me?" The psychic promised that she could help him become a success in his job and all other areas of life.

Rory fell for it, and he and Bernice began seeing the psychic on a regular basis. The psychic advised them to marry each other, which they did. They continued to seek and follow the psychic's advice as a couple.

Four years later Rory was in my office. His marriage to Bernice was a disaster, and the successful job which the psychic had promised never materialized. When I asked him how much money he had poured down the drain in his pursuit of "spiritual" knowledge, Rory answered, "I personally gave her almost 15,000 dollars, but Bernice lost over 65,000 dollars."

There's big money in these psychic/con artist operations, and a lot of magicians are raking it in. Many people crave to know something extra about their lives and their future, and they will pay handsomely for the inside information they desire.

The Down Side of Seeking the Dark Side

Not much is known about the biblical terms "medium" and "spiritist." Since "medium" (*ob*, meaning "witch or necromancer") is feminine, and "spiritist" (*yidd oni*, from the root "to know") is masculine, some students of the Bible think that they are male and female counterparts of the same role.

The Old Testament abounds with illustrations of kings, false prophets, and mediums leading the nation of Israel in rebellion against God. One of the more well-known cases was Israel's first king. Saul began well by seeking God's guidance and was appointed by Samuel as king of Israel (1 Samuel 9). He served well until his infamous rebellion against God's will (1 Samuel 15), a sin which God equates with the sin of divination (verse 23). Why did Saul sin and reject the word of the Lord? Because he feared the voice of the people more than the voice of God—a problem all too evident in our world today.

Although Saul was sorry that he sinned (or at least sorry that he was caught!), there is no evidence which suggests that he was truly repentant. Like many people who disobey God, he tried to rectify his mistake, but it was too late and "the Spirit of the LORD departed from Saul, and an evil spirit from the LORD terrorized him" (1 Samuel 16:14).

This is a difficult passage for two reasons. First, it seems to imply that a person can lose the Holy Spirit by an act of disobedience. But it must be understood that the presence of the Holy Spirit in the Old Testament was selective and temporary. The Spirit involved with Saul was probably the same Spirit involved with David in verse 13: a special equipping of the Spirit for ruling as God's anointed king. This unique equipping is not the same as the personal relationship in the Spirit that we enjoy with God as His children today.

Beginning after the cross, the church is identified by the indwelling presence of the Holy Spirit, who forever unites the children of God with their heavenly Father (Ephesians 1:13,14). Jesus promised that no one shall snatch us out of His hand (John 10:28), and Paul assured us that nothing—not even disobedience—can separate us from the love of God (Romans 8:35-39). We are secure in Christ and indwelt by His Spirit through faith in the work of Christ on the cross.

The second problem concerns the bothersome idea that an evil spirit could come from the Lord. But we must remember that God is supreme, and He can use Satan and his emissaries as a means to discipline His people as He did with Saul. This is no different from God using a godless nation like Assyria as "the rod of My anger" to discipline His people (Isaiah 10:5,6). It is not inconsistent with the nature or plan of God to use demons to accomplish His will. Even the church is advised to turn a grossly immoral member over to Satan "for the destruction of his flesh, that his spirit may be saved in the day of the Lord Jesus" (1 Corinthians 5:5).

It is interesting to note that whenever the evil spirit came upon Saul, David (the heir apparent to Israel's throne) would play his harp and the evil spirit would depart (1 Samuel 16:23). How pathetically unaware we are of the biblical prominence of music in the spiritual realm! When Elisha was about to inquire of God, he said, " 'Now bring me a minstrel.' And it came about, when the minstrel played, that the hand of the LORD came upon him" (2 Kings 3:15). During the reign of David, over 4000 musicians were assigned to sing in the temple night and day (1 Chronicles 9:33; 23:5). It is the mark of Spirit-filled Christians to sing and make melody in their hearts to the Lord and speak to each other in psalms, hymns, and spiritual songs (Ephesians 5:18-20).

On the other side of the truth lies the destructive power of secular music. The Satanist I led to the Lord showed me numerous symbols on popular record albums indicating the groups' association with Satanism. He believed that about 85 percent of today's heavy metal and punk music groups are "owned" by Satanists. They have unwittingly sold themselves to Satanism in exchange for fame and fortune. Few of these artists actually practice Satanism, but most are hopelessly lost and lead others astray through the godless message in their music.

After Samuel the prophet died, Saul's twisted thirst for spiritual knowledge led him to seek guidance from a medium. Having previously purged the nation of mediums and spiritists (1 Samuel 28:3), Saul decided to pay a visit to the witch of Endor, who had somehow escaped the purge. Coming to the witch in disguise, Saul persuaded her to call up Samuel (verses 8-19). But the scheme backfired when God permitted Samuel himself to return, terrifying the medium (who was expecting a counterfeit spirit). Samuel's message to Saul was nothing but bad news, foretelling the imminent capture of Israel by the Philistines and the death of Saul and his sons (verse 19).

God expressly forbids necromancy. "When they say to you, 'Consult the mediums and the spiritists who whisper and mutter,' should not a people consult their God? Should they consult the dead on behalf of the living? To the law and to the testimony! If they do not speak according to this word, it is because they have no dawn" (Isaiah 8:19,20).

The story of the rich man and Lazarus teaches the present-day impossibility of communicating with the dead (Luke 16:19-31). When a psychic claims to have contacted the dead, don't believe it. When a psychologist claims to have regressed a client back to a former existence through hypnosis, don't believe it. When a New Age medium purports to channel a person from the past into the present, realize that it is nothing more than a demonic spirit or the fraudulent work of a con artist.

An Old Idea in New Clothing

The New Age movement cloaks the occultic message of enlightenment: "You don't need God; you *are* God. You don't need to repent of your sins and depend on God to save you. Sin isn't a problem; you just need to turn off your mind and tune in to the great cosmic oneness through harmonic convergence." The New Age pitch is the oldest lie of Satan: "You will be like God" (Genesis 3:5).

This thirst for knowledge and power has lured a gullible public to seek guidance from mediums and spiritists, and from such occultic practices as fortune-telling, tarot cards, palm-reading, Ouija boards, astrology, magic charming, and automatic writing. "Is it because there is no God in Israel that you are going to inquire of Baal-zebub?" Elijah lamented (2 Kings 1:6). People all around us are ignoring the God who loves them and wants to guide their lives, and are instead seeking light and peace in the kingdom of darkness. We may well ask with Jehu, "What peace, so long as the harlotries of your mother Jezebel and her witchcrafts are so many?" (2 Kings 9:22). Peace can only be found in the Prince of Peace, not in the prince of darkness.

Don't be carried away by the prospect of knowledge and power which is luring so many people in our culture away from God. People such as the devotees of Simon in Acts 8:9,10 will continue to be astonished by those who practice New Age sorcery. Others, such as the customers of the demon-possessed slave girl in Acts 16:16-18 will contribute to the profit of those who exercise a spirit of divination. As in these examples from the early church, those who seek knowledge and power from the dark side will greatly interfere with the work of God, deceiving many by the counterfeit forces they employ. Other people will thirst after power to such an extent that they will sacrifice to the "goat demons" (Leviticus 17:7) and even sacrifice their own children to demons (Psalm 106:36-38). I can verify firsthand from my counseling experience that these kinds of things are actually happening today.

Let these words from Scripture sober us to the reality that even believers are vulnerable to being lured away from the knowledge and power of God by our enemy, who exaggerates our sense of independence and importance apart from God:

> But Jeshurun grew fat and kicked—you are grown fat, thick, and sleek—then he forsook God who made him, and scorned the Rock of his salvation. They made Him jealous with strange gods; with abominations they provoked Him to anger. They sacrificed to demons who were not God, to gods whom they have not known, new gods who came lately, whom your fathers did not dread. You neglected the Rock who begot you, and forgot the God who gave you birth (Deuteronomy 32:15-18).

Tempted to Do It Your Way

W HEN OUR CHILDREN WERE YOUNG we struggled through the ritual of family devotions. One harried evening we inadvertently overlooked our time of Bible reading and prayer with Heidi and Karl. Several minutes after we had put them to bed we heard Heidi's voice from down the hall: "Daddy, we forgot to do our commotions." "Commotions" is what our family devotions usually were in our family!

The devotional series I remember best was a continuing discussion with Karl about temptation. For several weeks all he wanted to talk about was temptation. I think he was mainly fascinated by the sound of the word. I remember liking the word "aluminum" when I was a child. But even after several weeks of discussion on the subject, Karl couldn't distinguish the concept of temptation from the act of sin itself.

I have found that many Christian adults struggle with that distinction. Bombarded by tempting thoughts, they conclude that there must be something pretty sick about them. They equate temptation with sin. But even Jesus was "tempted in all things as we are." But finish the verse: "Yet without sin" (Hebrews 4:15). As long as we are physically alive in this present world, we will be tempted just like Jesus was. But He didn't sin, and we don't have to sin either. In this chapter I want to define and describe temptation so you can easily recognize it and quickly refuse Satan's invitation to do things your own way.

135

The Basis of Temptation

Because Adam sinned, every person is born into this world physically alive and spiritually dead (Ephesians 2:1). Since from birth we had neither the presence of God nor the knowledge of His ways, we learned to live our lives independent of God. Rather than having our needs met through a living relationship with our loving heavenly Father, we sought to meet our own needs. We developed patterns of thought and habits of behavior which centered our interests on ourselves.

When we were born again we became spiritually alive, but our self-centered flesh patterns and mental strongholds remained opposed to the leading of the Holy Spirit. Consequently we are still tempted to look to the world, the flesh, and the devil to meet our basic needs and carnal desires instead of looking to Christ, who promises to meet all our needs according to His riches in glory (Philippians 4:19). Every temptation is an enticement to live independently of God.

The power of temptation is directly related to the strength of the mental strongholds and the carnal desires which were developed when we learned to live independently of God. For example, if you were raised in a Christian home where dirty magazines and television programs of questionable moral value were not allowed, the power of sexual temptations in your life will not be as great as for someone who grew up exposed to pornographic materials. The person who was raised in an environment of immorality and sexual permissiveness will experience a greater struggle with sexual temptation after becoming a Christian simply because these mental strongholds were well-established before he was born again. You are less likely be tempted to commit some gross immorality if your legitimate needs to be loved and accepted were met by caring parents who also protected you from exposure to the values of this fallen world.

Too Much of a Good Thing

Most of us won't often be tempted to commit obvious sins such as armed robbery, murder, or rape. Satan is too clever and subtle for that. He knows that we will recognize the flagrant wrong in such temptations and refuse to act on them. Instead, his tactic is to entice us to push something good beyond the boundary of the will of God until it becomes sin. He treats us like the proverbial frog in the pot of water: gradually turning up the heat of temptation, hoping we don't notice that we are approaching the boundary of God's will and jump out before something good becomes sin.

Paul wrote, "All things are lawful for me, but not all things are profitable. All things are lawful for me, but I will not be mastered by anything" (1 Corinthians 6:12). He saw nothing but green lights in every direction of the Christian life. Everything is good and lawful for us because we are free from sin and no longer under the condemnation of the law. But Paul also knew that if we irresponsibly floorboard our lives in any of these good and lawful directions we will eventually run the red light of God's will, and that's sin.

The following statements reveal the sinful results in a number of areas where we are tempted to take the good things that God created beyond the boundary of God's will:

- physical rest becomes laziness
- quietness becomes noncommunication
- ability to profit becomes avarice and greed
- enjoyment of life becomes intemperance
- physical pleasure becomes sensuality
- interest in the possessions of others becomes covetousness
- enjoyment of food becomes gluttony
- self-care becomes selfishness

- self-respect becomes conceit
- communication becomes gossip
- cautiousness becomes unbelief
- positiveness becomes insensitivity
- anger becomes rage and bad temper
- lovingkindness becomes overprotection
- judgment becomes criticism
- same-sex friendship becomes homosexuality
- sexual freedom becomes immorality
- conscientiousness becomes perfectionism
- generosity becomes wastefulness
- self-protection becomes dishonesty
- carefulness becomes fear

Sin Versus Growth

First John 2:12-14 describes three levels of Christian growth in relation to sin. The first level is compared to "little children" (verse 12). Little children in the faith are characterized by having their sins forgiven and possessing a knowledge of God. In other words, they are in the family of God and have overcome the penalty of sin, but they are not yet mature in Christ.

The second level is "young men" (verses 13,14), so characterized because they have overcome the evil one. These are maturing believers who are strong because the Word of God abides in them. They know the truth and have overcome the power of sin. They have overcome the evil one by winning the battle for their minds. They are no longer in bondage to uncontrollable habits, and they have resolved the personal and spiritual conflicts which keep many Christians from experiencing freedom in Christ. They are experiencing their freedom in Christ and they know how to stay free.

The third level is "fathers" (verses 13,14), those who have developed a deep personal knowledge of God and a deep personal relationship with their heavenly Father. Having challenged us to combat sin's power in our lives through a commitment to growth, John goes on to describe the avenues through which Satan tempts us.

Channels of Temptation

According to the Bible, there are only three channels through which Satan will entice you to act independently of God. They are summarized in John's instructions to believers concerning our relationship to this world:

> Do not love the world, nor the things in the world. If anyone loves the world, the love of the Father is not in him. For all that is in the world, the lust of the flesh and the lust of the eyes and the boastful pride of life, is not from the Father but is from the world. And the world is passing away, and also its lusts; but the one who does the will of God abides forever (1 John 2:15-17).

The three channels of temptation are the *lust of the flesh*, the *lust of the eyes*, and the *pride of life*. The lust of the flesh preys on our physical appetites and their gratification in this world. The lust of the eyes appeals to self-interest and tests the Word of God. The pride of life relates to self-promotion and self-exaltation. Satan confronted both the first Adam and the last Adam through each of these three channels of temptation. The first Adam failed miserably, and we still suffer the results of his failure. But the last Adam—Jesus Christ—met Satan's threefold temptation head-on and succeeded triumphantly. In Him we have the resources and the power to conquer every temptation which Satan throws at us (see Figure 9a).

Channel of Temptation (1 John 2:15-17)	Lust of the Flesh (animal appetites, cravings, passions) "the woman saw that the tree was good for food" (Genesis 3:6)	Lust of the Eyes (selfishness, self-interest) "and that it was a delight to the eyes" (Genesis 3:6)	Pride of Life (self-promotion, self-exaltation) "and that the tree was desirable to make one wise" (Genesis 3:6)
Draws us away from the	Will of God (Galatians 16:18)	Word of God (Matthew 16:24-26)	Worship of God (1 Peter 5:5-11)
Destroys our	Dependence upon God (John 15:5)	Confidence in God (John 15:7)	Obedience to God (John 15:8-10)
First Adam (Genesis 3:1-6)	"Indeed, has God said, 'You shall not eat from any tree of the garden'?" (Genesis 3:1)	"You surely shall not die!" (Genesis 3:4)	"You will be like God" (Genesis 3:5)
Last Adam (Matthew 4:1-11)	"Man does not live by bread alone, but man lives by everything that proceeds out of the mouth of the LORD" (Deuteronomy 8:3)	"You shall not put the LORD your God to the test" (Deuteronomy 6:16)	"You shall fear only the LORD your God; and you shall worship Him" (Deuteronomy 6:13)

Figure 9a

The Lust of the Flesh

Satan first appealed to the lust of the flesh in Eve. He planted a doubt in her mind about the fruit of the tree when he said: "Has God said, 'You shall not eat from any tree of the garden'? " (Genesis 3:1). Eve answered, "God has said, 'You shall not eat from it or touch it' "(verse 3). Notice that Eve added on to God's Word when she said "or touch it." But Satan had piqued her appetite for the forbidden fruit, and she "saw that the tree was good for food" (verse 6). Yielding to the lust of the flesh led to Adam and Eve's downfall.

Satan also appealed to the lust of the flesh when he tempted Jesus. Our Lord had been fasting for 40 days when Satan tempted Him in the wilderness at the point of His apparent vulnerability: "If You are the Son of God, command that these stones become bread" (Matthew 4:3). This strikes at the very heart of temptation. Satan wanted Jesus to use His divine attributes independently of His heavenly Father to save Himself. Satan is not omniscient, but he's not blind either. He learned about Jesus' apparent vulnerability to physical temptation by watching Him go without food for 40 days. He's watching you too, looking for soft spots of vulnerability in your physical appetites for food, rest, comfort, and sex. Temptation is greatest when hunger, fatigue, and loneliness are acute.

Yielding to the lust of the flesh will draw us away from the will of God. There is nothing sinful about eating. Eating is a legitimate physical need, and God created food so we could meet that need. But concerning the fruit of one tree God said, "Don't eat it," and by eating, Adam and Eve violated God's will and acted independently of Him.

Similarly, there was nothing wrong with Jesus eating bread at the end of His fast, except that it wasn't the Father's will for Him to do so. Jesus replied: "Man shall not live on bread alone, but on every word that proceeds out of the mouth of God" (Matthew 4:4). No matter how desirable a loaf of bread may have seemed to Jesus in His state of hunger, He was not about to act independently of the Father's will by accepting Satan's offer. The life that Jesus modeled was a life totally dependent on God the Father (John 5:30; 6:57; 8:42; 14:10; 17:7).

Eating is necessary and right, but eating too much, eating the wrong kinds of foods, and allowing food to rule your life are wrong. Sex as intended by God is beautiful and good, but sex outside of marriage, homosexuality, and selfish sex are out-of-bounds and lead to bondage. If you give in to the temptation to meet your own physical needs or carnal desires independent of God, you are yielding to the lust of the flesh.

The Lust of the Eyes

The second channel of temptation through which Satan came to Adam and Eve related to his lie concerning the consequences of disobeying God. God had said that death would accompany disobedience, but Satan said, "You surely shall not die!" (Genesis 3:4). He was appealing to Eve's sense of self-preservation by falsely assuring her that God was wrong on the issue of sin's consequences. "Don't listen to Him; do what's right in your own eyes," he urged. The forbidden fruit was a delight to her eyes (verse 6), so she and Adam ignored God's command in order to do what appeared to serve their own best interests.

The lust of the eyes subtly draws us away from the Word of God and eats away at our confidence in God. We see what the world has to offer and desire it above our relationship with God. We begin to place more credence in our own perspective of life than in God's commands and promises. Fueled by the lust for what we see, we grab for all we can get, believing that we need it and trying to justify the idea that God wants us to have it. Wrongly assuming that God will withhold nothing good from us, we lustfully pursue materialistic prosperity.

Instead of trusting God, we adopt a "prove it to me" attitude. That was the essence of Satan's second temptation of Jesus: "If You are the Son of God, throw Yourself down [from the pinnacle of the temple]; for it is written, 'He will give His angels charge concerning You'; and 'On their hands they will bear You up, lest You strike your foot against a stone'" (Matthew 4:6). But Jesus wasn't about to play Satan's "show me" game. He replied, "It is written, 'You shall not put the Lord your God to the test'" (verse 7).

When I was a pastor, some of the members of my church unwittingly yielded to the temptation to put God to the test. I had a dear friend who was dying of cancer. But word spread around the church that four independent "witnesses" all testified that Dick wasn't going to die because God had told them so. Several exclaimed, "Isn't it wonderful that God is going to heal Dick!" Three weeks later Dick was dead.

If God was the One who told these four people that Dick wasn't going to die, then what does that make God? A liar. But is God a liar? Of course not; He's the truth. The originator of this "good news" was obviously the father of lies. Deceiving spirits had circulated a lie about Dick in an attempt to create a false hope and destroy the congregation's confidence in God.

God is under no obligation to us; He is under obligation only to Himself. There is no way you can cleverly word a prayer so that God must respond to it. That not only distorts the meaning of prayer but puts us in the position of manipulating God. The righteous shall live by faith in the written Word of God and not demand that God prove Himself in response to our whims or wishes, no matter how noble they may be. We are the ones being tested, not God.

The Pride of Life

The third channel of temptation is at the heart of the New Age movement: the temptation to direct our own destiny, to rule our own world, to be our own god. Satan tantalized Eve concerning the forbidden fruit: "The day you eat from it your eyes will be opened, and you will be like God, knowing good and evil" (Genesis 3:5). Satan's offer was an exaggerated appeal to our God-instilled propensity to rule. "Don't be satisfied ruling *under* God, when you have the potential to be *like* God." When Eve was convinced that "the tree was desirable to make one wise" (verse 6), she and Adam ate.

Satan's promise that the couple would become like God was a lie. When Adam and Eve yielded to his temptation, they lost their life and their position with God. Satan usurped their role and became the god of this world.

Satan tried the same ploy with Jesus: "The devil took Him to a very high mountain, and showed Him all the kingdoms of the world and their glory; and he said to Him, 'All these things will I give You if You fall down and worship me'" (Matthew 4:8,9). Jesus didn't challenge Satan's right to offer Him the kingdoms of the world and their glory. Since he was the god of this world, they were his to offer after Adam and Eve had forfeited them. But Jesus was not about to settle for anything less than the defeat of Satan. So He replied, "Begone, Satan! For it is written, 'You shall worship the Lord your God, and serve Him only'" (verse 10).

By appealing to the pride of life, Satan intends to steer us away from the worship of God and destroy our obedience to God. Whenever you feel that you don't need God's help or direction, that you can handle your life without consulting Him, that you don't need to bow the knee to anyone, beware: That's the pride of life. You may think you are serving yourself, but whenever you stop worshipping and serving God you are in reality worshipping and serving Satan—which is what he wants more than anything else. Instead, the Christian life should be characterized by humble obedience to God in worship (John 15:8-10; Peter 5:5-11).

Remember, there are three critical issues reflected in these channels of temptation: 1) the will of God, as expressed through your dependence upon God; 2) the Word of God, as expressed through your confidence in God; and 3) the worship of God, as expressed through your humble obedience to God. Every temptation that Satan throws at you will challenge one or all of these values. He will watch you to learn where you are most vulnerable and will tempt you in any area that you leave unguarded.

Two of Our Biggest Appetites

Why do we entertain tempting thoughts which are contrary to God's Word and God's will? Let's face it—we do so because we want to. We're not tempted by foods we don't like, by unattractive members of the opposite sex, by unwanted promotions, and so on. Temptation's hook is the devil's guarantee that what we think we want and need outside God's will can satisfy us. Don't believe it. You can never satisfy the desires of the flesh. The more you feed your carnal desires the more they grow. You cannot satisfy the desires of the flesh, but you can be satisfied in Christ. "Blessed are those who hunger and thirst for righteousness, for they shall be satisfied" (Matthew 5:6). By sustaining right relationships, living by the power of the Holy Spirit, and experiencing the fruit of the Spirit, you will be satisfied.

Eat to Live or Live to Eat?

Food is the ultimate appetite, since it is necessary for survival. So we eat to live, but when we begin to live to eat, food no longer satisfies. Instead, it consumes us, and millions of people feel powerless to control their appetite for food. When your body is deprived of necessary nutrients, you naturally crave those foods which will keep you healthy and keep your immune system functioning. If you eat to satisfy those natural cravings, you will stay healthy and free. But when you turn to food to relieve anxiety or satisfy a lust for sweets, salt, and so on, you will lose control, and the results will negatively affect your health.

It is no coincidence that Paul mentioned misuse of food in conjunction with his sober warning that "in later times some will fall away from the faith, paying attention to deceitful spirits and doctrines of demons" (1 Timothy 4:1). One of the evidences of the last days will be those who "advocate abstaining from foods" (verse 3) which are intended to meet a legitimate need. Anorexia and bulimia are called eating disorders, but they have little to do with food. The primary issue is deception.

Have you ever wondered why young women cut themselves, binge and purge, or force themselves to defecate? They think there is evil in them and they have to get it out. Paul says, "I find then the principle that evil is present in me, the one who wants to do good" (Romans 7:21). Will cutting themselves, purging, or defecating get rid of the evil? Of course not. I encouraged one young lady (who was taking 75 laxatives a day) to say, "I renounce defecating as a means of cleansing myself; I trust only in the cleansing work of Christ." As soon as she said that she began to cry and continued to do so uncontrollably for ten minutes. When she regained her composure, I asked, "What were you thinking during that time?" She said, "I can't believe the lies I have been believing!" A pastor's wife wrote to me after a conference:

> I can't begin to tell you all that the Lord has done in my life through the truth you shared with us at the conference. I am now more aware of the deception of the enemy, and this makes my gratefulness for my powerful and gracious Savior real. I was bulimic for 11 years. But now I can be in the house alone all day with a kitchen full of food and be in peace. When a temptation or lie from Satan pops into my mind, I fend it off quickly with the truth. I used to be in bondage to those lies for hours and hours each day, always fearing food. Now I'm rejoicing in the freedom which the truth brings.

Sexual Passions Unleashed

Paul also mentioned deceivers who forbid marriage in the last days (1 Timothy 4:3). Paul taught that celibacy was good, "but because of immoralities, each man is to have his own wife, and each woman is to have her own husband" (1 Corinthians 7:2). Sexual sins seem to be in a class by themselves. Paul wrote, "Every other sin that a man commits is outside the body, but the immoral man [fornicator] sins against his own body" (1 Corinthians 6:18). Virtually every person I have counseled has confessed some kind of sexual aberration. Some were in bondage to uncontrollable lust. Others were the victims of sexual abuse.

Sex is a God-given part of our autonomic nervous system. Normal sexual functioning is a regular, rhythmic part of life. But when Jesus said, "Everyone who looks on a woman to lust for her has committed adultery with her already in his heart" (Matthew 5:28), He was describing something beyond the boundary of God's design for sex. The word for lust is *epithumos*. The prefix *epi* means "to add to," signifying that something is being added to a normal drive. Jesus challenged us not to add onto the God-given sexual drive by polluting our minds with lustful thoughts. The only way to control your sexual life is to control your thought life. The following testimony reveals how a polluted mind leads to devastation:

> I was raised in what everyone would think was the perfect home. My parents were Christians and were very involved in church. They went out of their way to demonstrate their love. When I reached puberty, I was interested in sex just like every other red-blooded boy. My father and mother were not very good at sharing at an intimate level, so most of what I learned was from a book they had in the house.
>
> From that book I figured out how to masturbate. Pretty soon I was a slave to it. I soon found pornography and became a slave to that. It was available in stores, and they didn't seem to care about a junior high kid buying it. I was in my own private little world. On the outside I was this Christian kid, involved in the youth group, a counselor at Christian camp, and a member of the "perfect family" at church. On the

inside I was in complete bondage to pornography and lustful thinking.

I went to a Christian college where I continued to feed my lustful habits. I married my beautiful Christian girlfriend, and to everyone around us we were the "perfect couple." But I still had this private world that even my wife didn't know about. My job took me on the road, where I got closer and closer to the big one (adultery). I always thought I could dabble with pornography and not commit adultery, but it finally happened and then it happened again and again. I would have guilt and remorse, but never true repentance.

Finally, events that I know were orchestrated by God led to my wife finding out, and I confessed my secret life of sexual addiction. With the help of your books *A Way of Escape*, *Victory Over the Darkness*, and *The Bondage Breaker*, I was able to discover my freedom in Christ. No more bondage! No more slavery to sin!

The Way of Escape

First Corinthians 10:13 says: "No temptation has overtaken you but such as is common to man; and God is faithful, who will not allow you to be tempted beyond what you are able, but with the temptation will provide the way of escape also, that you may be able to endure it." Where is the way of escape? In the same place temptation is introduced: in your mind. Every temptation is first a thought introduced to your mind by your own carnality or the tempter himself. If you ruminate on that thought and consider it an option, you will eventually act on it, and that's sin. Instead Paul instructs us to take every thought captive to the obedience of Christ (2 Corinthians 10:5). The first step for escaping temptation is to apprehend every thought before it steps through the doorway of your mind.

Once you have halted a penetrating thought, the next step is to evaluate it on the basis of Paul's eightfold criterion for what we should think about: "Whatever is true, whatever is honorable, whatever is right, whatever is pure, whatever is lovely, whatever is of good repute, if there is any excellence and if anything worthy of praise, let your mind dwell on these things" (Philippians 4:8). Ask yourself, "Does this thought line up with God's truth? Is it suggesting that I do something honorable? Right? Pure? If this thought becomes action, will the outcome be lovely and contribute to excellence in my life? Will other believers approve of my actions? Is it something for which I can praise God?" If the answer to any of those questions is no, dismiss that thought immediately by choosing the truth. If it keeps coming back, keep saying no. When you learn to respond to tempting thoughts by stopping them at the door of your mind, evaluating them on the basis of God's Word, and dismissing those which fail the test, you have found the way of escape that God's Word promises.

In contrast, if a thought enters your mind and it passes the Philippians 4:8 test of truth, honor, righteousness, and so on, "let your mind dwell on these things" (verse 8) and "practice these things" (verse 9). "And the God of peace shall be with you" (verse 9), which is an infinitely better result than the pain and turmoil that follow when we yield to tempting thoughts and become involved in sinful behavior.

Submit, Confess, Resist, and Change

People who are caught in the sin-confess-sin-confess-sin-confess cycle eventually begin to lose hope that they can experience any real victory over sin. Sheer willpower can't keep them from repeating the sin they just confessed, and Satan pours on the condemnation. Self-control seems like an illusion, and the Christian life is one of unending ups and downs.

God will enable us to overcome this sin cycle of defeat. "My little children, I am writing these things to you that you may not sin. And if anyone sins, we have an Advocate with the Father, Jesus Christ the righteous" (1 John 2:1). We also have an adversary who will accuse us of every wrong we have done. We must turn to our righteous Advocate and resist our perverted adversary if we are to experience victory and freedom over temptation and sin. "Submit therefore to God. Resist the devil and he will flee from you" (James 4:7).

Submitting to God involves more than confession. It requires genuine repentance which means a change of mind and way of life. The following testimony shows how one man overcame the power of sin:

> I had been involved in, a user of, and addicted to pornography for many years. I hit bottom when my wife finally caught me. Shortly after I was caught, my wife and I were in a restaurant which had a rack of Christian books. Among them was one of your books, *Helping Others Find Freedom in Christ* [published by Regal Books]. I knew it was for me. That began my recovery.
>
> I had come to a place of doubting my salvation. Did God really love me? Was I beyond hope? That book and *The Bondage Breaker* and *A Way of Escape* helped me realize that I had been lied to and deceived by the enemy of my soul— and I went through the Steps to Freedom in Christ. I am free today. I believe I have "redemption and forgiveness of sins," that I am "dead to sin and alive to God." I am taking my responsibility to stay free very seriously. I meet weekly with an accountability group of men at my church. I now have a regular daily devotion with my Lord. God is doing for me what I could not do for myself.

Accused by the Father of Lies

ONE OF THE MOST COMMON ATTITUDES I have discovered in Christians—even among pastors, Christian leaders, and their wives and children—is a deep-seated sense of self-deprecation. I've heard them say, "I'm not important, I'm not qualified, I'm no good." I'm amazed at how many Christians are paralyzed in their witness and productivity by thoughts and feelings of inferiority and worthlessness.

Next to temptation, perhaps the most frequent and insistent attack from Satan to which we are vulnerable is accusation. By faith we have entered into an eternal relationship with the Lord Jesus Christ. As a result, we are dead to sin and alive to God, and we now sit with Christ in the heavenlies. In Christ we *are* important, we *are* qualified, we *are* loved. Satan can do absolutely nothing to alter our position in Christ and our worth to God. But he can render us virtually inoperative if he can deceive us into listening to and believing his insidious lies accusing us of being of little value to God or other people.

Satan often uses temptation and accusation as a brutal one-two punch. He tempts us by saying, "Why don't you try it? Everybody does it. Besides, you can get away with it. Who's going to know?" Then as soon as we fall for his tempting line, he changes his tune to accusation: "What kind of a Christian are you to do such a thing? You're a pitiful excuse for a child of God. You'll never get away with it. You might as well give up because God has already given up on you."

Satan is called "the accuser of the brethren...who accuses them before our God day and night" (Revelation 12:10). We have all heard his lying, hateful voice in our hearts and consciences. He never seems to let up on us. Many Christians are perpetually discouraged and defeated because they believe his persistent lies about them. And those who give in to his accusations end up being robbed of the freedom that God intends His people to enjoy. One defeated Christian wrote:

> My old feelings that life isn't worth the trouble keep coming back. I'm scared, lonely, confused, and very desperate. I know deep down that God can overcome this, but I can't get past this block. I can't even pray. When I try, things get in my way. When I'm feeling good and I begin putting into action what I know God wants me to do, I'm stopped dead in my tracks by those voices and a force so strong I can't continue. I'm so close to giving in to those voices that I almost can't fight them anymore. I just want some peace.

Putting the Accuser in His Place

The good news is that we don't have to listen to Satan's accusations and live in despair and defeat. Zechariah 3:1-10 provides the essential truth we need in order to stand by faith against Satan's accusations and to live righteously in the service of God.

The Lord revealed to the prophet Zechariah a heavenly scene in which Satan's accusations of God's people are put into proper perspective:

> He showed me Joshua the high priest standing before the angel of the LORD, and Satan standing at his right hand to accuse him. And the LORD said to Satan, "The LORD rebuke you, Satan! Indeed, the

LORD who has chosen Jerusalem rebuke you! Is this
not a brand plucked from the fire?" Now Joshua was
clothed with filthy garments and standing before the
angel (verses 1-3).

The Lord Rebukes Satan

Look at the cast of characters in this scene which resembles
a heavenly courtroom. The judge is God the Father. The prosecuting attorney is Satan. The defense attorney is Jesus. And
the accused defendant is Joshua the high priest, who represents
all of God's people. Historically, when the high priest entered
God's presence in the holy of holies each year, it was a very
solemn occasion. The priest had to perform elaborate purifica-
tion rites and ceremonial cleansings before entering, because if
somehow he wasn't just right before God he could be struck
dead on the spot. The priest wore bells on the hem of his robe
so those outside the holy of holies could tell if he was still alive
and moving. A rope was tied around his ankle so he could be
dragged out of the inner sanctuary if he died in God's presence.

So here is a high priest named Joshua standing in God's
presence with filthy garments representing the sins of Israel.
Bad news! Satan the accuser says, "Look at him, God. He's
filthy. He deserves to be struck dead." But God rebukes the
accuser and puts him in his place. "You're not the judge, and
you cannot pass sentence on my people," God says in His
rebuke. "I have rescued Joshua from the flames of judgment,
and your accusations are groundless."

This courtroom scene continues night and day for every
child of God. Satan persists in pointing out our faults and
weaknesses to God and demands that He zap us for being
less than perfect. But our defense attorney in heaven is Jesus
Christ, and He has never lost a case before God the judge.
Satan can't make his charges stick because Jesus Christ has
justified us and lives to intercede for us (Romans 8:33,34).

At the same time Satan accuses us before God, his emissaries also accuse us personally by bombarding our minds with false thoughts of unworthiness and unrighteousness in God's sight: "How could you do that and be a Christian? You're not really a child of God." But Satan is not your judge; he is merely your *accuser*. Yet if you listen to him and believe him, you will begin to live out these accusations as if they were a sentence you must serve.

When Satan's accusations of unworthiness attack you, don't pay attention to them. Instead think to yourself, "I have put my trust in Christ, and I am a child of God in Him. Like Joshua the high priest, I have been rescued by God from the fire of judgment, and He has declared me righteous. Satan cannot determine a verdict or pronounce a sentence. All he can do is accuse me—and I don't buy it."

The Lord Removes Our Filthy Garments

The reason Satan's accusations are groundless is because God has solved the problem of our filthy garments. Zechariah's description of the heavenly scene continues:

> And he spoke and said to those who were standing before him saying, "Remove the filthy garments from him." Again he said to him, "See, I have taken your iniquity away from you and will clothe you with festal robes." Then I said, "Let them put a clean turban on his head." So they put a clean turban on his head and clothed him with garments, while the angel of the LORD was standing by (Zechariah 3:4,5).

God has not only declared us forgiven, but He has removed our filthy garments of unrighteousness and clothed us with His righteousness. Notice that the change of wardrobe is something that *God* does, not we ourselves. In ourselves we don't have any garments of righteousness to put on that will satisfy God. He must change us in response to our submission to Him in faith.

The Lord Admonishes Us to Respond

Having rebuked Satan and provided our righteousness, the Lord calls for a response of obedience: "If you will walk in My ways, and if you will perform My service, then you will also govern My house and also have charge of My courts, and I will grant you free access among these who are standing here" (Zechariah 3:7). God's condition here has nothing to do with your relationship with Him or your standing of righteousness, since they are already secure. And these admonitions have nothing to do with Satan's defeat, since he is already defeated. They have to do with your *daily victory*. In calling us to walk in His ways and perform His service, the Lord is simply calling us to live by faith as children of God. It means crucifying the flesh on a daily basis and walking according to the Spirit. It means considering ourselves dead to sin and alive to God and not allowing sin to reign in our mortal bodies. It means taking every thought captive to the obedience of Christ and being transformed by the renewing of our minds.

In response to our daily ministry to Him through obedience, God promises that we will govern His house and have charge of His courts. This means that we will actively experience our sharing in His authority in the spiritual world, able to daily live victoriously over Satan and sin. He also promises us free access in the heavenlies. We have an open line of communication with the Father. As we operate in His authority and live in fellowship and harmony with Him, our daily victory and fruitfulness are assured.

Recognizing a Critical Difference

You may wonder, "What's the difference between the devil's accusations and the Holy Spirit's conviction?" Paul provided a clear distinction between the two in 2 Corinthians 7:9,10:

> I now rejoice, not that you were made sorrowful, but that you were made sorrowful to the point of repentance; for you were made sorrowful according to the will of God, in order that you might not suffer loss in anything through us. For the sorrow that is according to the will of God produces a repentance without regret, leading to salvation; but the sorrow of the world produces death.

The false guilt of this world and the Holy Spirit's conviction both have the same feeling of sorrow. However, the sorrow resulting from Satan's accusation leads to death, while the sorrow of conviction leads to repentance and life without regret. Paul wasn't rejoicing that the Corinthians felt sorrowful; he was rejoicing that their sorrow would lead to repentance, a knowledge of the truth, and finally freedom.

Every Christian is faced with the choice of walking by the Spirit or by the flesh on a daily basis. The moment you choose to walk according to the flesh, the Holy Spirit brings conviction because what you have just chosen to do is not compatible with who you really are. If you continue in the flesh you will feel the sorrow of conviction.

"How do I know which kind of sorrow I'm experiencing?" you may ask. "They feel the same." Determine whether your feelings reflect thoughts of truth or error, and you will identify their source. Do you feel guilty, worthless, stupid, or inept? That's a sorrow provoked by accusation because those feelings don't reflect truth. Judicially, you are no longer guilty; you have been justified through your faith in Christ, and there is no condemnation for those who are in Christ Jesus. You are not worthless; Jesus gave His life for you. You are not stupid or inept; you have the mind of Christ, and you can do all things through Christ who strengthens you. When you find lies lurking beneath your feelings of sorrow—especially if your feelings persistently drive you into the ground—you are being falsely accused. Even if you changed you wouldn't feel any better, because Satan would then find something else to harass you about. To disarm the sorrow of accusation you must submit yourself to God and resist the devil and his lies.

But if you are sorrowful because your behavior doesn't reflect your true identity in Christ, that's the sorrow according to the will of God which is designed to produce repentance. It's the Holy Spirit calling you to admit on the basis of 1 John 1:9, "Dear Lord, I was wrong." As soon as you confess and repent, God says, "I'm glad you shared that with Me. You're cleansed; now get on with life." And you walk away from that confrontation free. The sorrow is gone, and you have a positive new resolve to obey God in the area of your failure.

A graphic example of the contrast between accusation and conviction is found in the lives of Judas Iscariot and Simon Peter. Somehow Judas allowed Satan to deceive him into betraying Jesus for 30 pieces of silver (Luke 22:3-5). When Judas realized what he had done, he succumbed to the sorrow of the world and hung himself. Was his suicide the result of Satan's accusation or of God's conviction? It had to be accusation because it drove Judas to kill himself. Accusation leads to death; conviction leads to repentance and life.

Peter also failed Jesus by denying Him. It apparently began with pride as the disciples argued over who was the greatest among them (Luke 22:24-30). Jesus told Peter, "Simon, Simon, behold, Satan has demanded permission to sift you like wheat" (verse 31). That's right—Jesus allowed Satan to put Peter through the mill because Peter had given the enemy a foothold through pride. But Jesus also looked at Peter and said, "I have prayed for you, that your faith may not fail; and you, when once you have turned again, strengthen your brothers" (verse 32).

Peter vowed to die with Jesus, but Jesus told him that he would deny Him three times (verses 33,34), which he did.

The remorse Peter felt was every bit as painful as that which Judas experienced. But Peter's sorrow was from conviction which led to repentance (John 21:15-17). When your feelings of remorse pound you into the ground and drive you from God, you are being accused by Satan. Resist it. But when your sorrow draws you to confront Christ and confess your wrong, you are being convicted by the Spirit. Yield to it through repentance.

According to Revelation 12:10, Satan's continuing work is to accuse the brethren. But the good news is that Christ's continuing work is to intercede for us as He did for Peter. The writer of Hebrews declared, "He is able to save forever those who draw near to God through Him, since He always lives to make intercession for them" (7:25). We have a persistent adversary, but we have an even more persistent, eternal advocate who defends us before the Father on the basis of our faith in Him (1 John 2:1).

The Quicksand of Accusation

How important is it that we learn to resist the persistent accusations of Satan? It is absolutely vital to our daily victory in Christ. We have all felt like worthless nobodies from time to time. And when we feel like worthless nobodies we act like worthless nobodies, and our lives and ministries suffer until we repent and choose to believe the truth. But Satan never gives up. He will try to get us down more often and keep us down longer by hurling one false accusation after another. If we fail to keep resisting him, we may become vulnerable to even more serious attacks from Satan. Janelle's story is an extreme case, but it illustrates what can happen to a Christian who fails to take a stand against the accuser of the brethren.

Janelle was a Christian woman with severe emotional problems who was brought to me by her elderly pastor. Janelle's fiancé, Curt, came with them. After introducing me to Janelle and Curt, the pastor started to leave. "Wait a minute," I said. "I'd prefer that you stay with us."

"I've got a bad heart," the pastor replied. He may have had heart trouble, but I really think he was fearful that our session might get a little bizarre.

"I don't think anything will happen here today that will affect your heart," I assured him. (Little did I realize what was about to happen!) "Besides, you're her pastor, and I would appreciate your prayer support." The pastor reluctantly agreed.

As Janelle told me her story I realized that the accuser of the brethren had really done a number on her. She had been the victim of one abuse after another as a child and adolescent. Her background also included a sick relationship with a previous boyfriend who was involved in the occult. Over the years she had come to believe Satan's lies that she was the cause of her troubles and that she was of no value to God or anybody else. Her self-perception was down in the mud.

Recognizing Satan's familiar strategy, I said, "Janelle, we can help you with your problems because there is a battle going on for your mind which God has given us authority to win." As soon as I spoke those words Janelle suddenly went catatonic. She sat as still as a stone, eyes glazed over and staring into space.

"Have you ever seen her behave like this?" I asked her pastor and fiancé.

"No," they answered, wide-eyed. They were more than a little frightened.

"Well, there's nothing to worry about. I've seen it before," I said. "We're going to take authority over it, but it's important that you two affirm your right standing with God."

I led the pastor in a prayer. When I turned to lead Curt, he started to shake.

"Curt, is there something between you and God that's not right?" I asked. "I suggest you get it cleared up right now."

Under the circumstances, Curt didn't need much prompting! He began confessing sin in his life, including the revelation that he and Janelle had been sleeping together. In response to my counsel, Curt committed himself to end that practice. All the while Janelle sat motionless.

After we had prayed together about getting his life straight with God, I gave Curt a sheet of paper with a prayer on it to read. As soon as Curt began to read the prayer, Janelle let out a menacing growl, then lashed out and slapped the paper out of Curt's hands. Satan tried to use the suddenness of her actions to frighten us, and for an instant we were startled. It was just a scare tactic. We would have elevated Satan to a position higher than God if we had feared him more. We exercised God's authority and agreed in prayer that the evil one be bound in the name of the Lord Jesus Christ.

I wish I could have videotaped my encounter with Janelle that day in order to show the skeptics what happens when Satan's attempt is confronted by God's authority. It was as if Wonder Woman had lassoed Janelle and tied her to the chair. She just sat there squirming, bound to the chair by the ropes of God's authority. Her eyes blazed at Curt with hatred, which was further evidence of the demonic power which was controlling her. Janelle didn't hate Curt; she loved him. They were going to be married. But Satan hated the fact that his strongholds in Curt and Janelle were being torn down, and his hatred was mirrored in Janelle's countenance.

Curt finished reading the prayer while Janelle continued to squirm in her chair. Then I prayed, "Lord, we declare our dependence on You, for apart from Christ we can do nothing. Now, in the name and authority of the Lord Jesus Christ, we command Satan and all his forces to release Janelle and to remain bound so she will be free to obey her heavenly

Father." Suddenly Janelle slumped in her chair and snapped out of her catatonic state.

"Do you remember anything we've been doing here?" I asked her.

"No, what happened?" she responded with a puzzled expression.

"It's nothing to worry about," I told her. "Somehow Satan has gained a foothold in your life, and we would like to take you through the Steps to Freedom in Christ." About an hour later Janelle was free.

What right did Satan have to control Janelle as he did? Only the right that she gave him by yielding to his lies and by living in sin. Satan had convinced her that she was of little value and that what she did was of little consequence. So she lived on the fringe of immorality and dabbled in the occult, allowing Satan even greater control. But once Janelle renounced her involvement with sin and Satan, his hold on her was canceled, and he had to leave.

For most of us, Satan's deceptive accusations will not result in the kind of bondage illustrated by Janelle's experience. But if he can cause you to doubt your worth to God or your effectiveness as His child through his accusations, he can neutralize your life for God. Put your feelings to the test. Take every thought captive. Don't believe anything Satan says about you; it's a lie. Believe everything God says about you; it's the truth which will set you free.

The Unpardonable Sin

Despite all the biblical assurances to the contrary, many believers struggle with the fear that they have committed the unpardonable sin. This is a critical matter to resolve, since one of the pieces of the armor of God is the helmet of salvation (Ephesians 6:17). Those who are tormented by this fear usually suffer in silence. They think they have committed the unpardonable sin by blaspheming the Holy Spirit. Usually this fear is born out of ignorance, or it is an attack of the enemy. Consider Mark 3:22-30:

> The scribes who came down from Jerusalem were saying, "He is possessed by Beelzebul," and "He casts out the demons by the ruler of the demons." And He called them to Himself and began speaking to them in parables, "How can Satan cast out Satan? And if a kingdom is divided against itself, that kingdom cannot stand. And if a house is divided against itself, that house will not be able to stand. And if Satan has risen up against himself and is divided, he cannot stand, but he is finished! But no one can enter the strong man's house and plunder his property unless he first binds the strong man, and then he will plunder his house. Truly I say to you, all sins shall be forgiven the sons of men, and whatever blasphemies they utter; but whoever blasphemes against the Holy Spirit never has forgiveness, but is guilty of an eternal sin"—because they were saying, "He has an unclean spirit."

It is the unique work of the Holy Spirit to draw all people to Christ. If you reject that witness, then you can never come to Christ and salvation. Those who do come to Christ are the sons of God, and their sins and blasphemies are forgiven because they are in Christ. If you reject the witness of God's Spirit, then you will never come to Christ in the first place. That is why no Christian can commit the unpardonable sin. Standing in front of the scribes and Pharisees was the Messiah, Jesus, the Son of God, and they attributed His ministry of delivering people from demonic bondage to the devil. They even accused Jesus of being possessed by Satan! They totally rejected the witness of the Spirit.

These were the same men who so hated Jesus that they maliciously orchestrated His betrayal, arrest, mock trial, scourging, beating, and crucifixion. They detested Jesus and cursed Him, spat upon Him, and sneered at Him when He hung on the cross. If you have come under the conviction of the Holy Spirit and have trusted in Christ, you have just done the *opposite* of committing the unpardonable sin.

We have talked with many believers who question their salvation and are under heavy conviction. The very fact that they are feeling convicted for their sins is the best evidence they are Christians or that the Holy Spirit is convicting them of their sinful nature and leading them to salvation. Such conviction is further evidence they have not committed the unpardonable sin. If the Holy Spirit was not at work in them, those things wouldn't even be bothering them.

The devil is an accuser. He is like a prosecuting attorney deceptively seeking to discredit and discourage a witness on the stand. He points his slimy finger and says, "Aha! You've done it now! There's no hope for you. You've blasphemed the Holy Spirit!" Perhaps you have questioned some spiritual gift, anointed preacher, or apparent supernatural manifestation. Is that blaspheming the Holy Spirit? Of course not. In fact it could be necessary discernment. Listen to John's instruction, "Beloved, do not believe every spirit, but test the spirits to see whether they are from God, because many false prophets have gone out into the world" (1 John 4:1). A Christian can grieve the Holy Spirit (Ephesians 4:30) and even quench the Holy Spirit (1 Thessalonians 5:19)—but neither of these is unpardonable.

The Danger of Deception

I HAD JUST FINISHED SPEAKING at a Sunday evening service when a friend of mine passed me a note: "I brought a family to church with me tonight. Will you please see them before you leave?" I was dead tired from a weekend of speaking, and I still had at least an hour of ministry ahead of me with people who wanted to talk after the service. But I agreed to see the family if they could wait until I was finished.

Unknown to me, my friend had practically dragged 26-year-old Alyce and her parents to the service against their will. They were Christians, but as I sat down with them it was obvious that they had a problem. Alyce was one of the most pathetic-looking young women I have ever met. She was dangerously thin. She had lost her job three days earlier, and her vacant eyes conveyed that she had lost all hope for her life.

Alyce's father told me that she had suffered terribly from PMS during adolescence and had become addicted to prescription painkillers. She was a very talented girl and a committed Christian in many ways, but she was also a Darvon junkie who had even been arrested once for illegal possession of prescription drugs. As her father told me her sad story, Alyce sat nodding to herself as if to say, "Yes, that's me, and life is the pits."

Finally I turned to Alyce, took her by the hands, and said, "I want you to tell me who you think you are."

"I'm just a no-good failure," she whimpered.

"You're not a failure," I responded. "You're a child of God." She continued to pour out the negative self-talk, and I continued to counter her negativism with the good news of who she was in Christ. The hour was late and I was tired, but the more we talked the more aware I became of Christ's presence ministering to Alyce. I encouraged her to pray, asking the Lord to show her the source and the true nature of all those negative thoughts.

After praying she said, "Do you mean to tell me that all these negative thoughts about myself are nothing but Satanic deception?"

"That's right, Alyce," I nodded in agreement. "You have been paying attention to a deceiving spirit. You don't have to believe those lies. When you discover who you are in Christ, and learn to take every thought captive to the obedience of Christ, you will be free from the bondage of Satan's lies."

Two weeks later Alyce was enrolled in an intensive 12-week, live-in spiritual growth course at the Julian Center near San Diego. By the end of the course Alyce had learned to take the initiative to believe the truth instead of being deceived by the father of lies. She got a job and gained about 25 pounds. Today she is free.

Satan's Number-One Strategy

If I tempted you, you would know it. If I accused you, you would know it. But if I deceived you, you wouldn't know it. If you knew you were being deceived, then you would no longer be deceived. Eve was deceived and she believed a lie. Deception has been the primary strategy of Satan from the beginning. That is why truth sets us free, and why Jesus prayed, "Sanctify them in the truth; Thy word is truth" (John

17:17). "Having girded [our] loins with truth" (Ephesians 6:14), we have available to us our first means of defense.

There are three primary avenues through which Satan will attempt to dissuade you from God's truth and deceive you into believing his lies: self-deception, false prophets/teachers, and deceiving spirits. We are vulnerable to Satan's lies if we fail to take every thought captive to the obedience of Christ (2 Corinthians 10:5).

Beware of Self-deception

There are several ways in which we can deceive ourselves:

We deceive ourselves when we hear the Word but don't do it (James 1:22; 1 Peter 1:13). I frequently come across pastors, missionaries, and Bible teachers who are preaching and teaching against the very sins they are committing themselves. Those of us who are called to preach or teach God's Word must apply the message to ourselves first. We need to get on our knees before God and ask, "Lord, is what I am about to teach true in *my* life?" If not, we had better be honest enough to say to those who hear us, "I wish I were a better example of this passage, but even though I'm not, I still need to preach the whole counsel of God. Would you pray for me as I pray for you, that we would all be able to live according to this truth?" To proclaim the Word of God as if it were true in our own lives when it's not is to live a lie, and we will be deceiving ourselves.

Those of us who receive the Word are also vulnerable to self-deception if we fail to put it into practice. We hear a sermon or a lesson and say, "Wow! What a great truth!" and share it with someone else without processing it ourselves and applying it to our own lives. James said that hearers of the Word who are not also doers of the Word deceive themselves (1:22).

Why are we afraid to admit it when our lives don't perfectly match up to Scripture? Don't we know we are forgiven and God accepts us for who we are? His unconditional love and acceptance are what set us free to be ourselves. Those who feel driven to earn God's love and acceptance will struggle with perfectionism and will find it difficult to admit failure. But we can't model perfection because we're not perfect; we can only model *growth*. The people around us need to know that we are real people who are in the process of becoming like Christ. They need to see how we handle failure as well as how we handle success. When we model this kind of honesty in the Christian community, we greatly reduce the possibility of the deceiver gaining a foothold.

We deceive ourselves when we say we have no sin (1 John 1:8). The Scripture doesn't say that we *are* sin; it says that it is possible for us to sin and for sin to reside in our mortal bodies (Romans 6:12). We are not sinless saints; we are saints who sin. It's important to keep honest account of our failures and pick up our cross daily. When we become aware of a discrepancy between our identity in Christ and our behavior, we must confess it and deal with it. The person who deceives himself by ignoring these sinful discrepancies and allowing them to accumulate is headed for a fall.

Those who live in earthquake-prone southern California keep hearing about "the big one," which is thought by many to be inevitable along the San Andreas fault. Minor earthquakes may shake up the residents of that area, but they do very little damage. Since these small quakes indicate the subterranean plates are shifting and adjusting to pressure, southern Californians like them. Slow, incremental changes are good. If they continue to happen, the "big one" may never occur.

The same is true for us. If we keep saying, "I don't have any sin," or if we fail to acknowledge our shortcomings and settle our differences with people and God, then "the big one" is coming. We can choose to humble ourselves; but if we don't, God will. "God is opposed to the proud, but gives grace to the humble" (James 4:6). Witness the alcoholic who will not admit he has a problem until he loses his health, family, job, and friendships. Unacknowledged sin is like cancer cells. If they are caught at an early stage of growth through regular checkups, the prognosis is good; but if they're left to grow undetected, the prognosis is bad. Living in the light and holding ourselves accountable to God on a daily basis prevents major spiritual crises.

We deceive ourselves when we think we are something we are not (Romans 12:3; Galatians 6:3). Scripture instructs us not to think of ourselves more highly than we ought to think. "But I know who I am," you say. "I'm a child of God, I'm seated with Christ in the heavenlies, I can do all things through Him. That makes me pretty special." Yes, you are very special in the eyes of God. But you are what you are by the grace of God (1 Corinthians 15:10). The life you live, the talents you possess, and the gifts you have received are not personal accomplishments; they are expressions of God's grace. Never take credit for what God has provided; rather, take delight in accomplishing worthwhile deeds which glorify the Lord.

We deceive ourselves when we think we are wise in this age (1 Corinthians 3:18,19). It is the height of intellectual arrogance to assume wisdom without the revelation of God. "Professing to be wise, they became fools" (Romans 1:22). Sometimes we are tempted to think we can match wits and intellect with the god of this world. But we are no match for him in the flesh. Whenever we think we can outsmart Satan on our own, we are prime candidates to be led astray by his craftiness. However, Satan is no match for God. It is important for us not to lean on our own understanding, but to employ the mind of Christ and acknowledge Him in all our ways (Proverbs 3:5,6; 1 Corinthians 2:16).

We deceive ourselves when we think we are religious but do not bridle our tongue (James 1:26). There is nothing that grieves God more than when we bad-mouth people instead of building them up. We are never to use our tongues to put others down. Instead we are to edify one another in what we say and thereby give grace to those who hear us (Ephesians 4:29,30). If your tongue is out of control, you're fooling yourself to believe that you have your spiritual life together.

We deceive ourselves when we think we will not reap what we sow (Galatians 6:7). As Christians we sometimes think we are exempt from this principle, but we are not. We will have to live with the consequences of our thoughts, words, and actions, whether good or bad.

We deceive ourselves when we think the unrighteous will inherit the kingdom of God (1 Corinthians 6:9,10). Kate, a young woman who was interning at a church I served, walked into the office one day completely devastated. She had just learned that her older sister, who had led her to Christ, had walked away from God and was living in a lesbian relationship. "My lifestyle doesn't make any difference," Kate's sister had argued. "God loves me and I'm forgiven." Kate was distraught and confused.

I directed her to 1 Corinthians 6: "Do not be deceived; neither fornicators, nor idolaters, nor adulterers, nor effeminate, nor homosexuals...shall inherit the kingdom of God" (verses 9,10). Somehow Kate's sister and others like her are deceived, failing to understand this truth: Living a brazenly sinful life is strong evidence of an unrighteous standing before God. This is not a works gospel; it is a matter of identifying true disciples by their fruit. You are deceived if you believe that your lifestyle does not need to line up with your profession of faith.

We deceive ourselves when we think we can continually associate with bad company and not be corrupted (1 Corinthians 15:33). When I was a young Christian I used to listen to records by an evangelist in New Orleans who was called "the Bourbon Street preacher." This man lived in the red-light district and claimed to have a ministry to prostitutes and other questionable characters. But according to 1 Corinthians 15:33, anyone who stays in that environment too long will get into trouble. And that's just what happened to this evangelist. He became so entangled with the seedy side of Bourbon Street that he eventually lost his ministry.

Does this mean that we shouldn't minister to those with bad morals? No, we must share Christ with them. But if we immerse ourselves in their environment, our ministry will eventually diminish and our morality will be affected for the worse.

Beware of False Prophets and Teachers

Recently a man in his thirties was referred to me. Alvin was discouraged and defeated. For several years he had believed he had a special gift of prophecy from God. He was invited to church after church to speak as an oracle for God by prophesying in his unique way. But over a period of months his personal life began to fall apart. Alvin eventually reached the point where he could no longer function in society, and he began to withdraw from people completely. By the time he came to see me he had been unemployed for two years, he was being cared for by his father, and he was a slave to prescription drugs.

Alvin and I read 1 Thessalonians 5:19-21: "Do not put out the Spirit's fire; do not treat prophecies with contempt. Test everything. Hold on to the good" (NIV). I said, "Alvin, the Bible does say there is a gift of prophecy. But Satan can counterfeit spiritual gifts and deceive us into believing they're from God. That's why the Scriptures instruct us to put everything to the test."

After a lengthy discussion about false prophets and teachers, Alvin admitted, "I think my problems began when I failed to test the 'gifts' of tongues and prophecy conferred on me by false teachers. Not only was I deceived, but I have deceived others."

"Would you be willing to put your gift of tongues to the test?" I asked. I assured Alvin that we were going to test the spirit, not him. He agreed, so I instructed him to begin praying aloud in his "spiritual language." As Alvin began praying in what he thought was his gift of tongues, I said, "In the name of Christ and in obedience to God's Word, I ask this spirit to identify itself."

Alvin stopped "praying" and said, "I am he."

In a situation like this, if you were inexperienced in these matters or lacked spiritual discernment, you might be tempted to take off your shoes, thinking you were on holy ground. But I continued testing the spirit: "Are you the Christ who was crucified under Pontius Pilate, buried, raised on the third day, and who now sits at the right hand of the Father?"

The response was, "No! Not he!"

Obviously the wrong spirit!

For those of you who are against certain gifts of the spirit, listen to Paul's instruction: "Desire earnestly to prophesy, and do not forbid to speak in tongues" (1 Corinthians 14:39), and "Do not quench the Spirit; do not despise prophetic utterances" (1 Thessalonians 5:19,20). For those who want the fullness of God but lack discernment, listen to Paul's instruction, "Examine everything carefully; hold fast to that which is good; and abstain from every form of evil" (1 Thessalonians 5:21,22). False prophets and teachers flourish simply because Christians accept their ministry without spiritual discernment.

Comparing the Counterfeit with the Real

Every true prophet of God in the Old Testament was essentially an evangelist. The true prophet drew people back to God and His Word. The call to righteousness was the standard which separated the genuine prophet from the imitation. Jeremiah wrote: "Thus says the LORD of hosts, 'Do not listen to the words of the prophets who are prophesying to you....I did not send these prophets, but they ran. I did not speak to them, but they prophesied. But if they had stood in My council, then they would have announced My words to My people, and would have turned them back from their evil way and from the evil of their deeds'" (23:16,21,22).

The Lord revealed through Jeremiah another criterion for distinguishing a true prophet from a false prophet: "I have heard what the prophets have said who prophesy falsely in My name, saying, 'I had a dream, I had a dream!'...The prophet who has a dream may relate his dream, but let him who has My word speak My word in truth. What does straw have in common with grain?" (verses 25,28). God is warning His people against prophets who value their dreams above His Word.

God often spoke to people in the Bible through dreams. But in comparison to the nutritious grain of His Word, dreams are mere straw. If you feed only straw to cattle, they'll die. They will sleep on it, but they won't eat it because it has no nutrients. Similarly, dreams are of some value, but they are never to be equated with God's Word nor serve as the basis for our faith. Dreams must be in agreement with God's Word—not the other way around.

Jeremiah continues: "'Is not My word like fire?' declares the LORD, 'and like a hammer which shatters a rock?'" (23:29). If you attend a Christian fellowship where prophecies are part of public worship, don't expect prophecies like "I love you, my children" or "I'm coming soon" if members of the congregation are living in sin (though such statements are true, and those who know their Bibles would already know that). The Spirit of God is not going to lull His people into an unrighteous complacency. Remember, judgment begins in the household of God (1 Peter 4:17).

A prophetic message should motivate people to righteousness, not placate them in their sin. According to Paul, the gift of prophecy will disclose the secrets of a person's heart, causing him to fall on his face and worship God (1 Corinthians 14:24,25). God is more concerned about church purity than about church growth, because church purity is an essential prerequisite for church growth. Comfort only comes to those who are suffering and persecuted for righteousness' sake.

Jeremiah relates other evidences of false prophets: "'Behold, I am against the prophets,' declares the LORD, 'who steal My words from each other'" (23:30). That's plagiarism: taking what God gave someone else and using it as if it were your own. "'I am against the prophets,' declares the LORD, 'who use their tongues and declare, "The Lord declares"'" (verse 31).

Declaring that your words are directly from the Lord when they aren't is an incredible offense to God. Manipulating people by claiming a word from the Lord is spiritual abuse. For instance, I have counseled several wives who were told by their husbands, "God revealed to me that we are supposed to get married." Any man who asked for my daughter's hand in marriage had better come with a humble request, not a mandate.

There is another subtle deception that we should be aware of. Has anybody ever said to you, "The Lord told me to tell you..."? I would probably respond, "No, He didn't!" If God wanted me to personally know or do something, why wouldn't He tell me directly? I believe in the priesthood of believers; God can and will encourage us and confirm His Word to us through others. For instance, another person could give me a prophetic message calling me to get right with God so He could lead me. But when God speaks to His children, "there is one God, and one mediator also between

God and men, the man Christ Jesus" (1 Timothy 2:5). No Christian is ever to function as a medium.

Signs and Wonders: Who's Being Tested?

A false prophet is revealed when his prophecies don't come true. Moses instructed us not to believe the prophet whose prophecies fail (Deuteronomy 18:22). But Deuteronomy 13:1-3 also warns us about the false prophet whose signs and wonders *do* come true: "If a prophet or a dreamer of dreams arises among you and gives you a sign or a wonder, and the sign or wonder comes true, concerning which he spoke to you, saying, 'Let us go after other gods (whom you have not known) and let us worship them,' you shall not listen to the words of that prophet or that dreamer of dreams; for the LORD your God is testing you to find out if you love the LORD your God with all your heart and with all your soul" (see also Matthew 24:4-11,23-25; Revelation 13:11-14).

It is wrong to assume that every miraculous experience is from God. God can use signs and wonders to confirm the Word, but the Bible also warns that "false Christs and false prophets will arise, and will show signs and wonders, in order, if possible, to lead the elect astray" (Mark 13:22). Satan can also perform signs and wonders, but he only does so to direct our worship away from God to himself. Deuteronomy 13:5-11 reveals the seriousness of attributing to God the activity of Satan. Persons who were involved in such things were to be executed, even if they were relatives. We are to love God, obey His Word, and test all signs, wonders, and dreams.

Counterfeits in the Church

What comes to mind when you hear the terms "false prophets" and "false teachers"? Many people tend to think of Eastern mystics and gurus, the spokespersons for other religions, or dynamic cult leaders—people who are recognizably outside the boundaries of the Christian church. But the apostle Peter devoted an entire chapter in one of his letters to false prophets and teachers who operate *within* the church: "But false prophets also arose among the people, just as there will be false teachers among you, who will secretly introduce destructive heresies, even denying the Master who bought them, bringing swift destruction upon themselves" (2 Peter 2:1). Apparently false prophets and false teachers disguised as workers of righteousness can be present in our churches.

Notice how false teachers lure you into their deceptive teaching: "Many will follow their sensuality, and because of them the way of the truth will be maligned" (verse 2). We "follow their sensuality" when we elevate appearance, performance, charm, and personality above the truth: "He's such a nice guy"; "She's a very charismatic person"; "He's a real dynamic speaker"; "She's so sweet and sounds so sincere." Being physically attractive and having a charismatic personality are not biblical criteria for validating a ministry or a teacher. The standards are *truth* and *righteousness*, and false teachers malign both.

Peter goes on to reveal two ways by which we can identify false prophets and false teachers who operate within the church. First, they will eventually reveal their immorality, indulging "the flesh in its corrupt desires" (verse 10). Or their teaching could be antinomian, claiming that God is all love and grace, so we don't need to abide by any moral absolutes. Their immorality may not be easy to spot, but it will eventually surface in their lives (2 Corinthians 11:13-15).

Second, false prophets and teachers "despise authority" and are "daring, self-willed" (2 Peter 2:10). These people have an independent spirit. They do their own thing and won't answer to anybody. They either won't submit to the authority of a denomination or board, or they will pick their own board which will simply rubber-stamp anything they want to do.

There are three Old Testament leadership roles which have functional equivalents in the church: prophet (preaching and teaching), priest (pastoring and shepherding), and king (administration). Only Jesus in His perfection is capable of occupying all three roles simultaneously. I believe we need the checks and balances of a plurality of elders in the church, distributing the three critical roles to more than one person. Absolute authority corrupts absolutely. Committed Christians in leadership roles need to submit themselves and their ideas to other mature believers who will hold them accountable. You need to find another church if your pastor is not under authority or if he doesn't display the heart of a shepherd and a servant.

Beware of Deceiving Spirits

In addition to deceiving ourselves and being deceived by false prophets and false teachers, we can pay attention to a deceiving spirit. "The Spirit explicitly says that in later times some will fall away from the faith, paying attention to deceitful spirits and doctrines of demons" (1 Timothy 4:1). John also cautioned us to test the spirits in order to unmask antichrists (1 John 2:18) and to distinguish the spirit of truth from the spirit of error (4:1-6). Satan's demonic forces are at work attempting to pollute your mind with lies in order to keep you from walking in the truth. Hannah Whitehall Smith wrote:

> There are the voices of evil and deceiving spirits, who lie in wait to entrap every traveler entering these higher regions of spiritual life. In the same epistle that tells us that we are seated in the heavenly places in Christ, we are also told that we shall have to fight with spiritual enemies. These spiritual enemies, whoever or whatever they may be, must necessarily communicate with us by means of our spiritual faculties, and their voices, as the voice of God, are an inward impression made upon

our spirit. Therefore, just as the Holy Spirit may tell us by impressions what the will of God is concerning us, so also will these spiritual enemies tell us by impression what is their will concerning us, though not, of course, giving it their name.[1]

Due to the deceptive nature of his impressions, Satan's voice may not always be detected objectively. The following prayer expresses the attitude we should have whenever we suspect a false prophet, false teacher, or deceiving spirit:

> *Heavenly Father, I commit myself unreservedly to Your will. I ask You to show me the true nature of this person or spirit. If I have been deceived in any way, I pray that You will open my eyes to the deception. I command in the name of the Lord Jesus Christ that all deceiving spirits depart from me, and I renounce and reject all counterfeit gifts (or any other spiritual phenomena). Lord, if it is from You, bless it and cause it to grow, that Your body may be blessed and edified through it. Amen.*

Spiritual Discernment

Spiritual discernment is our first line of defense against deception. The Holy Spirit has taken up residence in every believer, and He is not silent when we encounter the counterfeit. Discernment is that little "buzzer" that goes off inside when something is wrong. For example, have you ever visited someone's home where everybody is polite and everything external seems to be in order, but you can cut the air with a knife? Even though nothing visible confirms it, your spirit detects that something is wrong.

To have a discerning spirit, you need to examine your motives. In 1 Kings 3, Israel's young king cries out to God for help. God comes to Solomon in a dream and asks him what he wants. Solomon responds: "Give Thy servant an understanding heart to judge Thy people to discern between good and evil" (verse 9). God answers: "Because you have asked this thing and have not asked for yourself long life, nor have asked riches for yourself, nor have you asked for the life of your enemies, but have asked for yourself discernment to understand justice, behold, I have done according to your words. Behold, I have given you a wise and discerning heart" (verses 11,12).

The motive for true discernment is never self-promotion, personal gain, or to secure an advantage over another person—even an enemy. The Greek word for discernment—*diakrino*—simply means to make a judgment or a distinction. Discernment has only one function: to distinguish right from wrong so the right can be acknowledged and the wrong can be disregarded. In 1 Corinthians 12:10, discernment is the divinely enabled ability to distinguish a good spirit from a bad spirit. It is a manifestation of the Spirit, which is to be utilized to edify the church.

Spiritual discernment is not a function of the mind; it's a function of the spirit. Our union with God is what makes spiritual discernment possible. We rightly divide the word of truth with our minds, but the Spirit helps us know what cannot be objectively verified. We can spiritually discern whether something is right or wrong, but we can't always objectively verify what it is.

In many counseling cases I am able to sense in my spirit that something is wrong and subjectively know that the real issue has not surfaced. Sometimes I seem to even "know" what the issue is, but instead of saying it, I test it. For example, if I discern that the counselee may be in bondage to homosexuality, I don't say, "You're a homosexual, aren't you?" That would be judgment. Rather, I test the impression at the appropriate time by saying something like, "Have you ever struggled with homosexual thoughts or tendencies?" If my discernment matches the convicting work of the Holy Spirit in the counselee, the problem usually surfaces and is dealt with.

Satan can also counterfeit discernment, leading some to think they have God-given spiritual insight. Lana, an undergraduate student I counseled, was deceived by Satan's version of discernment. She had been seeing a counselor because she was deeply troubled. When she came to see me, Lana explained that she could walk through our campus and point out students who had problems with drugs and sex. She had no facts or substantiated information; she just "knew." And from what I could tell, she was right. Lana thought she had an unusual gift from God. She also told me how she played mental games with her counselor by telling him what he was going to do or say next.

When she said that, I knew there was something wrong with her spirit. "You like having power over people, don't you, Lana?" I said. The moment I exposed the false spirit it manifested itself in my office. When she finally found her freedom in Christ, she no longer had the "ability" to identify the sins of others. Lana's mind was so quiet that she had to learn to live without the noise from her "companions" which had cluttered her mind for years.

Evil spirits operate in the demonic realm like the Holy Spirit operates in the Christian realm. Have you ever "known" that someone was a Christian before he or she even said anything about it? Have you ever sensed a compatible spirit with other believers? There is nothing magical about that; it's just the presence of the Holy Spirit bearing witness with your spirit. At other times the Holy Spirit warns you that the spirit controlling another person is not a compatible spirit.

If we would learn to be more spiritually aware in our churches and homes, God could keep us from many disasters. In the Western world our cognitive, left-brain orientation all but excludes discernment as our essential guide for navigating through the spiritual world. But the writer of Hebrews identified those who had discernment: "Solid food is for the mature, who because of practice have their senses trained to discern good and evil" (5:14).

You cannot expose Satan's deception by human reasoning; you can only do it by God's Spirit and divine revelation. Jesus said, "If you abide in My word, then you are truly disciples of Mine; and you shall know the truth, and the truth shall make you free" (John 8:31,32). Jesus prayed, "Sanctify them in the truth; Thy word is truth" (John 17:17). It is critical that when you put on the armor of God you start with the belt of truth (Ephesians 6:14). The light of truth is the only valid weapon against the darkness of deception.

I close this chapter with an encouraging letter I received from a young woman who was trapped in deception until Jesus set her free when I took her through the Steps to Freedom:

> I will always remember the day I came to you for counsel and prayer. Ever since that day I have felt such freedom. There are no more voices or feelings of heaviness in my brain. I'm even enjoying a physical sense of release. Satan has returned many times trying to clobber me with those old thoughts, but his hold on me has been broken.
>
> I'll never forget what you told me. You said that those negative thoughts about God and myself were lies that Satan planted in my mind. You said I have the power through Jesus Christ to rebuke Satan and get rid of the evil thoughts. It has taken me awhile to really believe that with all my heart, but lately I've decided to fight back—and it works! It's been wonderful to deal with my problems with a clear head.

The Danger of Losing Control

I RECEIVED THE FOLLOWING LETTER from a young woman I have never met. Sheila attended a Saturday conference I conducted at her church on resolving personal and spiritual conflicts. On Sunday the pastor of the church handed me this letter from her:

> Dear Neil,
>
> I have been set free—praise the Lord! Yesterday, for the first time in years, the voices stopped. I could hear the silence. When we sang, I could hear myself sing.
>
> For the first 14 years of my life I lived with an oppressive, abusive mother who never said "I love you" or put her arms around me when I cried. I received no affection, no kind words, no affirmation, no sense of who I was—only physical and emotional abuse. At 15 I was subjected to three weeks of Erhard Seminar Training (EST), which really screwed up my mind. The year which followed was pure hell. My mother threw me out, so I went to live with another family. Eventually they also threw me out.
>
> Three years later I found Christ. My decision to trust Christ was largely based on my fear of Satan and the power of evil I had experienced in my life. Even though I knew Satan had lost his ownership of me, I was unaware of how vulnerable I

still was to his deception and control. For the first two years of my Christian life I was in bondage to a sin. I didn't even know it was a sin. Once I realized my sin, confessed it to God, and received forgiveness, I thought I was finally free of Satan's attempts to control me. I didn't realize that the battle had only begun.

I suffered from unexplainable rashes, hives, and welts all over my body. I lost my joy and closeness to the Lord. I could no longer sing or quote Scripture. I turned to food as my comfort and security. The demons attacked my sense of right and wrong, and I became involved in immorality in my search for identity and love.

But that all ended yesterday when I renounced Satan's control in my life. I have found the freedom and protection which comes from knowing I am loved. I'm not on a high; I'm writing with a clear mind, a clean spirit, and a calm hand. Even my previous bondage to food seems suddenly foreign to me.

I never realized that a Christian could be so vulnerable to Satan's control. I was deceived, but now I am free. Thank you, thank you, Jesus!

—Sheila

Sheila is a sobering example of a dimension of spiritual vulnerability that most Christians don't like to talk about: losing control. Yet every recovery ministry works with people who have lost control of their lives to food, sex, drugs, alcohol, or gambling. Life for Sheila had become unmanageable—and there are many who are just like her. She couldn't seem to exercise any control over her eating habits and sexual behavior. Actually she could, but she didn't know how. Christians generally agree that we are vulnerable to the enemy's temptation, accusation, and deception. But for some reason we hesitate to consider what would happen if we willfully surrender to those demonic influences.

There are consequences to sin—and our spiritual protection is partly dependent upon us. We are told to "put on the Lord Jesus Christ, and make no provision for the flesh in regard to its lusts" (Romans 13:14). But what will happen if we do make provision for the flesh? We are told to "[take] every thought captive to the obedience of Christ" (2 Corinthians 10:5). But what will happen if we don't do that and choose to believe a lie or pay attention to a deceiving spirit? We are told to put on the armor of God and stand firm. But what will happen if we don't? It is our responsibility to not let sin reign in our mortal bodies; we do that by not using our bodies as instruments of unrighteousness (Romans 6:12,13). But what if we do use our bodies as instruments of unrighteousness? We are told to submit to God and resist the devil (James 4:7). But what if we don't make a commitment to God and don't stand against the kingdom of darkness? Can we assume a spiritually neutral position without any negative consequences? To say nothing negative will happen to us or Satan won't take advantage of our indecision or indiscretion is scripturally wrong, and it creates a false hope for believers.

In this chapter we are going to look at some clear scriptural examples of what happens when believers succumb to temptation, accusation, and deception. Before we look at this level of vulnerability, I want to stress again that every believer belongs to God. We have been purchased by the blood of the Lamb, and not even the powers of hell can separate us from the love of God (Romans 8:35-39; 1 Peter 1:17-19). In his book *What Demons Can Do to Saints*, Dr. Merrill Unger wrote: "The demon enters...as a squatter and not as an owner or a guest or as one who has a right there. But he comes in as an intruder and as an invader and enemy. But come he does if the door is opened by serious and protracted sin."[1] Satan knows he can never own you. But if he can deceive you into yielding control of your life in any way, he can impede your growth and destroy your witness for Christ.

Kingdoms in Conflict

The usual argument against the level of spiritual vulnerability we are discussing is the assertion that an evil spirit and the Holy Spirit cannot coexist. There are several reasons why I don't believe this is true. First, Satan is the god of this world and "the prince of the power of the air" (Ephesians 2:2). Thus Satan and his demons are present in the atmosphere of this world, but so is the omnipresent Holy Spirit—which means they sometimes coexist. Second, Satan now has access to our Father in heaven, which means he and the Father are existing together—coexisting—for a time. Third, the Holy Spirit is in union—coexisting—with our spirit, and surely we don't consider our human spirit perfect. Fourth, spatial arguments don't apply to the spiritual realm. There are no natural barriers or physical boundaries for spirits. That is why we shouldn't think of a church building as a sanctuary. Our only sanctuary is "in Christ," not in some physical shelter. Fifth, if a person is paying attention to a deceiving spirit, it cannot be external only. The battle is in the mind. If an evil spirit and the Holy Spirit cannot operate at the same time and in the same sphere, then there is no need to be alert and put on the armor of God.

The term "demon-possessed" has also caused controversy in the church. The problem centers around the word "possessed," which actually doesn't exist in the Greek texts. The term "demon-possessed" is the English translation for only one word—*daimonizomai* (verb) or *daimonizomenos* (participle)—which is best transliterated "demonized" (Matthew 4:24; 9:32; 15:22; Mark 5:15). To be demonized means to be under the control of one or more demons. The term never occurs in the epistles, so we have no way of precisely knowing how it would apply in the church age. It is my belief that every believer is Holy Spirit–possessed. By that I mean we are indwelt by the Holy Spirit, who will never leave us nor forsake us.

Another Greek phrase in the Gospels is *echein daimonion*, which means to "have a demon." The religious leaders used this phrase when they accused both John the Baptist and Jesus of being demonized (Luke 7:33; John 7:20).

The influence that Satan and his demons can have on believers is a matter of degree. Since we live in a world whose god is Satan, the possibility of being tempted, deceived, and accused is continuously present. If you allow his schemes to influence you, you can lose control to the degree that you have been deceived. (For a more detailed discussion on our vulnerability, I encourage you to read *Three Crucial Questions About Spiritual Warfare* by Dr. Clinton Arnold, published by Baker Books.)

In my book *Released from Bondage* (Thomas Nelson) are several case studies written from the victims' perspective. Their problems varied from eating disorders to sexual abuse and addiction. All the victims struggled with their thought life, and sex always seemed to be an issue, regardless of what the surface problem was. They all professed to be Christians, and two were in full-time ministry. I wrote the book so the Christian community could hear their stories, because so many believers would simply pass these dear people off as unbelievers, which doesn't help them one bit.

Saints in Bondage

It is critical that Christians understand their vulnerability to demonic influence, so they may have an adequate biblical answer for any situation they face. Paul says we are not ignorant of Satan's schemes (2 Corinthians 2:11), and we shouldn't be. Those who don't understand their vulnerability will likely blame themselves or God for their problems. If we blame ourselves, we feel hopeless because we can't do anything to stop what we're doing. If we blame God, our confidence in Him as our benevolent Father is shattered. Either way, we have no chance to gain the victory which the Bible promises us. Then there is the tendency of the church in the

Western world to attribute all of Satan's activities to the flesh. This also leaves us with no way to resolve spiritual conflicts. Look at the following passages from Scripture, which show how destructive Satan can be to believers:

Luke 13:10-17. While Jesus was teaching in the synagogue, "there was a woman who for eighteen years had had a sickness caused by a spirit; and she was bent double, and could not straighten up at all" (verse 11). Verse 16 states that her physical disability was caused by satanic bondage. This woman was not an unbeliever. She was "a daughter of Abraham" (verse 16), a God-fearing woman of faith with a spiritual problem. As soon as Jesus released her from bondage, her physical problem was cured.

Notice that this woman wasn't protected from demonic control by being inside the synagogue. Neither the walls of a synagogue nor the walls of a church provide a sanctuary from demonic influence. Admittedly, this event occurred before the cross. But it is an indication that demons can physically affect believers.

Luke 22:31-34. The apostle Peter is an example of a believer who lost control of his life. Jesus said to him, "Simon, Simon, behold, Satan has demanded permission to sift you like wheat" (verse 31). What right did Satan have to make such a demand? Peter had apparently given Satan a foothold through pride when he debated with the disciples about which of them was the greatest (22:24). Even though Peter's heart desire was to stand by his Master even to the point of death or imprisonment (verse 33), Jesus announced that Peter would deny Him three times (verse 34), which he did. It's encouraging to note, however, that Jesus had already prayed for Peter's successful recovery from the incident (verse 32).

Ephesians 6:10-17. This passage contains Paul's familiar exhortation to believers to "put on the full armor of God, that you may be able to stand firm against the schemes of the devil" (verse 11). What is the purpose of armor? To prevent the enemy's arrows from penetrating the body and injuring the soldier. If it is impossible for Satan's arrows to penetrate us, there would be no need for us to put on the armor. The instructions regarding spiritual armor suggest that it is possible for the enemy to penetrate our lives and gain a measure of control.

James 3:14-16. James indicates that if we yield to jealousy and selfish ambition, we may open ourselves to being controlled by wisdom which is "earthly, natural, demonic" (verse 15). I had a seminary student whose logic regarding Scripture was completely confused. He had been completely orthodox in his faith until he encountered a prostitute who challenged his faith to the core. Then he started coming up with all kinds of new "insights," but nobody could understand them. His arguments sounded like they came from a book by Mary Baker Eddy, and none of the other students agreed with him. To my knowledge he never recovered from his experience with demonic logic.

1 Timothy 4:1-3. Paul wrote, "Some will fall away from the faith, paying attention to deceitful spirits and doctrines of demons" (verse 1). Paul illustrates how spiritual deception can affect our eating habits and marriages (verse 3). It is naive to say that Christians can't pay attention to a deceiving spirit. It is happening all over the world. In the past 15 years I have counseled well over a thousand professing Christians who were struggling with their thought life. Some just have difficulty praying or reading their Bible. Others are hearing voices. To pass this off as some kind of a chemical imbalance is to remove the church from the ministry of setting captives free. If all those negative thoughts are just flesh patterns, then why did the thoughts leave when these believers submitted to God and resisted the devil? Flesh patterns are ingrained and don't instantly leave upon command.

1 Corinthians 5:1-13. This passage contains Paul's instructions concerning a man in the Corinthian church who was living in an incestuous relationship with his father's wife (verse 1). He was a man so deluded by Satan and controlled by immorality that he apparently flaunted his illicit relationship before the whole church. Paul's judgment on the matter was severe: "I have decided to deliver such a one to Satan for the destruction of his flesh, that his spirit may be saved in the day of the Lord Jesus" (verse 5). Paul was ready to allow Satan to have his way with the man for awhile in hopes that he would finally say "I've had enough" and repent.

Some wonder if a person at this level of immorality is really a Christian. Paul would not have disciplined him if he were not a Christian, because the church is only required to discipline those within its membership. This man was a believer (at least Paul treated him like one) who had allowed himself to become trapped in immorality. Paul's hope was that he experience the natural consequences of his sin, repent, and be set free from his bondage.

Ephesians 4:26,27. Paul instructed, "'In your anger do not sin': Do not let the sun go down while you are still angry, and do not give the devil a foothold" (NIV). The word "foothold" literally means "place." Paul is saying that we may allow the devil a place in our lives if we fail to speak the truth in love and be emotionally honest. Anger which turns to bitterness and unforgiveness is an open invitation to demonic control (2 Corinthians 2:10,11).

1 Peter 5:6-9. Peter warned, "Your adversary, the devil, prowls about like a roaring lion, seeking someone to devour" (verse 8). The word "devour" means to consume or to swallow up. It is the same word used in 1 Corinthians 15:54: "Death is swallowed up in victory." To be swallowed up by something certainly conveys the thought of being controlled by it. If believers are not vulnerable to being controlled by Satan, Peter would not need to alert us to the possibility.

The context of Peter's warning suggests two conditions which may predispose a believer to vulnerability. In verse six we are encouraged to humble ourselves before the Lord. Perhaps with the painful memory of the consequences of his own self-exaltation in mind, Peter indicates that whenever we resist pride we resist Satan. And verses seven and eight suggest that if we don't learn how to cast our anxieties on the Lord, we make ourselves easy prey for Satan.

Acts 5:1-11. This is perhaps the most definitive passage on Satan's ability to control believers. The members of the young Jerusalem church were voluntarily selling property and giving the proceeds to the apostles for use in ministry (Acts 4). "But a certain man named Ananias, with his wife Sapphira, sold a piece of property, and kept back some of the price for himself, with his wife's full knowledge, and bringing a portion of it, he laid it at the apostles' feet. But Peter said, 'Ananias, why has Satan filled your heart to lie to the Holy Spirit, and to keep back some of the price of the land?...You have not lied to men, but to God' "(verses 1-4).

The issue was not that Ananias and Sapphira withheld part of the proceeds, but that they lied about it, apparently saying that what they gave was the total amount they received. The consequence of the couple's sin was immediate and sobering: They died on the spot (verses 5,10).

Some people who have difficulty with the idea of satanic control of believers have argued that Ananias and Sapphira were unbelievers. I don't believe that argument. First, Acts 4:32 states that this event took place within the context of the Christian community, of which Ananias and Sapphira were members. Second, Acts 5:11 records, "And great fear came upon the whole church." If God were judging someone *outside* the church, why would great fear come upon those *within* the church? There was great fear among *believers* because God had dramatically displayed His attitude toward *believers* who live a lie. Third, the severity of the punishment indicates that God was underscoring the importance of truth in the community of believers. Unbelievers lie all the time, and they usually are not as swiftly and thoroughly judged as were Ananias and Sapphira. I believe that God was sending a powerful message to the church. He knew that if Satan could deceive believers, he could control their lives.

Ananias' problem was that he had allowed Satan's deception to fill (control) his heart. The word "filled" in Acts 5:3 (*pleroo*) is the same word used in Ephesians 5:18: "Be filled with the Spirit." It is possible for the believer to be filled with satanic deception or filled by the Spirit. To whichever source you yield, by that source you shall be filled (that is, controlled). When you allow Satan to deceive you in any area of your life, you are vulnerable to his control in that area.

The Devil Did Not Make You Do It

Lest we tend to lay the total blame for Ananias and Sapphira's demise on Satan, we must remember that these two believers were willing participants in the lie which led to their deaths. Peter confronted Ananias and Sapphira respectively: "Why is it that you have conceived this deed in your heart?…Why is it that you have agreed together to put the Spirit of the Lord to the test?" (Acts 5:4,9). Yes, Satan filled their hearts with deception and exerted a measure of control over them in their misdeed. But he was only able to do so because at some point Ananias and Sapphira opened the door for him.

For the sake of those who come to me for help, I never accept the excuse, "The devil made me do it." We are all responsible for our own attitudes and actions. Satan simply takes advantage of the opportunities we give him. We have all the resources and protection we need to live a victorious life in Christ. If we're not living it, it's our choice. When we leave a door open for the devil by not resisting temptation, accusation, or deception, he will enter it. And if we continue to allow him access, he will assume squatter's rights. We won't lose our salvation, but we will lose our daily victory.

If we go into battle without some of our armor, we will suffer casualties! If we fail to cover ourselves with the armor God has provided, we are vulnerable in those exposed areas. Dr. Unger comments:

> If the Christian fails to use his armor, will he [Satan] stop short of invading the believer's citadel? If he does invade, this is precisely why the believer may become enslaved having been "taken captive by him at his will" (2 Timothy 2:26). The believer is invaded and overrun by the enemy, who, like any invading foe, does not permit the use of weapons of any sort by the citizens of the country overrun. As a result there is no struggle, only enforced submission and subservience.[2]

James 4:1 reveals that the source of our quarrels and conflicts is the pleasures that "wage war in your members." Paul instructed, "Do not let sin reign in your mortal body that you should obey its lusts" (Romans 6:12). The world, the flesh, and the devil are continually at war against the life of the Spirit within us. But what if we don't stand firm in our faith? Will we still be victorious over the pleasures and lusts which strive to reign over us?

Choosing truth, living a righteous life, and donning the armor of God are each believer's individual responsibility. I cannot be responsible for you, and you cannot be responsible for me. I can pray for you, encourage you in the faith, and counsel you, but if you go into the battle without your armor on, you may get hurt. As much as that may be a matter of concern for me, I still cannot make those decisions of responsibility for you. Those choices are yours alone, but you do have a choice—and that is what the rest of this book is about.

Finally, let me share with you one of my favorite testimonies. As this woman tells her story, ask yourself some questions: Is what she is describing normal? Is this just a severe case of the negative "self-talk" which we all have? Does she have a split personality? Is she psychotic? Does she have multiple personalities or an inner child of her past? A counselor could make any one of those diagnoses depending on his education or experience. What do you think her problem is? She called her testimony:

Silence

When I sit and think, I think of many things—my life, what I want to do, what I think about issues and people. I have conversations with myself inside my head. I talk to myself and answer myself...I am my own best friend. We get along great! Sometimes I talk to myself so much during the day that I am really tired at the end of the day. But I keep myself occupied, and it helps me to think things through.

Sometimes I think of myself as two people: the one who is me every day of the week...the one I want to change. The one who has a low self-esteem and is afraid to really be herself in front of everyone. And then there's the one inside me...the confident me who I wish would come out but for some reason won't. I call that part of me "her." She is a "she," and I refer to her as such. She is very bold, and everybody loves her—at least that's what I think would happen if I would just let her out. If I could just be myself...life would be so much easier and happier.

But until then, I talk to her inside of me. We talk about what we will do today, where we will go to eat, what we will wear, who we will talk to. Sometimes she comes up with very good ideas, and I am impressed with myself that I am so smart and clever. "If only people knew the real me," I think, "they would really love me." And sometimes I hear her say things to me that don't make sense. "I shouldn't really do that," I think. "That's not very nice. That would hurt someone. That is a stupid thing to do." I don't listen to her those times. But I don't mind. I like talking to her, so I continue talking.

One day, things changed between us. My life was going okay, but I wanted a closer walk with God. I wanted to be free from the past and to be healed in my heart from the pain that I have been carrying. Someone told me I should go through something called the "Steps to Freedom in Christ," and I made an appointment with a counselor. I wasn't thinking about my friend inside me, I was thinking about myself.

In the counseling session, I was asked to read some prayers and Scripture out loud. While I was doing this, my mind became fuzzy, and I couldn't concentrate. Most of all, when I tried to speak to her in my mind, I became confused. I couldn't hear her clearly. I became scared, my heart raced, and I became enraged inside. I shook. Where was my friend inside me? Why all of a sudden was she mad? What was going on? What was wrong with me?

Then I found out. She wasn't my friend. She wasn't really me. She didn't want me to get right with God. It didn't make sense, because these were things that I wanted to do. I thought she was on my side. But I was wrong. I had to tell her to leave...out loud. Out loud? It seemed weird when I was told that she couldn't read my thoughts. But it made sense...she wasn't God, and she wasn't omniscient. So I told her out loud to leave...and she was gone.

And there was silence. There were no more conversations going on in my mind anymore. And I missed her. I knew I shouldn't, but I did. I knew that she wasn't good for me and that God wanted me to talk to Him and not her. I struggled with the thought of not talking to her. I couldn't stand the silence...I felt alone. She tried to come back, and when she did, it scared me. She was angry and hostile. I felt betrayed. But after a time, I got used to the silence. I used it to remind me to talk to God, and I did. He didn't answer like she did. I couldn't hear His voice like I could hers. But I began to love talking to Him, singing to Him. I really felt close to Him...like He cared. And after a while, I forgot about the silence.

After some time I found myself lonely again. I forgot about the silence and found myself in conversation without even realizing it. My life was in confusion, and I couldn't figure out why, until one day I had to pray. My friend who had been discipling me wanted to help me, and I wanted help. She talked to me about my rebellion and how I needed to stop living independent of God. It was then that I heard a loud voice inside of me say, "I AM INDEPENDENT OF GOD." It scared me. Was that me? Did I really feel that way? No, I didn't...she was back. Then I got angry because I had let her back. I wanted her gone, but I couldn't move, and I couldn't say anything. My friend prayed with me, and I bowed my head. She told me to picture heaven with a light, the lampstands, and the throne of God. I started to really see it and to feel calm again. But then the voice started yelling, "No! No! No!" So I opened my eyes and gave up. My heart became hard, and I didn't really want to give everything to God. I still wanted control. There were some things that I did not want to give up.

But inside I longed for the silence again. "How ironic," I thought. "Something that I didn't like at first had become my freedom." How I fought inside trying to struggle with praying to God or running away from Him. It is so easy to run, so easy to put off what I can do right now. But I didn't FEEL repentant. I didn't FEEL like letting go, even though I knew I needed to. I wondered if I would ever feel like it again.

And that is when I saw the words from the "Steps to Freedom in Christ" jump out at me from the page. They read, "Faith is something you decide to do, not something you feel like doing." So I did it.

And now I live in wonderful silence.

Part Three

Walk Free!

Steps to Freedom in Christ

CHRIST HAS SET YOU FREE through His victory over sin and death on the cross. But if you have failed to stand firm in the faith or you have willfully sinned, it is your responsibility to do whatever is necessary to maintain a right relationship with Him. Your eternal destiny is not at stake, but your daily victory is. You will be tempted to skip this chapter, or read it without doing it, but for your sake, I pray that you won't.

In this chapter I want to share seven specific issues that every Christian needs to resolve. You may already have dealt with one or more of these issues, but you couldn't possibly hurt yourself by going through every step. Even if nothing else is accomplished, you will really be ready for communion the next time your church offers it.

As you go through these steps to freedom, remember that Satan is under no obligation to obey your thoughts. Find a private place where you can verbally process each step. These are critical issues between you and God, and it is possible to process them on your own because Jesus is the Wonderful Counselor. However, some of you may be unable to get through each step on their own. In this case, please call for help. Ask your pastor or Christian counselor to lead you through the Steps, or call our office, and we will try to help you find a qualified person.

Even if your problems stem from a source other than those covered in these steps, you have nothing to lose by going through them. It is just a comprehensive process of submitting to God and resisting the devil (James 4:7). It doesn't make any difference whether or not there are evil spirits present. The real issue is your relationship with God, and the lack of resolution of any one of these issues will affect your intimacy with Him.

Each step is explained so you will have no problem knowing what to do. If you experience any resistance, stop and pray. If you experience some mental opposition, just ignore it. It is just a thought, and it can have no power over you unless you believe it. Throughout the process, you will be asking God to lead you. He is the only One who can grant repentance leading to a knowledge of the truth which will set you free (2 Timothy 2:24-26). Start the steps with the following prayer and declaration. (You don't have to read the words in the parentheses. These are just for clarification or reference.)

Prayer

> *Dear heavenly Father, I acknowledge Your presence in this room and in my life. You are the only omniscient (all-knowing), omnipotent (all-powerful), and omnipresent (always present) God. I am dependent upon You, for apart from You I can do nothing. I stand in the truth that all authority in heaven and on earth has been given to the resurrected Christ, and because I am in Christ, I share that authority in order to make disciples and set captives free. I ask You to fill me with Your Holy Spirit and lead me into all truth. I pray for your complete protection and ask for Your guidance. In Jesus' name I pray. Amen.*

Declaration

In the name and authority of the Lord Jesus Christ, I command Satan and all evil spirits to release me in order that I can be free to know and to choose to do the will of God. As a child of God who is seated with Christ in the heavenlies, I command every evil spirit to leave my presence. I belong to God and the evil one cannot touch me.

Step 1: Counterfeit vs. Real

The first step toward experiencing your freedom in Christ is to renounce (verbally reject) all past or present involvement with occult practices, cult teachings, and rituals, as well as non-Christian religions.

You must renounce any activity or group which denies Jesus Christ or offers guidance through any source other than the absolute authority of the Bible. Any group that requires dark, secret initiations, ceremonies, promises, or pacts should also be renounced. Begin this step by praying aloud:

Dear heavenly Father, I ask You to bring to my mind anything and everything that I have done knowingly or unknowingly that involves occult, cult, or non-Christian teachings or practices. I want to experience Your freedom by renouncing these things right now. In Jesus' name I pray, amen.

Even if you took part in something and thought it was just a game or a joke, you need to renounce it. Satan will try to take advantage of anything he can in our lives, so it is always wise to be as thorough as possible. Even if you were just standing by and watching others do it, you need to renounce your passive involvement. You may not have even realized at the time that what was going on was evil. Still, go ahead and renounce it.

If something comes to your mind and you are not sure what to do about it, trust that the Spirit of God is answering the prayer you just prayed, and go ahead and renounce it.

Note the following "Non-Christian Spiritual Checklist." This inventory covers many of the more common occult, cult, and non-Christian religious groups and practices. It is not a complete list, however. Feel free to add others that you were personally involved with.

After that checklist, there are some additional questions designed to help you become aware of other things you may need to renounce. Below those questions is a short prayer of confession and renunciation. Pray it out loud, filling in the blanks with the groups, teachings, or practices that the Holy Spirit has prompted you to renounce during this time of personal evaluation.

Non-Christian Spiritual Checklist

(Check all those that you have participated in)
- ❏ Out of body experience (astral projection)
- ❏ Ouija board
- ❏ Bloody Mary
- ❏ Light as a feather (or other occult games)
- ❏ Table lifting
- ❏ Magic Eight Ball
- ❏ Spells or curses
- ❏ Mental telepathy or mental control of others
- ❏ Automatic writing
- ❏ Trances
- ❏ Spirit guides
- ❏ Fortune telling/divination (e.g., tea leaves)
- ❏ Tarot cards
- ❏ Levitation
- ❏ Magic—The Gathering
- ❏ Witchcraft/sorcery

- ❏ Satanism
- ❏ Palm reading
- ❏ Astrology/horoscopes
- ❏ Hypnosis (amateur or self-induced)
- ❏ Seances
- ❏ Black or white magic
- ❏ Dungeons & Dragons® (and similar games)
- ❏ Blood pacts or cutting yourself on purpose
- ❏ Objects of worship/crystals/good luck charms
- ❏ Sexual spirits
- ❏ Martial arts (mysticism/devotion to sensei)
- ❏ Superstitions
- ❏ Mormonism (Latter-day Saints)
- ❏ Jehovah's Witness (Watchtower)
- ❏ New Age (books, objects, seminars, medicine)
- ❏ Masons
- ❏ Christian Science
- ❏ Mind Science cults
- ❏ The Way International
- ❏ Unification Church (Moonies)
- ❏ The Forum (est)
- ❏ Church of the Living Word
- ❏ Children of God (Children of Love)
- ❏ Church of Scientology
- ❏ Unitarianism/Universalism
- ❏ Roy Masters
- ❏ Silva Mind Control
- ❏ Transcendental meditation (TM)
- ❏ Yoga
- ❏ Hare Krishna
- ❏ Bahaism
- ❏ Native American spirit worship
- ❏ Islam
- ❏ Hinduism
- ❏ Buddhism (including Zen)
- ❏ Black Muslim
- ❏ Rosicrucianism

❏ Other non-Christian religions or cults
❏ Occult or violent video and computer games
❏ Movies, TV shows, music, books, magazines, or comics that the Lord is bringing to your mind (especially those that glorified Satan, caused fear or nightmares, were gruesomely violent, or stimulated the flesh). List them below:

Below are some additional questions designed to help you become aware of other things you may need to renounce.

1. Have you ever seen, heard, or felt a spiritual being in your room?

2. Do you have recurring nightmares? Specifically renounce any accompanying fear.

3. Do you now have, or have you ever had, an imaginary friend, spirit guide, or "angel" offering you guidance or companionship? (If it has a name, renounce it by name.)

4. Have you ever heard voices in your head or had repeating, nagging thoughts such as "I'm dumb," "I'm ugly," "Nobody loves me," "I can't do anything right"—as if there were a conversation going on inside your head? (List any specific nagging thoughts.)

5. Have you ever consulted a medium, spiritist, or channeler?

6. Have you ever seen or been contacted by beings you thought were aliens?

7. Have you ever made a secret vow or pact?

8. Have you ever been involved in a satanic ritual of any kind or attended a concert in which Satan was the focus?

9. What other spiritual experiences have you had that were evil, confusing, or frightening?

Once you have completed your checklist and the questions, confess and renounce *each* item you were involved in by praying the following prayer *out loud:*

> *Lord, I confess that I have participated in _____. I know it was evil and offensive in Your sight. Thank You for Your forgiveness. I renounce any and all involvement with _____, and I cancel out any and all ground that the enemy gained in my life through this activity. In Jesus' name, amen.*

Renouncing Wrong Priorities

Who or what is most important to us becomes that which we worship. Our thoughts, love, devotion trust, adoration, and obedience are directed to this object above all others. This object of worship is truly our God or god(s).

We were created to worship the true and living God. In fact, the Father seeks those who will worship Him in spirit and in truth (John 4:23). As children of God, "we know also that the Son of God has come and has given us understanding, so that we may know him who is true. And we are in him who is true—even in his Son Jesus Christ. He is the true God and eternal life" (1 John 5:20 NIV).

The apostle John follows the above passage with a warning: "Little children, guard yourselves from idols" (1 John 5:21). An idol is a false god, any object of worship other than the true God. Though we may not bow down to statues, it is easy for people and things of this world to subtly become more important to us than the Lord. The following prayer expresses the commitment of a heart that chooses to "worship the Lord your God, and serve Him only" (Matthew 4:10).

> *Dear Lord God, I know how easy it is to allow other things and other people to become more important to me than You. I also know*

that this is terribly offensive to Your holy eyes as You have commanded that I "shall have no other gods" before You.

I confess to You that I have not loved You with all my heart and soul and mind. As a result, I have sinned against You, violating the first and greatest commandment. I repent of and turn away from this idolatry and now choose to return to You, Lord Jesus, as my first love.

Please reveal to my mind now any and all idols in my life. I want to renounce each of them and, in so doing, cancel out any and all ground Satan may have gained in my life through my idolatry. In the name of Jesus, the true God, amen.

(See Exodus 20:3; Matthew 22:37;
Revelation 2:4,5.)

The checklist below may help you recognize those areas where things or people have become more important to you than the true God, Jesus Christ. Notice that most (if not all) of the areas listed below are not evil in themselves; they become idols when they usurp God's rightful place as Lord of our lives.

- ❏ Ambition
- ❏ Food or any substance
- ❏ Money/possessions
- ❏ Computers/games/software
- ❏ Financial security
- ❏ Rock stars/media celebrities/athletes
- ❏ Church activities
- ❏ TV/movies/music/other media
- ❏ Sports or physical fitness

- ❏ Fun/pleasure
- ❏ Ministry
- ❏ Appearance/image
- ❏ Work
- ❏ Busyness/activity
- ❏ Friends
- ❏ Power/control
- ❏ Boyfriend/girlfriend
- ❏ Popularity/opinion of others
- ❏ Spouse
- ❏ Knowledge/being right
- ❏ Children
- ❏ Hobbies
- ❏ Parents

Use the following prayer to renounce any areas of idolatry or wrong priority the Holy Spirit brings to your mind.

> *In the name of the true and living God, Jesus Christ, I renounce my worship of the false god of (<u>name the idol</u>). I choose to worship only You, Lord. I ask You, Father, to enable me to keep this area of (<u>name the idol</u>) in its proper place in my life.*

If you have been involved in satanic rituals or heavy occult activity (or you suspect it because of blocked memories, severe and recurring nightmares, or sexual bondage or dysfunction), we strongly urge you to say out loud the "Special Renunciations for Satanic Ritual Involvement." Read across the page, renouncing the first item in the column under "Domain of Darkness" and then announcing the first truth in the column

Special Renunciations for Satanic Ritual Involvement

Domain of Darkness

1. I renounce ever signing or having my name signed over to Satan.

2. I renounce any ritual where I was wed to Satan.

3. I renounce any and all covenants, agreements, or promises that I made to Satan.

4. I renounce all satanic assignments for my life including duties, marriage, and children.

5. I renounce all spirit guides assigned to me.

6. I renounce any giving of my blood in the service of Satan.

7. I renounce ever eating flesh or drinking blood in satanic worship.

8. I renounce all guardians and satanist parents that were assigned to me.

9. I renounce any baptism whereby I am identified with Satan.

10. I renounce any sacrifice made on my behalf by which Satan may claim ownership of me.

Kingdom of Light

1. I announce that my name is now written in the Lamb's Book of Life.

2. I announce that I am the bride of Christ.

3. I announce that I have made a new covenant with Jesus Christ alone that supersedes any previous agreements.

4. I announce and commit myself to know and do only the will of God, and I accept only His guidance for my life.

5. I announce and accept only the leading of the Holy Spirit.

6. I trust only in the shed blood of my Lord, Jesus Christ.

7. By faith, I take Holy Communion, the body and blood of the Lord Jesus.

8. I announce that God is my heavenly Father and the Holy Spirit is my guardian by whom I am sealed.

9. I announce that I have been baptized into Christ Jesus and my identity is now in Him alone.

10. I announce that only the sacrifice of Christ has any claim on me. I belong to Him. I have been purchased by the blood of the Lamb.

under "Kingdom of Light." Continue down the page in that manner.

In addition to the "Special Renunciations" list, all other satanic rituals, covenants (promises), and assignments must be specifically renounced as the Lord brings them to your mind.

Some people who have been subjected to Satanic Ritual Abuse (SRA) develop multiple or alter personalities in order to cope with their pain. If this is true in your case, you need someone who understands spiritual conflict to help you work through this problem. For now, walk through the rest of the "Steps to Freedom in Christ" as best you can. It is important that you remove any demonic strongholds in your life *before* trying to integrate the personalities. Eventually, *every* alter personality (if this is the case with you) must be identified and guided into resolving the issues that caused its formation. Then, all true personalities can agree to come together in Christ.

Step 2: Deception vs. Truth

God's Word is true and we need to accept His truth in the innermost part of our being (Psalm 51:6). Whether or not we *feel* it is true, we need to *believe* it is true! Since Jesus is the truth, the Holy Spirit is the Spirit of truth, and the Word of God is truth, we ought to speak the truth in love. (See John 14:6; 16:13; 17:17; Ephesians 4:15.)

The believer in Christ has no business deceiving others by lying, telling "white" lies, exaggerating, stretching the truth, or anything relating to falsehoods. Satan is the father of lies, and he seeks to keep people in bondage through deception, but it is the truth in Jesus that sets us free. (See John 8:32-36,44; 2 Timothy 2:26; Revelation 12:9.) We will find real joy and freedom when we stop living a lie and walk openly in the truth. After confessing his sin, King David wrote, "How blessed [happy] is the man...in whose spirit there is no deceit!" (Psalm 32:2).

How can we find the strength to walk in the light (1 John 1:7)? When we are sure God loves and accepts us, we can be free to own up to our sins and face reality instead of running and hiding from painful circumstances.

Start this step by praying the following prayer out loud. Don't let any opposing thoughts, such as "This is a waste of time" or "I wish I could believe this stuff but I just can't," keep you from praying and choosing the truth. Even if this is difficult for you, work your way through this step. God will strengthen you as you rely on Him.

> *Dear heavenly Father, I know that You want me to know the truth, believe the truth, speak the truth, and live in accordance with the truth. Thank You that it is the truth that will set me free. In many ways I have been deceived by Satan, the father of lies, and I have deceived myself as well.*
>
> *Father, I pray in the name of the Lord Jesus Christ, by virtue of His shed blood and resurrection, asking You to rebuke all of Satan's demons that are deceiving me.*
>
> *I have trusted in Jesus alone to save me, and so I am Your forgiven child. Therefore, since You accept me just as I am in Christ, I can be free to face my sin and not try to hide. I ask for the Holy Spirit to guide me into all truth. I ask You to "search me, O God, and know my heart; try me and know my anxious thoughts; and see if there be any hurtful way in me, and lead me in the everlasting way." In the name of Jesus, who is the Truth, I pray. Amen.*

> (See Psalm 139:23,24.)

There are many ways in which Satan, "the god of this world," seeks to deceive us. Just as he did with Eve, the devil tries to convince us to rely on ourselves and to try to get our needs met through the world around us, rather than trusting in the provision of our Father in heaven.

The following exercise will help open your eyes to the ways you have been deceived by the world system. Check each area of deception that the Lord brings to your mind and confess it, using the prayer following the list.

Ways you can be deceived by the world

❏ Believing that acquiring money and things will bring lasting happiness (Matthew 13:22; 1 Timothy 6:10)

❏ Believing that consuming food and alcohol excessively will make me happy (Proverbs 20:1; 23:19-21)

❏ Believing that a great body and personality will get me what I want (Proverbs 31:10; 1 Peter 3:3,4)

❏ Believing that gratifying sexual lust will bring lasting satisfaction (Ephesians 4:22; 1 Peter 2:11)

❏ Believing that I can sin and get away with it and not have it affect my heart (Hebrews 3:12,13)

❏ Believing that I need more than what God has given me in Christ (2 Corinthians 11:2-4,13-15)

❏ Believing that I can do whatever I want and no one can touch me (Proverbs 16:18; Obadiah 3; 1 Peter 5:5)

❏ Believing that unrighteous people who refuse to accept Christ go to heaven anyway (1 Corinthians 6:9-11)

❏ Believing that I can hang around bad company and not become corrupted (1 Corinthians 15:33,34)

❏ Believing that there are no consequences on earth for my sin (Galatians 6:7,8)

❏ Believing that I must gain the approval of certain people in order to be happy (Galatians 1:10)

❏ Believing that I must measure up to certain standards in order to feel good about myself (Galatians 3:2,3; 5:1)

> *Lord, I confess that I have been deceived by _____. I thank You for Your forgiveness, and I commit myself to believing only Your truth. In Jesus' name, amen.*

It is important to know that in addition to being deceived by the world, false teachers, and deceiving spirits, we can also deceive ourselves. In addition, now that you are alive in Christ, completely forgiven and totally accepted, you don't need to defend yourself the way you used to. Christ is now your defense. Confess the ways the Lord shows you that you have deceived yourself or defended yourself wrongly by using the following lists and prayers of confession:

Ways to deceive yourself

❏ Hearing God's Word but not doing what it says (James 1:22)

❏ Saying I have no sin (1 John 1:8)

❏ Thinking I am something I'm really not (Galatians 6:3)

❏ Thinking I am wise in this worldly age (1 Corinthians 3:18,19)

❏ Thinking I can be truly religious but not bridle my tongue (James 1:26)

> *Lord, I confess that I have deceived myself by _____. Thank You for Your forgiveness. I commit myself to believing only Your truth. In Jesus' name, amen.*

Ways to wrongly defend yourself

❏ Denial of reality (conscious or unconscious)

❏ Fantasy (escaping reality by daydreaming, TV, movies, music, computer or video games, drugs, alcohol, etc.)

❏ Emotional insulation (withdrawing from people or keeping people at a distance to avoid rejection)

❏ Regression (reverting back to less threatening times)

❏ Displaced anger (taking out frustrations on innocent people)

❏ Projection (blaming others for my problems)

❏ Rationalization (making excuses for my own poor behavior)

> *Lord, I confess that I have defended myself wrongly by _____. Thank You for Your forgiveness. I now commit myself to trusting in You to defend and protect me. In Jesus' name, amen.*

Choosing the truth may be hard for you if you have been believing lies for many years. You may need some ongoing counseling to help weed out any defense mechanisms you have relied on to cope with life. Every Christian needs to learn that Christ is the only defense he or she needs. Realizing that you are already forgiven and accepted by God through Christ will help free you up to place all your dependence on Him.

Ways That We Can Be Deceived About God

Faith is the biblical response to the truth, and believing what God says is a choice we all can make. If you say, "I wish I could believe God, but I just can't," you are being deceived. Of course you can believe God because what God says is always true.

Sometimes we are greatly hindered from walking by faith in our Father God because of lies we have believed about Him. We are to have a healthy fear of God (awe of His holiness, power, and presence), but we are not to be afraid of Him. Romans 8:15 says, "For you have not received a spirit of slavery leading to fear again, but you have received a spirit of adoption as sons by which we cry out, 'Abba! Father!'" The following exercise will help break the chains of those lies and enable you to begin to experience that intimate "Abba, Father" relationship with Him.

Work your way down the lists on page 215, one by one, left to right. Begin each one with the statement in bold at the top of that list. Read through the lists *out loud*.

Ways That Our Fears Deceive Us

A central part of walking in the truth and rejecting deception is to deal with the fears that plague our lives. First Peter 5:8 says that our enemy, the devil, prowls around like a roaring lion, seeking people to devour. Just as a lion's roar strikes terror in the hearts of those who hear it, so Satan uses fear to try to paralyze Christians. His intimidation tactics are designed to rob us of faith in God and drive us to try to get our needs met through the world or the flesh.

I renounce the lie that my Father God is...	I joyfully accept the truth that my Father God is...
1. distant and uninterested	1. intimate and involved (Psalm 139:1-18)
2. insensitive and uncaring	2. kind and compassionate (Psalm 103:8-14)
3. stern and demanding	3. accepting and filled with joy and love (Zephaniah 3:17; Romans 15:7)
4. passive and cold	4. warm and affectionate (Isaiah 40:11; Hosea 11:3,4)
5. absent or too busy for me	5. always with me and eager to be with me (Jeremiah 31:20; Ezekiel 34:11-16; Hebrews 13:5)
6. never satisfied with what I do, impatient, or angry	6. patient and slow to anger (Exodus 34:6; 2 Peter 3:9)
7. mean, cruel, or abusive	7. loving, gentle, and protective of me (Psalm 18:2; Jeremiah 31:3; Isaiah 42:3)
8. trying to take all the fun out of life	8. trustworthy and wants to give me a full life; His will is good, perfect, and acceptable (Lamentations 3:22,23; John 10:10; Romans 12:1,2)
9. controlling or manipulative	9. full of grace and mercy; He gives me freedom to fail (Luke 15:11-16; Hebrews 4:15,16)
10. condemning or unforgiving	10. tenderhearted and forgiving; His heart and arms are always open to me (Psalm 130:1-4; Luke 15:17-24)
11. nit-picking, exacting, or perfectionistic	11. committed to my growth and proud of me as His growing child (Romans 8:28,29; 2 Corinthians 7:4; Hebrews 12:5-11)

I am the apple of His eye!
(Deuteronomy 32:10 NIV)

Fear weakens us, causes us to be self-centered, and clouds our minds so that all we can think about is the thing that frightens us. But fear can only control us if we let it.

God, however, does not want us to be mastered by anything, including fear (1 Corinthians 6:12). Jesus Christ is to be our only Master (John 13:13; 2 Timothy 2:21). In order to begin to experience freedom from the bondage of fear and the ability to walk by faith in God, pray the following prayer from your heart:

> *Dear heavenly Father, I confess to You that I have listened to the devil's roar and have allowed fear to master me. I have not always walked by faith in You but instead have focused on my feelings and circumstances. Thank You for forgiving me for my unbelief. Right now I renounce the spirit of fear and affirm the truth that You have not given me a spirit of fear but of power, love, and a sound mind. Lord, please reveal to my mind now all the fears that have been controlling me so I can renounce them and be free to walk by faith in You.*
>
> *I thank You for the freedom You give me to walk by faith and not by fear. In Jesus' powerful name, I pray. Amen.*
>
> (See 2 Corinthians 4:16-18; 5:7;
> 2 Timothy 1:7.)

The following list may help you recognize some of the fears the devil has used to keep you from walking by faith. Check the ones that apply to your life. Write down any others that the Spirit of God brings to your mind. Then, one-by-one, renounce those fears out loud, using the suggested renunciation after the list.

- ❏ Fear of death
- ❏ Fear of Satan
- ❏ Fear of failure
- ❏ Fear of rejection by people
- ❏ Fear of disapproval
- ❏ Fear of becoming/being homosexual
- ❏ Fear of financial problems
- ❏ Fear of never getting married
- ❏ Fear of the death of a loved one
- ❏ Fear of being a hopeless case
- ❏ Fear of losing salvation
- ❏ Fear of having committed the unpardonable sin
- ❏ Fear of not being loved by God
- ❏ Fear of never loving or being loved by others
- ❏ Fear of embarrassment
- ❏ Fear of being victimized by crime
- ❏ Fear of marriage
- ❏ Fear of divorce
- ❏ Fear of going crazy
- ❏ Fear of pain/illness
- ❏ Fear of the future
- ❏ Fear of confrontation
- ❏ Fear of specific individuals (list)
- ❏ Other specific fears that come to mind now:

I renounce the (name the fear) because God has not given me a spirit of fear. I choose to live by faith in the God who has promised to protect me and meet all my needs as I walk by faith in Him.

(See Psalm 27:1; Matthew 6:33,34;
2 Timothy 1:7.)

After you have finished renouncing all the specific fears you have allowed to control you, pray the following prayer:

> *Dear heavenly Father, I thank You that You are trustworthy. I choose to believe You, even when my feelings and circumstances tell me to fear. You have told me not to fear, for You are with me; to not anxiously look about me, for You are my God. You will strengthen me, help me, and surely uphold me with Your righteous right hand. I pray this with faith in the name of Jesus my Master. Amen.*
>
> (See Isaiah 41:10.)

(To further understand how the fear of the Lord is the beginning of wisdom, and the one fear that expels all other fears, see the book I coauthored with Rich Miller, *Freedom from Fear*, published by Harvest House.)

Faith Must Be Based on the Truth of God's Word

The New Age movement has twisted the concept of faith by saying that we make something true by believing it. No, we can't create reality with our minds; only God can do that. We can only *face* reality with our minds. Faith is choosing to believe and act upon what God says, regardless of feelings or circumstances. Believing something, however, does not make it true. *It's true; therefore, we choose to believe it.*

Just "having faith" is not enough. The key question is whether the object of your faith is trustworthy. If the object of your faith is not reliable, then no amount of believing will change it. That is why our faith must be on the solid rock of God and His Word. That is the only way to live a responsible and fruitful life. On the other hand, if what you believe in is not true, then how you end up living will not be right.

For generations, Christians have known the importance of publicly declaring what they believe. Read aloud the following "Statement of Truth," thinking about what you are saying.

You may find it very helpful to read it daily for several weeks to renew your mind with the truth and replace any lies you may be believing.

Statement of Truth

1. *I recognize that there is only one true and living God who exists as the Father, Son, and Holy Spirit. He is worthy of all honor, praise, and glory as the One who made all things and holds all things together.* (See Exodus 20:2,3; Colossians 1:16,17.)

2. *I recognize that Jesus Christ is the Messiah, the Word who became flesh and dwelt among us. I believe that He came to destroy the works of the devil, and that He disarmed the rulers and author-ities and made a public display of them, having tri-umphed over them.* (See John 1:1,14; Colossians 2:15; 1 John 3:8.)

3. *I believe that God demonstrated His own love for me in that while I was still a sinner, Christ died for me. I believe that He has delivered me from the domain of darkness and transferred me to His kingdom, and in Him I have redemption, the forgiveness of sins.* (See Romans 5:8; Colossians 1:13,14.)

4. *I believe that I am now a child of God and that I am seated with Christ in the heavenlies. I believe that I was saved by the grace of God through faith, and that it was a gift and not a result of any works on my part.* (See Ephesians 2:6,8,9; 1 John 3:1-3.)

5. *I choose to be strong in the Lord and in the strength of His might. I put no confidence in the flesh, for the weapons of warfare are not of the flesh but are divinely powerful for the destruction of strongholds. I put on the full armor of God. I*

resolve to stand firm in my faith and resist the evil one. (See 2 Corinthians 10:4; Ephesians 6:10-20; Philippians 3:3.)

6. *I believe that apart from Christ I can do nothing, so I declare my complete dependence on Him. I choose to abide in Christ in order to bear much fruit and glorify my Father. I announce to Satan that Jesus is my Lord. I reject any and all counterfeit gifts or works of Satan in my life.* (See John 15:5,8; 1 Corinthians 12:3.)

7. *I believe that the truth will set me free and that Jesus is the truth. If He sets me free, I will be free indeed. I recognize that walking in the light is the only path of true fellowship with God and man. Therefore, I stand against all of Satan's deception by taking every thought captive in obedience to Christ. I declare that the Bible is the only authoritative standard for truth and life.* (See John 8:32,36; 14:6; 2 Corinthians 10:5; 2 Timothy 3:15-17; 1 John 1:3-7.)

8. *I choose to present my body to God as a living and holy sacrifice and the members of my body as instruments of righteousness. I choose to renew my mind by the living Word of God in order that I may prove that the will of God is good, acceptable, and perfect. I put off the old self with its evil practices and put on the new self. I declare myself to be a new creation in Christ.* (See Romans 6:13; 12:1,2; 2 Corinthians 5:17; Colossians 3:9,10 NIV.)

9. *By faith, I choose to be filled with the Spirit so that I can be guided into all truth. I choose to walk by the Spirit so that I will not carry out the desires of the flesh.* (See John 16:13; Galatians 5:16; Ephesians 5:18.)

10. *I renounce all selfish goals and choose the ultimate goal of love. I choose to obey the two greatest*

*commandments: to love the Lord my God with all
my heart, soul, mind, and strength and to love my
neighbor as myself.* (See Matthew 22:37-39; 1 Timothy 1:5.)

11. *I believe that the Lord Jesus has all authority in
heaven and on earth, and He is the head over all
rule and authority. I am complete in Him. I believe
that Satan and his demons are subject to me in
Christ since I am a member of Christ's body. Therefore, I obey the command to submit to God and
resist the devil, and I command Satan in the name
of Jesus Christ to leave my presence.* (See Matthew
28:18; Ephesians 1:19-23; Colossians 2:10; James
4:7.)

Step 3: Bitterness vs. Forgiveness

We need to forgive others so Satan cannot take advantage
of us (2 Corinthians 2:10,11). We are commanded to get rid
of all bitterness in our lives and forgive others as we have been
forgiven (Ephesians 4:31,32). Ask God to bring to your mind
the people you need to forgive by praying the following prayer
out loud:

> *Dear heavenly Father, I thank You for the
> riches of Your kindness, forbearance, and
> patience toward me, knowing that Your kindness has led me to repentance. I confess that
> I have not shown that same kindness and
> patience toward those who have hurt me.
> Instead, I have held on to my anger, bitterness, and resentment toward them. Please
> bring to my mind all the people I need to forgive in order that I may do so now. In Jesus'
> name, amen.*
>
> (See Romans 2:4.)

On a separate sheet of paper, list the names of people who come to your mind. At this point don't question whether you need to forgive them or not. If a name comes to mind, just write it down.

Often we hold things against ourselves as well, punishing ourselves for wrong choices we've made in the past. Write "myself" at the bottom of your list so you can forgive yourself. Forgiving yourself is accepting the truth that God has already forgiven you in Christ. If God forgives you, you can forgive yourself!

Also write down "thoughts against God" at the bottom of your list. Obviously, God has never done anything wrong so we don't have to forgive Him. Sometimes, however, we harbor angry thoughts against Him because He did not do what we wanted Him to do. Those feelings of anger or resentment against God can become a wall between us and Him so we must let them go.

Before you begin working through the process of forgiving those on your list, take a few minutes to review what forgiveness is and what it is not.

Forgiveness is not forgetting. People who want to forget all that was done to them will find they cannot do it. Don't put off forgiving those who have hurt you, hoping the pain will one day go away. Once you choose to forgive someone, *then* Christ can come and begin to heal you of your hurts. But the healing cannot begin until you first forgive.

Forgiveness is a choice, a decision of your will. Since God requires you to forgive, it is something you can do. Sometimes it is very hard to forgive someone because we naturally want revenge for the things we have suffered. Forgiveness seems to go against our sense of what is right and fair. So we hold on to our anger, punishing people over and over again in our minds for the pain they've caused us.

But we are told by God never to take our own revenge (Romans 12:19). Let God deal with the person. Let him or her off your hook because as long as you refuse to forgive someone, you are still hooked to that person. You are still chained to your past, bound up in your bitterness. By forgiving, you let the other person off your hook, but he or she is not off God's hook. You must trust that God will deal with the person justly and fairly, something you simply cannot do.

"But you don't know how much this person hurt me!" you say. You're right. We don't, but Jesus does, and He tells you to forgive. And don't you see? Until you let go of your anger and hatred, the person is still hurting you. You can't turn back the clock and change the past, but you can be free from it. You can stop the pain, but there is only one way to do it—forgive.

Forgive others for your sake so you can be free. Forgiveness is mainly a matter of obedience to God. God wants you to be free; there is no other way.

Forgiveness is agreeing to live with the consequences of another person's sin. You are going to live with those consequences anyway whether you like it or not, so the only choice you have is whether you will do so in the *bondage of bitterness* or in the *freedom of forgiveness*. No one truly forgives without accepting and suffering the pain of another person's sin. That can seem unfair and you may wonder where the justice is in it, but justice is found at the cross, which makes forgiveness legally and morally right.

Jesus took the *eternal* consequences of sin upon Himself. God "made Him who knew no sin to be sin on our behalf, that we might become the righteousness of God in Him" (2 Corinthians 5:21). We, however, often suffer the temporary consequences of other people's sins. That is simply a harsh reality of life all of us have to face.

Do not wait for the other person to ask for your forgiveness. Remember, Jesus did not wait for those who were crucifying Him to apologize before He forgave them. Even while they mocked and jeered at Him, He prayed,

"Father, forgive them; for they do not know what they are doing" (Luke 23:34).

Forgive from your heart. Allow God to bring to the surface the painful emotions you feel toward those who've hurt you. If your forgiveness doesn't touch the emotional core of your life, it will be incomplete. Too often we're afraid of the pain so we bury our emotions deep down inside us. Let God bring them to the surface so He can begin to heal those damaged emotions.

Forgiveness is choosing not to hold someone's sin against him or her any more. It is common for bitter people to bring up past issues with those who have hurt them. They want them to feel bad. But we must let go of the past and choose to reject any thought of revenge. This doesn't mean you continue to put up with the future sins of others. God does not tolerate sin and neither should you. Don't allow yourself to be continually abused by others. Take a stand against sin while continuing to exercise grace and forgiveness toward those who hurt you. If you need help setting wise limits and boundaries to protect yourself from further abuse, talk to a trusted friend, counselor, or pastor.

Don't wait until you feel like forgiving. You will never get there. Make the hard choice to forgive even if you don't feel like it. Once you choose to forgive, Satan will have lost his power over you in that area, and God's healing touch will be free to move. Freedom is what you will gain right now, not necessarily an immediate change in feelings.

Now you are ready to begin. Starting with the first person on your list, make the choice to forgive him or her for every painful memory that comes to your mind. Stay with that individual until you are sure you have dealt with all the remembered pain. Then work your way down the list in the same way.

As you begin forgiving people, God may bring to your mind painful memories you've totally forgotten. Let Him do this even if it hurts. God wants you to be free; forgiving those people is the only way. Don't try to excuse the offender's behavior, even if it is someone you are really close to.

Don't say, "Lord, please help me to forgive." He is already helping you and will be with you all the way through the process. Don't say, "Lord, I want to forgive..." because that bypasses the hard choice we have to make. Say, "Lord, I *choose* to forgive..."

For every painful memory you have for each person on your list, pray out loud:

> *Lord, I choose to forgive (name the person) for (what they did or failed to do) because it made me feel (share the painful feelings).*

After you have forgiven each person for all the offenses that came to your mind, and after you have honestly expressed how you felt, conclude your forgiveness of that person by praying out loud:

> *Lord, I choose not to hold onto my resentment. I thank You for setting me free from the bondage of my bitterness. I relinquish my right to seek revenge and ask you to heal my damaged emotions. I now ask You to bless those who have hurt me. In Jesus' name, I pray. Amen.*

Step 4: Rebellion vs. Submission

We live in a rebellious age. Many people only obey laws and authorities when it is convenient for them. There is a general lack of respect for those in government, and Christians are often as guilty as the rest of society in fostering a critical, rebellious spirit. Certainly, we are not expected to agree with our leaders' policies that are in violation of Scripture, but we are to "honor all men; love the brotherhood, fear God, honor the king" (1 Peter 2:17).

It is easy to believe the lie that those in authority over us are only robbing us of the freedom to do what we want. The truth is that God has placed them there for our protection and liberty. Rebelling against God and the authorities He has set up is a very serious sin for it gives Satan a wide open avenue to attack. Submission is the only solution. God requires more, however, than just the outward appearance of submission; He wants us to sincerely submit from the heart to those in authority. When you stand under the authority of God and those He has placed over you, you cut off this dangerous opening for demonic attacks.

The Bible makes it clear that we have two main responsibilities toward those in authority over us: to pray for them and to submit to them (Romans 13:1-7; 1 Timothy 2:1,2). To commit yourself to that godly lifestyle, pray the following prayer out loud from your heart:

> *Dear heavenly Father, You have said in the Bible that rebellion is the same thing as witchcraft and as bad as idolatry. I know I have not obeyed You in this area and have rebelled in my heart against You and against those You have placed in authority over me. Thank You for Your forgiveness of my rebellion. By the shed blood of the Lord Jesus Christ, I pray that all ground gained by evil spirits in my life due to my rebellion would be canceled. I pray that You would show me all the ways I have been rebellious. I choose now to adopt a submissive spirit and a servant's heart. In Jesus' precious name, I pray. Amen.*
>
> (See 1 Samuel 15:23.)

Being under authority is clearly an act of faith! By submitting, you are trusting God to work through His established lines of authority, even when they are harsh or unkind or tell you to do something you don't want to do. There may be times when those over you abuse their authority and break the laws that are ordained by God for the protection of innocent people. In those cases, you will need to seek help from a *higher authority* for your protection. The laws in your state may require that such abuse be reported to the police or other governmental agency. If there is continuing abuse (physical, mental, emotional, or sexual) where you live, you may need further counseling help to deal with that situation.

If authorities abuse their position by requiring you to break God's law or compromise your commitment to Him, then you need to óbey God rather than man (Acts 4:19,20). Be careful though. Don't assume that an authority is violating God's Word just because they are telling you to do something you don't like. We all need to adopt a humble, submissive spirit to one another in the fear of Christ (Ephesians 5:21). In addition, however, God has set up specific lines of authority to protect us and to give order to our daily lives.

As you prayerfully look over the next list, allow the Lord to show you any *specific* ways in which you have been rebellious to authority. Then, using the prayer of confession that follows the list, specifically confess whatever the Lord brings to your mind.

- ❏ Civil government (including traffic laws, tax laws, attitude toward government officials) (Romans 13:1-7; 1 Timothy 2:1-4; 1 Peter 2:13-17)
- ❏ Parents, stepparents, or legal guardians (Ephesians 6:1-3)
- ❏ Teachers, coaches, school officials (Romans 13:1-4)

❑ Employers (past and present) (1 Peter 2:18-23)
❑ Husband (1 Peter 3:1-4) [*Note to Husbands:*
Take a moment and ask the Lord if your lack of
love for your wife could be fostering a rebellious
spirit within her. If so, confess that now as a vio-
lation of Ephesians 5:22-33.]
❑ Church leaders (Hebrews 13:7)
❑ God (Daniel 9:5,9)

For each way in which the Spirit of God brings to your
mind that you have been rebellious, use the following prayer
to specifically confess that sin:

> *Lord, I confess that I have been rebellious*
> *toward (name) by (say what you did specifi-*
> *cally). Thank You for forgiving my rebellion.*
> *I choose now to be submissive and obedient to*
> *Your Word. In Jesus' name, I pray. Amen.*

Step 5: Pride vs. Humility

Pride kills. Pride says, "I don't need God or anyone else's
help. I can handle it by myself." Oh no, you can't! We absolutely need God, and we desperately need each other. The
apostle Paul wisely wrote, "[we] worship in the Spirit of God
and glory in Christ Jesus and put *no confidence in the flesh*"
(Philippians 3:3 emphasis added). That is a good definition of
humility: putting no confidence in the flesh, that is in ourselves; but, rather, being *"strong in the Lord, and in the*
strength of His might" (Ephesians 6:10 emphasis added).
Humility is confidence properly placed in God.

Proverbs 3:5-7 expresses a similar thought: "Trust in the
LORD with all your heart, and do not lean on your own understanding. In all your ways acknowledge Him, and He will
make your paths straight. Do not be wise in your own eyes;
fear the LORD and turn away from evil." (James 4:6-10 and

1 Peter 5:1-10 also warn us that serious spiritual problems will result when we are proud.) Use the following prayer to express your commitment to living humbly before God:

> *Dear heavenly Father, You have said that pride goes before destruction and an arrogant spirit before stumbling. I confess that I have been thinking mainly of myself and not of others. I have not denied myself, picked up my cross daily, and followed You. As a result, I have given ground to the devil in my life. I have sinned by believing I could be happy and successful on my own. I confess that I have placed my will before Yours, and I have centered my life around myself instead of You.*
>
> *I repent of my pride and selfishness and pray that all ground gained in my members by the enemies of the Lord Jesus Christ would be canceled. I choose to rely on the Holy Spirit's power and guidance so I will do nothing from selfishness or empty conceit. With humility of mind, I will regard others as more important than myself. And I choose to make You, Lord, the most important of all in my life.*
>
> *Please show me now all the specific ways in which I have lived my life in pride. Enable me through love to serve others and in honor to prefer others. I ask all of this in the gentle and humble name of Jesus, my Lord. Amen.*
>
> (See Proverbs 16:18; Matthew 6:33; 16:24; Romans 12:10; Philippians 2:3.)

Having made that commitment to God in prayer, now allow Him to show you any specific ways in which you have lived in a proud manner. The following list may help you. As the Lord brings to your mind areas of pride, use the prayer on the next page to guide you in your confession.

❏ Having a stronger desire to do my will than God's will

❏ Leaning too much on my own understanding and experience rather than seeking God's guidance through prayer and His Word

❏ Relying on my own strengths and abilities instead of depending on the power of the Holy Spirit

❏ Being more concerned about controlling others than in developing self-control

❏ Being too busy doing "important" things to take time to do little things for others

❏ Having a tendency to think that I have no needs

❏ Finding it hard to admit when I am wrong

❏ Being more concerned about pleasing people than pleasing God

❏ Being concerned about getting the credit I feel I deserve

❏ Thinking I am more humble, spiritual, religious, or devoted than others

❏ Being driven to obtain recognition by attaining degrees, titles, or positions

❏ Often feeling that my needs are more important than another person's needs

❏ Considering myself better than others because of my academic, artistic, or athletic abilities and accomplishments

❏ Other ways I have thought more highly of myself than I should

For each of the above areas that has been true in your life, pray out loud:

> *Lord, I agree I have been proud in (name the area). Thank You for forgiving me for my pride. I choose to humble myself before You and others. I choose to place all my confidence in You and none in my flesh. In Jesus' name, amen.*

Dealing with Prejudice and Bigotry

Pride is the original sin of Lucifer. It sets one person or group against another. Satan's strategy is always to divide and conquer, but God has given us a ministry of reconciliation (2 Corinthians 5:19). Consider for a moment the work of Christ in breaking down the long-standing barrier of racial prejudice between Jew and Gentile:

> For [Christ] is our peace, who has made the two one and has destroyed the barrier, the dividing wall of hostility, by abolishing in his flesh the law with its commandments and regulations. His purpose was to create in himself one new man out of the two, thus making peace, and in this one body to reconcile both of them to God through the cross, by which he put to death their hostility. He came and preached peace to you who were far away and peace to those who were near. For through him we both have access to the Father by one Spirit (Ephesians 2:14-18 NIV).

Many times we deny that there is prejudice or bigotry in our hearts, yet "nothing in all creation is hidden from God's sight. Everything is uncovered and laid bare before the eyes of him to whom we must give account" (Hebrews 4:13 NIV). The following is a prayer, asking God to shine His light upon your heart and reveal any area of proud prejudice:

Dear heavenly Father, I know that You love all people equally and that You do not show favoritism. You accept people from every nation who fear You and do what is right. You do not judge them based on skin color, race, economic standing, ethnic background, gender, denominational preference, or any other worldly matter. I confess that I have too often prejudged others or regarded myself superior because of these things. I have not always been a minister of reconciliation but have been a proud agent of division through my attitudes, words, and deeds. I repent of all hateful bigotry and proud prejudice, and I ask You, Lord, to now reveal to my mind all the specific ways in which this form of pride has corrupted my heart and mind. In Jesus' name, amen.

(See Acts 10:34; 2 Corinthians 5:16.)

For each area of prejudice, superiority or bigotry that the Lord brings to mind, pray the following prayer out loud from your heart:

I confess and renounce the prideful sin of prejudice against (name the group). I thank You for Your forgiveness, Lord, and ask now that You would change my heart and make me a loving agent of reconciliation with (name the group). In Jesus' name, amen.

Step 6: Bondage vs. Freedom

Many times we feel trapped in a vicious cycle of "sin-confess-sin-confess" that never seems to end. We can become very discouraged and end up just giving up and giving in to the sins of our flesh. To find freedom we must follow James

4:7: "Submit therefore to God. Resist the devil and he will flee from you." We submit to God by confession of sin and repentance (turning away from sin). We resist the devil by rejecting his lies. Instead, we walk in the truth and put on the full armor of God (see Ephesians 6:10-20).

Sin that has become a habit often requires help from a trusted brother or sister in Christ. James 5:16 says, "Confess your sins to one another, and pray for one another, so that you may be healed. The effective prayer of a righteous man can accomplish much." Sometimes the assurance of 1 John 1:9 is enough: "If we confess our sins, He is faithful and righteous to forgive us our sins and to cleanse us from all unrighteousness."

Remember, confession is not saying, "I'm sorry"; it is openly admitting, "I did it." Whether you need help from other people or just the accountability of walking in the light before God, pray the following prayer out loud:

> *Dear heavenly Father, You have told me to put on the Lord Jesus Christ and make no provision for the flesh in regard to its lust. I confess that I have given in to fleshly lusts that wage war against my soul. I thank You that in Christ my sins are already forgiven, but I have broken Your holy law and given the devil a chance to wage war in my body. I come to You now to confess and renounce these sins of the flesh so that I might be cleansed and set free from the bondage of sin. Please reveal to my mind now all the sins of the flesh I have committed and the ways I have grieved the Holy Spirit. In Jesus' holy name, I pray. Amen.*
>
> (See Proverbs 28:13 NIV; Romans 6:12,13; 13:14; 2 Corinthians 4:2; 1 Peter 2:11; 5:8.)

There are many sins of the flesh that can control us. The following list contains many of them, but a prayerful examination of Mark 7:20-23, Galatians 5:19-21, Ephesians 4:25-31, and other Scripture passages will help you to be even more thorough. Look over the list below and the Scriptures just listed and ask the Holy Spirit to bring to your mind the ones you need to confess. He may reveal to you others as well. For each one the Lord shows you, pray a prayer of confession from your heart. There is a sample prayer following the list. (*Note:* Sexual sins, divorce, eating disorders, substance abuse, abortion, suicidal tendencies, and perfectionism will be dealt with later in this step. Further counseling help may be necessary to find complete healing and freedom in these and other areas.)

- ❏ Stealing
- ❏ Quarreling/fighting
- ❏ Jealousy/envy
- ❏ Complaining/criticism
- ❏ Lustful actions
- ❏ Gossip/slander
- ❏ Swearing
- ❏ Apathy/laziness
- ❏ Lying
- ❏ Hatred
- ❏ Anger
- ❏ Lustful thoughts
- ❏ Drunkenness
- ❏ Cheating
- ❏ Procrastination
- ❏ Greed/materialism
- ❏ Others:

> *Lord, I confess that I have committed the sin of (name the sin). Thank You for Your forgiveness and cleansing. I now turn away*

> *from this sin and turn to You, Lord.*
> *Strengthen me by Your Holy Spirit to obey You.*
> *In Jesus' name, amen.*

Wrong Sexual Use of Our Body

It is our responsibility not to allow sin to have control over our bodies. We must not use our bodies or another person's body as an instrument of unrighteousness (see Romans 6:12,13). Sexual immorality is sin against your body, the temple of the Holy Spirit (1 Corinthians 6:18,19). To find freedom from sexual bondage, begin by praying the following prayer:

> *Lord, I ask You to bring to my mind every sexual use of my body as an instrument of unrighteousness so I can renounce these sins right now. In Jesus' name, I pray. Amen.*

As the Lord brings to your mind every wrong sexual use of your body, whether it was done to you (rape, incest, sexual molestation) or willingly by you (pornography, masturbation, sexual immorality), renounce *every* occasion:

> *Lord, I renounce (<u>name the specific use of your body</u>) with (<u>name any other person involved</u>). I ask You to break that sinful bond with (<u>name</u>).*

After you are finished, commit your body to the Lord by praying:

> *Lord, I renounce all these uses of my body as an instrument of unrighteousness, and I admit to any willful participation. I choose now to present my eyes, mouth, mind, heart, hands, feet, and sexual organs to You as*

instruments of righteousness. I present my whole body to You as a living sacrifice, holy and acceptable. I choose to reserve the sexual use of my body for marriage only.

I reject the devil's lie that my body is not clean or that it is dirty or in any way unacceptable to You as a result of my past sexual experiences. Lord, thank You that You have totally cleansed and forgiven me and that You love and accept me just the way I am. Therefore, I choose now to accept myself and my body as clean in Your eyes. Amen.

(See Hebrews 13:4.)

Special Prayers for Special Needs

Divorce

Lord, I confess to You any part that I played in my divorce (ask the Lord to show you specifics). Thank You for Your forgiveness, and I choose to forgive myself as well. I renounce the lie that my identity is now in "being divorced." I am a child of God, and I reject the lie that says I am a second-class Christian because of the divorce. I reject the lie that says I am worthless, unlovable, and that my life is empty and meaningless. I am complete in Christ who loves me and accepts me just as I am. Lord, I commit the healing of all hurts in my life to You as I have chosen to forgive those who have hurt me. I also place my future into Your hands and trust You to provide the human companionship You created me to need through Your church and, if it be Your will, through another spouse. I pray all this in the healing name of Jesus, my Savior, Lord, and closest friend. Amen.

Homosexuality

Lord, I renounce the lie that You have created me or anyone else to be homosexual, and I agree that in Your Word You clearly forbid homosexual behavior. I choose to accept myself as a child of God, and I thank You that You created me as a man (woman). I renounce all homosexual thoughts, urges, drives, and acts, and cancel out all ways that Satan has used these things to pervert my relationships. I announce that I am free in Christ to relate to the opposite sex and my own sex in the way that You intended. In Jesus' name, amen.

Abortion

Lord, I confess that I was not a proper guardian and keeper of the life You entrusted to me, and I admit that as sin. Thank You that because of Your forgiveness, I can forgive myself. I recognize the child is in Your caring hands for all eternity. In Jesus' name, amen.

Suicidal Tendencies

Lord, I renounce all suicidal thoughts and any attempts I've made to take my own life or in any way injure myself. I renounce the lie that life is hopeless and that I can find peace and freedom by taking my own life. Satan is a thief and comes to steal, kill, and destroy. I choose life in Christ who said He came to give me life and give it abundantly. Thank You for Your forgiveness that allows me to forgive myself. I choose to believe that there is always hope in Christ. In Jesus' name, I pray. Amen.
(See John 10:10.)

Drivenness and Perfectionism

Lord, I renounce the lie that my self-worth is dependent upon my ability to perform. I announce the truth that my identity and sense of worth is found in who I am as Your child. I renounce seeking the approval and acceptance of other people, and I choose to believe that I am already approved and accepted in Christ because of His death and resurrection for me. I choose to believe the truth that I have been saved, not by deeds done in righteousness, but according to Your mercy. I choose to believe that I am no longer under the curse of the law because Christ became a curse for me. I receive the free gift of life in Christ and choose to abide in Him. I renounce striving for perfection by living under the law. By Your grace, heavenly Father, I choose from this day forward to walk by faith in the power of Your Holy Spirit according to what You have said is true. In Jesus' name, amen.

Eating Disorders or Self-Mutilation

Lord, I renounce the lie that my value as a person is dependent upon my appearance or performance. I renounce cutting or abusing myself, vomiting, using laxatives or starving myself as a means of being in control, altering my appearance, or trying to cleanse myself of evil. I announce that only the blood of the Lord Jesus cleanses me from sin. I realize I have been bought with a price and my body, the temple of the Holy Spirit, belongs to God. Therefore, I choose to glorify God in my body. I renounce the lie that I am evil or that any part of my body is evil. Thank You that You accept me just the way I am in Christ. In Jesus' name, I pray. Amen.

Substance Abuse

Lord, I confess that I have misused substances (alcohol, tobacco, food, prescription or street drugs) for the purpose of pleasure, to escape reality, or to cope with difficult problems. I confess that I have abused my body and programmed my mind in a harmful way. I have quenched the Holy Spirit as well. Thank You for forgiving me. I renounce any satanic connection or influence in my life through my misuse of food or chemicals. I cast my anxieties onto Christ who loves me. I commit myself to yield no longer to substance abuse, but instead I choose to allow the Holy Spirit to direct and empower me. In Jesus' name, amen.

After you have confessed all known sin, pray:

Lord, I now confess these sins to You and claim through the blood of the Lord Jesus Christ my forgiveness and cleansing. I cancel out all ground that evil spirits have gained through my willful involvement in sin. I pray this in the wonderful name of my Lord and Savior, Jesus Christ. Amen.

Step 7: Curses vs. Blessings

The next step to freedom is to renounce the sins of your ancestors as well as any curses which may have been placed on you by deceived and evil people or groups. In giving the Ten Commandments, God said,

> You shall not make for yourself an idol, or any
> likeness of what is in heaven above or on the earth
> beneath or in the water under the earth. You shall not
> worship them or serve them; for I, the LORD your
> God, am a jealous God, visiting the iniquity of the
> fathers on the children, on the third and the fourth
> generations of those who hate Me, but showing lov-
> ingkindness to thousands, to those who love Me and
> keep My commandments (Exodus 20:4-6).

Iniquities can be passed on from one generation to the
next if you don't renounce the sins of your ancestors and
claim your new spiritual heritage in Christ. You are not guilty
for the sin of any ancestor, but because of their sin, you may
be vulnerable to Satan's attack.

Because of the fall, you are genetically predisposed to certain strengths or weaknesses and are influenced by the physical and spiritual atmosphere in which you were raised. These
conditions can contribute toward causing someone to
struggle with a particular sin. Ask the Lord to show you
specifically what sins are characteristic of your family by
praying the following prayer:

> *Dear heavenly Father, I ask You to reveal
> to my mind now all the sins of my ancestors
> that are being passed down through family
> lines. I want to be free from those influences
> and walk in my new identity as a child of
> God. In Jesus' name, amen.*

As the Lord brings those areas of family sin to your mind,
list them below. You will be specifically renouncing them later
in this step.

1. _____

2. _____

3. _____

4. _____

5. _____

6. _____

7. _____

8. _____

9. _____

10. _____

In order to walk free from the sins of your ancestors and any curses and assignments targeted against you, read the following declaration and pray the following prayer out loud. Remember, you have all the authority and protection you need in Christ to take your stand against such activity.

Declaration

I here and now reject and disown all the sins of my ancestors. I specifically renounce the sins of (list here the areas of family sin the Lord revealed to you). As one who has now been delivered from the domain of darkness into the kingdom of God's Son, I cancel out all demonic working that has been passed down to me from my family. As one who has been crucified and raised with Jesus Christ and who sits with Him in heavenly places, I renounce all satanic assignments that are directed toward me and my ministry. I cancel out every curse that Satan and his workers have put on me. I announce to Satan and all his forces that Christ became a curse for me when He died for my sins on the cross. I reject any and every way in which Satan may claim ownership of me. I belong to the Lord Jesus Christ who purchased me with His own blood. I reject all blood sacrifices whereby Satan may claim ownership of me. I declare myself to be fully and eternally signed over and committed to the Lord Jesus Christ. By the authority I have in Christ, I now command every familiar spirit and every enemy of the Lord Jesus that is influencing me to leave my presence. I commit myself to my heavenly Father to do His will from this day forward.

(See Galatians 3:13.)

Prayer

Dear heavenly Father, I come to You as Your child, bought out of slavery to sin by the blood of the Lord Jesus Christ. You are the Lord of the universe and the Lord of my life. I submit my body to You as an instrument of righteousness, a living and holy sacrifice that I may glorify You in my body. I now ask You to fill me with the Holy Spirit. I commit myself to the renewing of my mind in order to prove that Your will is good, acceptable, and perfect for me. All this I pray in the name and authority of the risen Lord Jesus Christ. Amen.

Maintaining Your Freedom

Even after finding freedom in Christ by going through these seven steps, you may still be attacked by demonic influences trying to regain control of your mind, hours, days, or even weeks later. But you don't have to let them. As you continue to walk in humble submission to God, you can resist the devil and he *will* flee from you (James 4:7).

The devil is attracted to sin like flies are attracted to garbage. Get rid of the garbage and the flies will depart for smellier places. In the same way, walk in the truth, confessing all sin and forgiving those who hurt you, and the devil will have no place in your life to set up shop.

Realize that one victory does not mean the battles are over. Freedom must be maintained. After completing these steps to freedom, one happy lady asked, "Will I always be like this?" I told her she would stay free as long as she remained in right relationship with God. "Even if you slip and fall," I encouraged, "you know how to get right with God again."

One victim of horrible atrocities shared this illustration:

> It's like being forced to play a game with an ugly stranger in my own home. I kept losing and wanting to quit but the ugly stranger wouldn't let me. Finally, I called the police (a higher authority), and they came and escorted the stranger out. He knocked on the door trying to regain entry, but this time I recognized his voice and didn't let him in.

What a beautiful picture of gaining and keeping your freedom in Christ! We call upon Jesus, the ultimate authority, and He escorts the enemy of our souls out of our lives.

How to Maintain Your Freedom

Your freedom must be maintained. We cannot emphasize that enough. You have won a very important battle in an ongoing war. Freedom will continue to be yours as long as you keep choosing the truth and standing firm in the strength of the Lord. If you become aware of lies you have believed, renounce them and choose the truth. If new, painful memories surface, forgive those who hurt you. If the Lord shows you other areas of sin in your life, confess those promptly. This tool can serve as a constant guide for you in dealing with the things God points out to you. Some people have found it helpful to walk through the "Steps to Freedom in Christ" again. As you do, read the instructions carefully.

For your encouragement and growth, we recommend these additional books: *Victory Over the Darkness* (or the youth version, *Stomping Out the Darkness*), *Walking in Freedom* (a 21-day follow-up devotional), and *Living Free in Christ*. To maintain your freedom in Christ, we strongly suggest the following as well.

1. Be involved in a loving, caring church fellowship where you can be open and honest with others and where God's truth is taught with grace.

2. Read and meditate on the Bible daily. Memorize key verses from the "Steps to Freedom in Christ." You may want to read the "Statement of Truth" (see Step 2) out loud daily and study the verses mentioned.

3. Learn to take every thought captive to the obedience of Christ. Assume responsibility for your thought life. Don't let your mind become passive. Reject all lies, choose to focus on the truth, and stand firm in your true identity as a child of God in Christ.

4. Don't drift back to old patterns of thinking, feeling, and acting. This can happen very easily if you become spiritually and mentally lazy. If you are struggling with walking in the truth, share your battles openly with a trusted friend who will pray for you and encourage you to stand firm.

5. Don't expect other people to fight your battles for you, however. They can help you, but they can't think, pray, read the Bible, or choose the truth for you.

6. Commit yourself to daily prayer. Prayer demonstrates a life of trusting in and depending on God. You can pray the following prayers often and with confidence. Let the words come from your heart as well as your lips and feel free to change them to make them *your* prayers.

Daily Prayer and Declaration

Dear heavenly Father, I praise You and honor You as my Lord. You are in control of all things. I thank You that You are always with me and will never leave me nor forsake me. You are the only all-powerful and only wise God. You are kind and loving in all Your ways. I love You and thank You that I am united with Christ and spiritually alive in Him. I choose not to love the world or the things in the world, and I crucify the flesh and all its passions.

Thank You for the life I now have in Christ. I ask You to fill me with the Holy Spirit so I may say no to sin and yes to You. I declare my total dependence upon You and I take my stand against Satan and all his lying ways. I choose to believe the truth of God's Word despite what my feelings may say. I refuse to be discouraged; You are the God of all hope. Nothing is too difficult for You. I am confident that You will supply all my needs as I seek to live according to Your Word. I thank You that I can be content and live a responsible life through Christ who strengthens me.

I now take my stand against Satan and command him and all his evil spirits to depart from me. I choose to put on the full armor of God so I may be able to stand firm against all the devil's schemes. I submit my body as a living and holy sacrifice to God, and I choose to renew my mind by the living Word of God. By so doing I will be able to prove that the will of God is good, acceptable, and perfect for me. In the name of my Lord and Savior, Jesus Christ. Amen.

Bedtime Prayer

Thank You, Lord, that You have brought me into Your family and have blessed me with every spiritual blessing in the heavenly places in Christ Jesus. Thank You for this time of renewal and refreshment through sleep. I accept it as one of Your blessings for Your children, and I trust You to guard my mind and my body during my sleep.

As I have thought about You and Your truth during the day, I choose to let those good thoughts continue in my mind while I am asleep. I commit myself to You for Your protection against every attempt of Satan and his demons to attack me during sleep. Guard my mind from nightmares. I renounce all fear and cast every anxiety upon You, Lord. I commit myself to You as my rock, my fortress, and my strong tower. May Your peace be upon this place of rest now. In the strong name of the Lord Jesus Christ, I pray. Amen.

Prayer for Cleansing Home/Apartment/Room

After removing and destroying all objects of false worship, pray this prayer aloud in every room if necessary:

> *Heavenly Father, I acknowledge that You are the Lord of heaven and earth. In Your sovereign power and love, You have given me all things to enjoy. Thank You for this place to live. I claim my home as a place of spiritual safety for me and my family, and ask for Your protection from all the attacks of the enemy. As a child of God, raised up and seated with Christ in the heavenly places, I command every evil spirit claiming ground in this place, based on the activities of past or present occupants, including me, to leave and never return. I renounce all curses and spells directed against this place. I ask You, heavenly Father, to post Your holy, warring angels around this place to guard it from any and all attempts of the enemy to enter and disturb Your purposes for me and my family. I thank You, Lord, for doing this in the name of the Lord Jesus Christ. Amen.*

Prayer for Living in a Non-Christian Environment

After removing and destroying all objects of false worship from your possession, pray this aloud in the place where you live:

> *Thank You, heavenly Father, for a place to live and to be renewed by sleep. I ask You to set aside my room (or portion of this room) as a place of spiritual safety for me. I renounce any allegiance given to false gods or spirits by other*

occupants. I renounce any claim to this room (space) by Satan based on the activities of past or present occupants, including me. On the basis of my position as a child of God and joint-heir with Christ, who has all authority in heaven and on earth, I command all evil spirits to leave this place and never return. I ask You, heavenly Father, to station Your holy, warring angels to protect me while I live here. In Jesus' mighty name, I pray. Amen.

Continue to walk in the truth that your identity and sense of worth comes through who you are in Christ. Renew your mind with the truth that your *acceptance, security,* and *significance* are in Christ alone.

We recommend that you meditate on the following truths daily, perhaps reading the entire list out loud, morning and evening, for the next few weeks. Think about what you are reading and let your heart rejoice in the truth.

In Christ

I renounce the lie that I am rejected, unloved, dirty, or shameful because in Christ *I am completely accepted. God says...*

I am God's child (John 1:12)
I am Christ's friend (John 15:5)
I have been justified (Romans 5:1)
I am united with the Lord and I am one spirit with Him (1 Corinthians 6:17)
I have been bought with a price: I belong to God (1 Corinthians 6:19,20)
I am a member of Christ's body (1 Corinthians 12:27)
I am a saint, a holy one (Ephesians 1:1)
I have been adopted as God's child (Ephesians 1:5)

I have direct access to God through the Holy Spirit
(Ephesians 2:18)
I have been redeemed and forgiven of all my sins
(Colossians 1:14)
I am complete in Christ (Colossians 2:10)

I renounce the lie that I am guilty, unprotected, alone, or abandoned because in Christ *I am totally secure. God says...*

I am free forever from condemnation (Romans
8:1,2)
I am assured that all things work together for good
(Romans 8:28)
I am free from any condemning charges against me
(Romans 8:31-34)
I cannot be separated from the love of God
(Romans 8:35-39)
I have been established, anointed, and sealed by
God (2 Corinthians 1:21,22)
I am confident that the good work God has begun
in me will be perfected (Philippians 1:6)
I am a citizen of heaven (Philippians 3:20)
I am hidden with Christ in God (Colossians 3:3)
I have not been given a spirit of fear, but of power,
love, and a sound mind (2 Timothy 1:7)
I can find grace and mercy to help in time of need
(Hebrews 4:16)
I am born of God and the evil one cannot touch me
(1 John 5:18)

I renounce the lie that I am worthless, inadequate, helpless, or hopeless because in Christ *I am deeply significant. God says...*

I am the salt of the earth and the light of the world
(Matthew 5:13,14)

I am a branch of the true vine, Jesus, a channel of
His life (John 15:1,5)

I have been chosen and appointed by God to bear
fruit (John 15:16)

I am a personal, Spirit-empowered witness of
Christ's (Acts 1:8)

I am a temple of God (1 Corinthians 3:16)

I am a minister of reconciliation for God (2 Corinthians 5:17-21)

I am God's coworker (2 Corinthians 6:1)

I am seated with Christ in the heavenly realm
(Ephesians 2:6)

I am God's workmanship, created for good works
(Ephesians 2:10)

I may approach God with freedom and confidence
(Ephesians 3:12)

I can do all things through Christ who strengthens
me! (Philippians 4:13)

I am not the great "I Am,"
but by the grace of God I am what I am.
(See Exodus 3:14; John 8:24,28,58; 1 Corinthians 15:10.)

Seeking the Forgiveness of Others

Therefore, if you bring your gift to the altar, and
there remember that your brother has something
against you, leave your gift there before the altar, and
go your way. First be reconciled to your brother, and
then come and offer your gift. Agree with your
adversary quickly, while you are on the way with him,
lest your adversary deliver you to the judge, the judge
hand you over to the officer, and you are thrown into
prison. Assuredly, I say to you, you will by no means

get out of there till you have paid the last penny (Matthew 5:23-26 NKJV).

The Motivation for Seeking Forgiveness

Matthew 5:23-26 is the key passage on seeking forgiveness. Several points in these verses bear emphasizing. The worshiper coming before God to offer a gift *remembers* that someone has something against him. The Holy Spirit is the One who brings to his or her mind the wrong that was done.

Only the actions which have hurt another person need to be confessed to them. If you have had jealous, lustful, or angry thoughts toward another, and they don't know about it, these are to be confessed to God alone.

An exception to this principle occurs when restitution needs to be made. If you stole or broke something, damaged someone's reputation, and so on, you need to go to that person and make it right, even if he or she is unaware of what you did.

The Process of Seeking Forgiveness

1. Write out what you did wrong and why you did it.

2. Make sure you have already forgiven them for whatever they may have done to you.

3. Think through exactly how you will ask them to forgive you. Be sure to:
   a. Label your action as "wrong."

   b. Be specific and admit what you did.

   c. Make no defenses or excuses.

d. Do not blame the other people, and do not expect or demand that they ask for your forgiveness.

e. Your confession should lead to the direct question: "Will you forgive me?"

4. Seek the right place and the right time to approach the offended person.

5. Ask for forgiveness in person with anyone with whom you can talk face-to-face with the following exception: *Do not go alone* when your safety is in danger.

6. Except where no other means of communication is possible, *do not write a letter* because: a letter can be very easily misread or misunderstood; A letter can be read by the wrong people (those having nothing to do with the offense or the confession); a letter can be kept when it should have been destroyed.

7. Once you sincerely seek forgiveness, you are free—whether the other person forgives you or not (Romans 12:18).

8. After forgiveness, fellowship with God in worship (Matthew 5:24).

Helping Others Find Freedom in Christ

AFTER I HAD SHARED SOME testimonies of people finding their freedom in Christ, a woman asked, "Are you an exorcist?"

"No, I'm not an exorcist," I replied. "I don't think there is such a thing as an exorcist, and I don't believe there is a gift of exorcism. I'm just a concerned brother in Christ."

Over the years I have been privileged to see thousands find their freedom in Christ. I believe every committed Christian, especially pastors and counselors, can do what I do to help others resolve their personal and spiritual conflicts. Helping others find their freedom in Christ does not require the exercise of a special gift; it requires the loving application of truth.

Our ministry has trained thousands of Christian workers all over the world. In this chapter I want to briefly describe how you can help others, whether you are a "professional" helper, such as a pastor or counselor, or a Christian who is committed to personal ministry and is willing to be used by God. One church I know of has a "Freedom Ministry" (which has led hundreds of people to freedom in Christ) in which most of the ministry is done by trained laypeople.

Whatever your position, the following pages will give you some practical and very basic guidelines for ministry.*

Principles of Spiritual Conflict Resolution

People's lives are like houses. Suppose a family hasn't taken the garbage out of their house for months, and they have spilled food and beverages without cleaning up. That will attract a lot of flies. To resolve this problem, I don't think it is necessary to study the flight patterns of the flies and determine their names and rank structure in the insect hierarchy. There may be some value in doing this which I am not aware of, but I don't think the answer is primarily found in gaining knowledge about and getting rid of the flies. Similarly, to "focus on the flies" in our lives is to allow the devil to set the agenda for us and distract us from the real issue—which is to get rid of the garbage. Repentance and faith in God have been and will continue to be the answer in this present church age.

To resolve personal and spiritual conflicts, we need to understand that God is the Wonderful Counselor, and that He will minister to the whole person and take into account all reality. Seldom if ever does a Christian have just a spiritual problem or just a psychological problem. God relates to us as *whole people,* and He takes into account all reality.

I would like to suggest the four following principles as we consider the spiritual side of conflict resolution:

---

* For a more detailed discussion of the theological basis and practical application of this approach to counseling, see my book *Helping Others Find Freedom in Christ* (Regal Books). There is also a video series which leads you step by step through the process. For professional counselors and therapists, see *Christ-Centered Therapy* (Zondervan) which I coauthored with two professional therapists, Terry and Julie Zuehlke. This book is on the integration of theology and psychology. It also deals with values, world view, methodology, strategy, and the relationship between the professional counselor and the church.

1. We should derive our methodology for dealing with the kingdom of darkness primarily from the epistles rather than the Gospels and the Book of Acts.

It is easy to see why some have derived their methodology for deliverance from the Gospels and the Book of Acts, because they are the only authoritative source for examples of demonic expulsion. Why not follow the example of Jesus and His disciples? Their example does clearly reveal the battle between the kingdom of darkness and the kingdom of God and proves that Jesus came to "destroy the works of the devil" (1 John 3:8). However, the Gospels record the life and ministry of Christ before the cross. All authority had not yet been given to Him "in heaven and on earth" (Matthew 28:18). Satan had not yet been defeated and disarmed (Colossians 2:15). So to confront Satan and his demons, a specially endowed agent of authority was required. That is why Jesus "called the twelve together, and gave them power and authority over all the demons" (Luke 9:1).

All conservative systematic theologies (covenant as well as dispensational) teach clear distinctions between living under the old covenant (law) and the new covenant (grace). The historical life of Christ was lived under the law. The new covenant was not effective until after His death and resurrection. This means that Christ, who was born under the law, had to live under it as well. Jesus said, "Do not think that I came to abolish the Law or the Prophets; I did not come to abolish but to fulfill" (Matthew 5:17).

For example, if a wealthy leader in your community asked you how he could have eternal life, would you tell him to keep the commandments? That is how Jesus instructed the rich young ruler (Matthew 19:16,17). Before the cross and under the law, God's covenant people demonstrated their faith in God by living according to the law. But after the cross and under grace you would proclaim the gospel to such a person. Obviously our approach to evangelism changed after

Pentecost, and so has our approach to resolving spiritual conflicts.

The Book of Acts is the historical account of the period of transition between the cross and the completion of the canon. There is some disagreement among Christians about how much method and theology we should extract from this important book. Therefore I stress caution in using examples of demonic expulsion from Acts as the sole basis for methodology. Form follows function, but hosts of problems arise when we derive function from form. However, the Book of Acts does clearly reveal that demonic encounters continued after the cross and that evil forces continue to exist in opposition to the growth of the church. But this book of history does not constitute the final word on dealing with those forces.

2. Because there are no instructions in the epistles to cast out demons does not mean that Christians cannot have spiritual problems. It means that the responsibility for living free in Christ has shifted from the specially endowed agent of authority to the individual believer.

The individual believer under the law had no authority over the kingdom of darkness. Now by the grace of God every born-again believer is seated with Christ in the heavenlies. Freedom for believers is based on what Christ has already done and on how they individually respond to Him in repentance and faith. There *are* instructions throughout the epistles for living free in Christ and dealing with the demonic, but the ultimate responsibility rests on the individual believer, not on some outside agent. I can't repent or believe for you, nor can I submit to God and resist the devil for you, but I can *help* you do those things. When we see the issue from this perspective, there is a very definitive passage in the pastoral epistles which instructs us how to help one another (2 Timothy 2:24-26):

> The Lord's bond-servant must not be quarrelsome, but be kind to all, able to teach, patient when wronged, with gentleness correcting those who are in opposition, if perhaps God may grant them repentance leading to the knowledge of the truth, and they may come to their senses and escape from the snare of the devil, having been held captive by him to do his will.

This passage clearly teaches that truth sets people free and that the one who grants repentance is God. Christian counseling is far more than some technique which we learn. Christian counseling is an encounter with God. He is the Wonderful Counselor. Only God can bind up the brokenhearted and set the captive free. God does, however, work through His bond-servants who are dependent upon Him.

If you were successful in casting a demon out of someone without his or her involvement, what is to keep the demon from coming back when you leave? Unless the individual assumes responsibility for his own freedom, he may end up like the poor fellow who was freed from one spirit only to be occupied by seven others who were worse than the first (Matthew 12:43-45).

I graduated from a seminary which offered very little instruction for helping the spiritually oppressed. So I was ill-prepared to help those who were spiritually afflicted. The only method I knew was to call up the demons, get their name and rank, and cast them out. With this approach, the pastor or counselor is the deliverer, and he or she is getting information from a demon. Why would you believe a demon? They are all liars. "Whenever he speaks a lie, he speaks from his own nature, for he is a liar and the father of lies" (John 8:44).

I think the epistles paint a different picture. First, the deliverer is Christ, and He has already come. Second, we should get our information from the Word of God and the Holy

Spirit, who will lead us into all truth, and that truth will set us free.

I have not attempted to cast a demon out of someone for several years. But I have seen hundreds of people find their freedom in Christ as I helped them resolve their personal and spiritual conflicts through genuine repentance and faith in God. I no longer deal directly with demons or dialogue with them. Nor do I permit their manifestation in counseling sessions. I only work with the person by helping him or her assume responsibility to submit to God and resist the devil (James 4:7).

I have learned from experience if you try to resist the devil without first submitting to God, you will have a dogfight. On the other hand, you can submit to God without resisting the devil and stay in bondage. The tragedy is that most recovery ministries aren't doing either one.

3. *Dealing with the demonic should be seen as a truth encounter rather than a power encounter.*

Truth sets people free (John 8:32). There is not a verse in the Bible which instructs us to pursue power, because we as believers already have all the power we need in Christ (Ephesians 1:18,19). The power for Christian living is found in the truth; the power of Satan is in the lie. Satan does not want you to know your power and authority as a believer in Christ because his power is only effective in the dark. And all the darkness in the world cannot extinguish the light of one candle. Christians are to pursue the truth because they already have the power and authority to do His will. Truth is what makes an encounter with Satan effective because his primary strategy is deception. Satan's scare tactics are intended to provoke a response of fear. When fear is controlling a believer, the Spirit of God is not, and Satan has the upper hand. Fear of the enemy and faith in God are mutually exclusive.

Satan fears detection more than anything else. Whenever the light of truth comes on, he and his demons, like cockroaches, head for the shadows. I have had people tell me that the demons who are tormenting them are afraid of me. If you are helping someone, don't let that sort of lie go to your head. The demons are really afraid of *God* and of being exposed to the *truth*. I have also had people tell me that the demons were laughing at me. They were mocking my feeble efforts! This is just a strategy of intimidation, designed to put us on the defensive and discourage our efforts. As soon as you expose the strategy, the mocking stops.

I do everything I can to prevent Satan from manifesting himself and glorifying himself through a power encounter. We are to glorify *God* by allowing *His* presence to be manifested. God does everything "properly and in an orderly manner" (1 Corinthians 14:40). God is glorified if you maintain control of the whole process. If you lose control, Satan is glorified.

4. *The primary prerequisites for helping others find freedom are godly character and the ability to teach.*

The church has sometimes assumed that giftedness, or calling, or having some official position in the church is what qualifies one to help others. According to 2 Timothy 2:24-26, the primary qualification is to be "the Lord's bond-servant." To be an instrument in God's hand, we have to be totally dependent upon Him. Beyond that requirement, the Lord's bond-servant must be kind, patient, gentle, and able to teach. In other words we need to speak the truth in love, because truth sets us free. It took me years to realize that people are not in bondage because of past traumas—they are in bondage to the *lies* they believed as a result of past traumas.

A resolution of personal and spiritual conflicts which is a *truth encounter* has specific advantages. First, it keeps a ministry from polarizing itself into a psychotherapeutic approach that doesn't take into account the reality of the spiritual world, or into some kind of deliverance ministry that doesn't take into account psychological issues and personal responsibility. Second, the method is transferable because it doesn't depend on any unusual gifts or calling. Third, it produces lasting results—because the people who are counseled are the ones making the decisions and assuming personal responsibility, rather than allowing the pastor or counselor to do it for them.

Guidelines for Helping Others Find Freedom

The truth encounter requires the same personal skills that any other counseling procedure does. You must be compassionate, nonjudgmental, and understanding. You must be a good listener and able to practice empathy. Solomon warned, "He who gives an answer before he hears, it is folly and shame to him" (Proverbs 18:13). Therefore you need to hear the story before you attempt to resolve anything. If you don't know what the problem is, you can't know what the answer is.

1. Gather Background Information

If possible, have the person you're helping fill out a Confidential Personal Inventory (see appendix) before the first counseling session. In churches, we prefer to use the word "encourager" instead of counselor, and "freedom appointment" instead of counseling. You have permission to copy the inventory or adapt it for your own use. Many people, however, will not disclose certain confidential information on a written sheet of paper.

First, you should get a brief history of the person's family. What was the religious experience of their parents or grandparents? Were they involved in the occult or a counterfeit religion? Was there harmony in the home? Have there been any divorces or affairs in the family history? Dysfunctional families breed false beliefs. For example, many children wrongly blame themselves for their parents' divorce. Others harbor bitterness toward their parents for years because of something which happened in the home.

You will want to know if the family has any history of alcoholism, drug abuse, or sexual addiction. Is there a history in the family of mental illness? What type of exercise and eating habits characterized the family? What was the moral climate in the home?

In order to hear their stories, I ask the people I'm helping to share their childhood and school experiences. You are not trying to resolve anything by hearing their personal and family histories. The purpose is to understand what happened to them and what may have caused them to have certain beliefs. The intimate details will come out when you take them through the Steps, and the Confidential Personal Inventory will also provide important information concerning their physical, mental, emotional, and spiritual lives.

2. Determine False Beliefs

Most people caught in a spiritual conflict have a distorted concept of God. In Figure 14a, the true concepts of God shown on the left side have been distorted by a number of negative experiences which result in false concepts of God.

A pastor's wife told me about her rigidly moral home which was dominated by her demanding mother. The father was a wimp who knew better than to interrupt the mother's tirades against their daughter. Thirty minutes into our session, I asked, "You really love Jesus, don't you?"

"Oh, yes," she responded.

"And you really love the Holy Spirit."

"Yes, I do."

"But you don't even like God the Father, do you?"

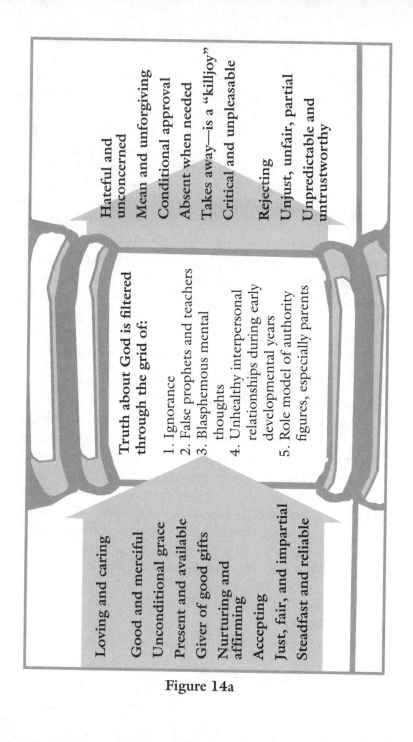

Loving and caring

Good and merciful

Unconditional grace

Present and available

Giver of good gifts

Nurturing and affirming

Accepting

Just, fair, and impartial

Steadfast and reliable

Truth about God is filtered through the grid of:

1. Ignorance
2. False prophets and teachers
3. Blasphemous mental thoughts
4. Unhealthy interpersonal relationships during early developmental years
5. Role model of authority figures, especially parents

Hateful and unconcerned

Mean and unforgiving

Conditional approval

Absent when needed

Takes away—is a "killjoy"

Critical and unpleasable

Rejecting

Unjust, unfair, partial

Unpredictable and untrustworthy

Figure 14a

She could only respond with tears. Her concept of the heavenly Father was distorted by the image of her earthly father. She perceived Jesus and the Holy Spirit as being actively involved in her life, but in her mind God the Father, like her earthly father, just sat around passively and uncaring while she was being verbally abused by her mother. Emotionally she was on the right side of the diagram even though she knew the left side was theologically correct. I gave her a set of tapes by A.W. Tozer on the attributes of God. She listened to them three times, and the impact was zero. But after she resolved her conflicts and found her freedom in Christ, the Spirit bore witness with her spirit that she was a child of her Father, and she emotionally lined up with the truth.

People in conflict also very commonly have false beliefs about *themselves*. Most don't know who they are in Christ, nor do they understand what it means to be a child of God. Consequently, they question their salvation. Many think they are different from others—that the Christian life doesn't work for them as it does for others. Some fear a mental breakdown and are filled with anxiety. Almost all feel unloved, worthless, and rejected. They have tried everything they can think of to improve their self-image, but nothing works. Some even suspect that their problem is spiritual, but they don't know how to resolve their conflicts.

Stephanie was struggling with anorexia. She was admitted to an eating-disorder clinic and underwent extensive counseling, but with little progress. One of my students suspected a spiritual problem and brought Stephanie to see me. After two counseling sessions she was free of the oppression. Stephanie returned to the clinic to tell her counselor about her freedom in Christ. The counselor told her she was only on a temporary high. If so, Stephanie is still on it, because today she enjoys her freedom in Christ while serving the Lord on the mission field!

Finally, people in conflict often have a *distorted concept of the two kingdoms.* They think they are caught between two equal but opposite powers: "bad old Satan" on one side, "good old God" on the other, and "poor me" caught in the middle. This of course is not the truth, and such people are defeated if that is what they believe. The truth is, God is omnipresent, omnipotent, and omniscient. Satan is a defeated foe—and we are in Christ, seated with Him in the heavenlies.

3. Deal with the Individual, Not the Demons

In the case of some people, Satan seems to be more present, real, and powerful to them than God. These types of people usually hear opposing arguments in their heads. They are constantly confronted with lies; they are told to get out of the counseling sessions; or they are threatened with harm or embarrassment.

One dear lady I was counseling suddenly bolted for the door. "Tell me what you're hearing," I said.

"You're going to hurt me," she answered fearfully.

I assured her what she had heard was a lie, and she slowly returned to her chair.

Such mental interference is not uncommon. That is why I always explain to the people I'm counseling that the mind is the control center. If they don't lose control of their minds, then we will not lose control in the session. I don't care whether the negative or condemning thoughts are coming from a speaker on the wall, from their own memories, or from the pit of hell. The only way these thoughts can have any control over them is if they believe them. To help them maintain mental control, I ask them to share with me what is going on in their minds. I want them to bring those deceptive thoughts into the light. As soon as the lies are exposed, the power of the devil is broken.

Sometimes people may be reluctant to share with you for two reasons. First, if they sense that you won't believe them, they won't tell you. If a client is hearing voices, secular counselors and many Christian counselors would not consider the voices demonic. And we all know what happens next. The client is given a psychological label and a prescription for medication. Realizing this, troubled people may share what has happened *to* them, but will be very reluctant to share what is happening *inside* them. Second, these voices can be very intimidating. They could be threatening harm to the clients, the counselors, or to the families and friends of the clients.

That is why you should watch the eyes of the people you counsel very carefully. If they start to become dizzy, or glassy-eyed, or start looking around the room, stop what you are doing and ask them to share what is going on inside. If you aren't paying attention, you could lose control of a session. When I see people really struggling, I may have them get up and go for a walk. I want them to know they have a choice and they can exercise their will.

Highly subjective people have a thought, and they act on it. They seem to live as though they have no will. I tell them, "If you have a thought, don't just do it. Share it with me." That is revolutionary for some people. Highly subjective people are the hardest to help because they have never really assumed responsibility for their own thoughts.

To help maintain control in the counseling session, the Steps to Freedom begin with a very specific prayer and declaration. If the people you are helping have made a declaration of faith in God, Satan cannot touch them because he has no authority over them.

I never touch the person during a freedom appointment, and I caution you against it also. This is hard for me because I am a hugger by nature. But until the person is free, the demonic forces in him or her will be repelled by the Holy Spirit in you. You typically can't get very close to a demonized person. I touched one woman on the arm to get her attention, and she later told me she felt as though she had been violated.

I never try to restrain people physically, because the weapons of our warfare are not of the flesh (2 Corinthians 10:3,4). If they run out of my office, I let them go. I wait and pray, and invariably they come back, usually within five minutes. I am not going to violate their minds or try to control them. They are free to leave or stay.

If the person you are trying to help has been actively involved in Satanism, be prepared for major opposition. Step 2 has special renunciations for those who have worshipped Satan. Everything they do is an antithesis of Christianity, because Satan is the anti-Christ. It could take you several hours to work through those renunciations. Resolving spiritual conflicts is not the only step to freedom needed by ritual-abuse victims. Paul says, "Let us cleanse ourselves from all defilement of flesh and spirit, perfecting holiness in the fear of God" (2 Corinthians 7:1). Rebuilding their fractured God-concepts and self-concepts takes time, lots of love and acceptance, and the support of an understanding Christian community. Paul summarizes this ministry in 2 Corinthians 4:1-4:

> Since we have this ministry, as we received mercy, we do not lose heart, but we have renounced the things hidden because of shame, not walking in craftiness or adulterating the word of God, but by the manifestation of truth commending ourselves to every man's conscience in the sight of God. And even if our gospel is veiled, it is veiled to those who are perishing, in whose case the god of this world has blinded the minds of the unbelieving so that they might not see the light of the gospel of the glory of Christ, who is the image of God.

4. Lead Them Through the Steps to Freedom

I came to believe years ago that the process of submitting to God and resisting the devil cannot be that difficult. I *do* believe that God made some of us smart and some of us not so smart; but I *don't* believe that His grace is available only to the smart. Those who think they are smart should make the plan of Christian living so simple that the simplest of God's creatures should be able to enter into it—though we dare not be simplistic.

Think of it this way. Suppose you were hopelessly lost in a maze. Would you want a mazeologist explaining to you all the intricacies of the maze and teaching you coping skills so you could survive in the maze? Would you want a sick legalistic preacher calling you a jerk for getting lost in the maze? No—I think you would want to know the way, the truth, and the life. The paths back to God can't be that numerous! There are a million ways to sin, but the same one answer for all sins. You could have been abused in a thousand different ways, but for your own sake you would still need to forgive the abuser.

In the same way, there is only One who sets you free—Christ. The Steps to Freedom don't set you free; they are just a tool that can be used rightly or wrongly. What sets you free is your response to Christ in repentance and faith. The primary focus of the Steps is your relationship with God. Many people can and do go on through the Steps on their own. The process is unique to each person, because the one who is praying is the one who needs the help, and that person is praying to the only One who can help him or her.

In the case of freedom appointments, where we are involved in helping people through the Steps, we often include a prayer partner. (Many times we do this for the purpose of training others.) Out of necessity, I often deal alone with the people I counsel, and the truth still sets them free. However, I always try to have a third party present when the person I'm counseling is of the opposite sex.

When we begin the sessions, the people I'm working with have a copy of the Steps, as do I. As we go along, I explain what they are doing and why they are doing it. I try to go through all seven steps with every person in one session.

People may not need every step, but I want to be thorough for their sakes. I have them read every prayer and doctrinal affirmation aloud. Hopefully they will share any mental opposition or physical discomfort. When they do, I thank them for sharing it with me. Once these things are acknowledged, simply go on. In most cases there is very little opposition. If there is, it is usually in the first two steps.

The step dealing with unforgiveness is the most important one. Every person I have counseled had a person, or many people, to forgive. I believe that unforgiveness offers Satan the biggest door into the church. If we can't help a person forgive from the heart, we can't help that person be free from the past. Someone said, "Forgiveness is to set a captive free, only to realize that you were the captive."

When these people pray and ask God whom they need to forgive, rest assured that God does reveal names to their minds. I have sometimes had people say, "Well, there's no one." In this case I say, "Would you just share the names that are coming to your mind right now?" Without exception, out come several names, and I record them. It is not uncommon that the people I'm talking with have names come to mind which surprise them. (And it is not uncommon for them to recall forgotten painful memories while they are in the process of forgiving.)

I explain what forgiveness is and how to do it. The key issues are highlighted in the Steps. Then I hand the list of names back to them and ask if, for their own sake, they would be willing to forgive those people. Their forgiving of others is primarily an issue between them and their heavenly Father. Reconciliation with the people they have forgiven may or may not follow.

Very little opposition occurs during Steps 4 through 6. In Step 6, I always deal with sexual sin separately. It is amazing how much sex plays a part in human bondage. (If you are actively helping others, I would encourage you to read *A Way of Escape* (Harvest House) so you understand how to help others be sexually free.)

In most cases, complete freedom isn't realized until after the final declaration and prayer in Step 7. When they are finished, I usually ask the people I counsel to sit comfortably and close their eyes. Then I ask, "What do you hear in your mind? Is it quiet?" After a pause they usually respond with relieved smiles and say, "Nothing. It's finally quiet in my mind." I often ask those who had difficulty reading the doctrinal affirmation in Step 2 to read it again. They can hardly believe the ease with which they can now read and understand the truth. The countenance of many people often changes so markedly that I encourage them to look at themselves in a mirror.

Getting free in Christ is one thing—staying free is another. Paul says in Galatians 5:1, "It was for freedom that Christ set us free; therefore keep standing firm and do not be subject again to a yoke of slavery." The Steps include several follow-up suggestions that will help people maintain their freedom in Christ. (We have also made available a 21-day devotional book entitled *Walking in Freedom,* published by Regal Books, which we encourage everyone to work through. Every third day they repeat one of the steps. This helps reinforce what they have done.)

Special Circumstances for Seeking Freedom

I am often asked if little children can come under attack. The answer is yes. If you are concerned for your children, I would encourage you to read either *The Seduction of Our Children* (Harvest House) or *Spiritual Protection For Our Children* (Regal Books). The latter book has age-graded Steps for children; I coauthored it with Pete and Sue Vander Hook. Pete is an Evangelical Free Church pastor—he and Sue seemed to be doing everything right, when suddenly their children started to have major spiritual attacks. Finding an answer about these attacks for their children led them to freedom for themselves and for many others in their church.

I should mention two more books. *Leading Teens to Freedom in Christ* (Regal Books), which I coauthored with my colleague, Rich Miller, is for parents and youth workers. Steps for setting your church free and setting your marriage free, as well as all our age-graded individual Steps, are available in one volume entitled, *Ministering the Steps to Freedom in Christ* (Regal Books). Each Step can be duplicated for use in your church or private ministry.

I have received several calls from people who claim that their houses are haunted by evil spirits. Usually these types of spiritual conflicts are personal in nature rather than geographic, but sometimes there may be problems in a home as the result of evil activities which were practiced there. If the house or location belongs to you, then renounce any activities that may have gone on before you purchased the property, and commit the property to the Lord. Doing this is just being a good steward of what God has entrusted to our care.

A Final Encouragement

CHAPTER 15

D EAR CHRISTIAN READER, we are involved in a winnable war. Your name is written in the Lamb's Book of Life, and the victory has already been won. Your freedom in Christ, and the freedom of those to whom you minister, has already been secured. All you need to do is appropriate it and be a good steward of what God has entrusted to you.

I want to close with one more encouraging account of victory in Jesus. Cindy attended a Christian school and married a wonderful Christian man, but they were prevented from consummating their marriage by a series of problems. First it was an infection in Cindy's female organs. Before that could be cleared up, she began suffering horrible memories of being raped as a child by her father. She entered intense counseling but was not able to gain any real victory. Then she began remembering additional experiences of abuse, and she went into an emotional tailspin.

In desperation Cindy flew to Los Angeles and showed up on my doorstep unexpectedly. I was able to spend nearly six hours with her in one long evening session. Then she flew home. Six weeks later I received this letter:

Dear Neil:

I want to thank you again for being so gracious and available to counsel me a few weeks ago. I can truly say that God has performed a miraculous healing in me.

My entire life has been one of intense inner conflict as well as physical, emotional, and mental pain. I have lived with constant fears, recurring nightmares, continual harassment from inner voices, and an obsessive fear of death. Even though I am a committed, obedient Christian, I was convinced that Christ would certainly reject me at the gates of heaven.

A year-and-a-half ago I found that I could no longer hold the pieces of my life together. I sought counseling, and God began to provide people to minister to me and instruct me in His truth. I gained strength as I learned to claim my position in Christ as a child of God. My eyes were opened to the battle in which I was engaged.

Then last summer God allowed me to remember the horrible ritual abuse in my past, and the battle became much more intense. I had to spend hours every day and night in God's Word, in prayer and meditation, and in direct confrontation and resistance of the enemy. After two months of very little sleep and virtually no peace or rest, I was certain that only Christ could deliver me from my internal hell.

Before I left for Los Angeles to see you, God encouraged me with several passages of Scripture: Psalm 11:7; Micah 7:7,8; Job 23:10. Our counseling session was a vital tool that God used in my healing process. After several hours of reliving the horrors of my past and forgiving the 22 people who had sexually abused me, I was finally free from Satan's bondage. Praise God that He went before me and defeated Satan at the cross (Hebrews 2:14,15).

Neil, I'm so happy that I am free and that I have a sound mind! I no longer have to hide the hell inside with a happy Christian facade. God gave me Isaiah 51:3 as a picture of what He has done in me: "Indeed, the LORD will comfort...all her waste places. And her wilderness He will make like Eden, and her desert like the garden of the LORD; joy and gladness will be found in her, thanksgiving and sound of a melody."

With love,
Cindy

Have you met the Bondage Breaker? Jesus Christ will set you free!

Appendix

Further Help!

Confidential Personal Inventory

I. Personal Information

Name _____

Telephone _____

Address _____

Church affiliation _____

_____

Schools attended _____

_____

Highest grade completed; degrees earned_____

Marital status _____

Previous marriage/divorce _____

Vocation:

      Present _____

      Past _____

II. Family History

A. Religious

1. To your knowledge, have any of your parents, grandparents, or great-grandparents ever been involved in any occultic, cultic, or non-Christian religious practices? Please use the Non-Christian Spiritual Checklist (see pages 202–204) and indicate what their involvement was.

2. Briefly explain your parents' Christian experience (that is, were they Christians, and did they profess and live their Christianity?).

B. Marital Status

1. Are your parents presently married or divorced? Explain.

2. Was there a sense of security and harmony in your home during the first 12 years of your life?

3. Was your father clearly the head of the home, or was there a role reversal in which your mother ruled the home? Explain.

4. How did your father treat your mother?

5. To your knowledge, were any of your parents or grandparents ever involved in an adulterous affair?

C. Health

1. Are there any addictive problems in your family (alcohol, drugs, and so on)?

2. Is there any history of mental illness?

3. Is there any history of the following ailments in your family? (Please circle.)

tuberculosis (TB)	heart disease
diabetes	cancer
ulcers	glandular problems
other	

4. How would you describe your family's concern for:

a) diet

b) exercise

c) rest

D. Were your parents strict or permissive?

III. History of Personal Health
A. Physical
1. Describe your eating habits (that is, junk food addict, eat regularly or sporadically, balanced diet, and so on).

2. Do you have any addictions or cravings that you find difficult to control (sweets, drugs, alcohol, food in general, other)?

3. Are you presently under any kind of medication for either physical or psychological reasons?

4. Do you have any problem sleeping? Are you having recurring nightmares or disturbances?

5. Does your present schedule allow for regular periods of rest and relaxation?

6. Are you adopted?

7. Have you ever been physically beaten or sexually molested? Explain.

B. Mental

1. Which of the following have you struggled with in the past or are you struggling with presently? (Please check.)

❑ daydreaming   ❑ lustful thoughts

❑ thoughts of inferiority   ❑ thoughts of inadequacy

❑ worry   ❑ doubts

❑ fantasy   ❑ obsessive thoughts

❑ insecurity   ❑ blasphemous thoughts

❑ compulsive thoughts   ❑ dizziness

❑ headaches

2. Do you spend much time wishing you were somebody else or fantasizing that you were a different person? Do you imagine yourself living at a different time, in a different place, or under different circumstances? Explain.

3. How many hours of TV do you watch per week? List your five favorite programs.

4. How many hours do you spend each week reading? What do you read primarily (newspaper, magazines, books, other)?

5. Would you consider yourself to be an optimist or a pessimist (that is, do you have a tendency to see the good in people and life or the bad)?

6. Have you ever thought that maybe you were "cracking up"? Do you presently fear that possibility? Explain.

7. Do you have regular devotions in the Bible? Where and when, and to what extent?

8. Do you find prayer difficult mentally? Explain.

9. When attending church or other Christian ministries, are you plagued by foul thoughts, jealousies, or other mental harassment? Explain.

10. Do you listen to music a lot? What type do you enjoy most?

C. Emotional

1. Which of the following emotions do you struggle with? (Please circle.)

frustration	fear of death
anger	fear of losing your mind
anxiety	fear of being hurt
depression	fear of man
bitterness	fear of failure
hatred	fear of Satan
worthlessness	

2. Which of the above listed emotions do you feel are sinful? Why?

3. Concerning your emotions, whether positive or negative, which of the following best describes you? (Please check.)

❑ readily express my emotions

❑ express some of my emotions, but not all

❑ readily acknowledge their presence, but am reserved in expressing them

❑ tend to suppress my emotions

❑ find it safest not to express how I feel

❑ tend to disregard how I feel since I cannot trust my feelings

❑ consciously or subconsciously deny them; it's too painful to deal with them

4. Do you presently know someone with whom you could be emotionally honest (that is, you

could tell this person exactly how you feel about yourself, life, and other people)?

5. How important is it that we are emotionally honest before God? Do you feel that you are? Explain.

IV. Spiritual History

A. If you were to die tonight, do you know where you would spend eternity?

B. Suppose you die tonight and appear before God in heaven, and He asks you, "By what right should I allow you into My presence?" How would you answer Him?

C. First John 5:11,12 says, "God has given us eternal life, and this life is in His Son. He who has the Son has the life; he who does not have the Son of God does not have the life."

1. Do you have the Son of God in you?

2. When did you receive Him (John 1:12)?

3. How do you know that you received Him?

D. Are you plagued by doubts about your salvation?

E. Are you presently enjoying fellowship with other believers, and if so, where and when?

F. Are you under the authority of a local church where the Bible is taught? Do you regularly support it with your time, talent, and treasure? If not, why not?

Notes

Chapter 1—You Don't Have to Live in the Shadows
1. Conversation with Dr. Paul Hiebert, who teaches at Trinity Evangelical Divinity School in Deerfield, Illinois.

Chapter 3—You Have Every Right to Be Free
1. Neil T. Anderson, *Living Free in Christ* (Ventura, California: Regal Books, 1993).

Chapter 4—You Can Win the Battle for your Mind
1. F.F. Bruce, *Commentary on the Book of Acts* (Grand Rapids, Michigan: Eerdmans, 1954), p. 114.
2. Ernst Haenchen, *The Acts of the Apostles* (Philadelphia: Westminster Press, 1971), p. 237.
3. Luther, *Table Talk,* IV, 5097, cited by Father Louis Coulange, [pseud. Joseph Turmell], *The Life of the Devil* (London: Alfred A. Knopf, 1929), pp. 147, 148.
4. Coulange [Turmel], pp. 150ff.
5. David Powlison, *Power Encounters: Reclaiming Spiritual Warfare* (Grand Rapids, Michigan: Baker, 1995), p. 135.
6. Thomas Brooks, *Precious Remedies Against Satan's Devices* (Carlisle, Pennsylvania: Banner of Truth, 1984).

Chapter 6—Jesus Has You Covered
1. Jessie Penn-Lewis, *War on the Saints*, 9th ed. (New York: Thomas E. Lowe, Ltd., 1973).
2. Theodore H. Epp *Praying with Authority* (Lincoln, NE: Back to the Bible Broadcast, 1965), p.98.
3. C. Fred Dickason, *Demon Possession and the Christian* (Chicago: Moody Press, 1987), p.255.

Chapter 7—Manipulating Spirits
1. C.S. Lewis, *The Screwtape Letters* (Old Tappan, NJ: Fleming H. Revell, 1978).
2. As cited by Michael Scanlan, T.O.R., and Randall J. Cirner, *Deliverance from Evil Spirits* (Ann Arbor, MI: Servant Books, 1980), p.16.

3. As cited by Everett Ferguson, *Demonology of the Early Christian World*, Symposium Series, vol.12 (New York: Edwin Mellen Press, 1984), p.118.

Chapter 8—The Lure of Knowledge and Power

1. Neil T. Anderson and Steve Russo, *The Seduction of Our Children* (Eugene, Oregon: Harvest House, 1991), pp. 34, 39.

Chapter 11—The Danger of Deception

1. As cited by Martin Wells Knapp, *Impressions* (Wheaton, IL: Tyndale House, 1984), p.14-15.

Chapter 12—The Danger of Losing Control

1. Merrill F. Unger, *What Demons Can Do to Saints* (Chicago: Moody Press, 1977), p. 51.
2. Ibid.

Topical Reference

About the Author

Dr. Neil T. Anderson, founder and president emeritus of Freedom in Christ Ministries, is an author, counselor, public speaker, and former associate professor at Biola University and Talbot School of Theology in La Mirada, California. He is the former chairman of the Practical Theology Department at Talbot School of Theology and has more than 30 years of pastoral experience.

Anderson is the author of *Freedom from Fear* and *Getting Anger Under Control* (both coauthored with Rich Miller) and *God's Power at Work in You* (coauthored with Dr. Robert Saucy). His other works include *Victory Over the Darkness, The Christ-Centered Marriage, Freedom from Addiction, Finding Hope Again, Walking in the Light, The Seduction of Our Children,* and *Daily in Christ.* Several of his books, including *The Bondage Breaker,* are available in youth editions coauthored with youth expert Dave Park; he and Park have also developed the Freedom in Christ 4 Teens devotional series.

Anderson has appeared on dozens of radio and television talk shows including *Focus on the Family, The 700 Club, Point of View, CBN Radio, Truths that Transform, Action Sixties, Hope for the Heart, 100 Huntley Street,* and many others.

Widely known for his work in resolving personal and spiritual conflicts, Anderson maintains a brisk counseling, consulting, and speaking schedule. His "Living Free in Christ" church conferences, as well as his several video training series for church and Sunday school leaders and discipleship ministries, have led thousands to freedom in Christ. This life-changing message has also been translated into many languages, making training possible for countless pastors, missionaries, and laypeople worldwide. Anderson also conducts seminars on marriage, family, spiritual identity, church management, and leadership renewal.

Anderson earned his B.S. in electrical engineering from Arizona State University and formerly worked as an aerospace engineer. At Talbot School of Theology, he earned his M.A. in Christian Education, along with his M.Div. and D.Min. His second doctorate, in education, is from Pepperdine University. He and his wife Joanne have been married for more than 34 years and have two grown children and two grandchildren.

Freedom in Christ is an international ministry which exists to glorify God by equipping churches, Christian organizations, and mission groups in obedience to the Great Commandment in order to accomplish the Great Commission.

Thousands have found their freedom in Christ; your group can, too! Here are some conferences you can host, which would be led by Freedom in Christ staff, that can change your community:

Living Free in Christ

A Bible conference on resolving personal and spiritual conflicts

Discipleship Counseling

A two-day advanced seminar on helping others find freedom in Christ

Setting Your Church Free

A leadership conference on corporate freedom for churches, ministries, or mission groups

Stomping Out the Darkness

A youth conference for parents, youth workers, and young people

Resolving Spiritual Conflicts and Cross-Cultural Ministry

A conference for leaders, missionaries, and all believers desiring to see the Great Commission fulfilled

Setting Your Marriage Free

A two-day event for engaged couples, newlyweds, or those who have been married many years

The above conferences are also available on video-and audiocassettes, except for *Setting Your Marriage Free.* To order these and other resources, write or call us at the address below.

To host a conference, feel free to contact us:
Freedom in Christ
9051 Executive Park Dr. Ste. 503
Knoxville TN 37923
Phone: (865) 342-4000 – Fax: (865) 342-4001
Email: info@ficm.org
Website: www.ficm.org

Other Books by Neil Anderson

Bondage Breaker®—Youth Edition

Bondage Breaker®, Youth Edition Study Guide

Bondage Breaker® Audiobook

Stomping Out the Darkness

Stomping Out the Darkness, Study Guide

Busting Free, Youth Curriculum

FREEDOM IN CHRIST 4 TEENS
Devotional Series

Awesome God
by Neil Anderson and Rich Miller

Extreme Faith
by Neil Anderson and Dave Park

Purity Under Pressure
by Neil Anderson and Dave Park